ENGLISH
FOR ACADEMIC
AND TECHNICAL PURPOSES

ENGLISH FOR ACADEMIC AND TECHNICAL PURPOSES

Studies in Honor of Louis Trimble

Larry Selinker
University of Michigan

Elaine Tarone
University of Minnesota

Victor Hanzeli
University of Washington

Editors

Newbury House Publishers, Inc. / Rowley / Massachusetts /01969
ROWLEY ● LONDON ● TOKYO

1981

Library of Congress Cataloging in Publication Data
Main entry under title:

English for academic and technical purposes.

"Bibliography of Louis Trimble's works": p.
1. English language--Study and teaching--Foreign students--Addresses, essays, lectures. 2. English language--Technical English--Addresses, essays, lectures. 3. Trimble, Louis, 1917–   I. Trimble, Louis, 1917–   II. Selinker, Larry, 1937–   III. Tarone, Elaine, 1945–   IV. Hanzeli, Victor Egon, 1925–
PE1128.A2E473   420'.7   80-15531
ISBN 0-88377-178-0

Cover design by Barbara Frake

NEWBURY HOUSE PUBLISHERS, INC.

Language Science
Language Teaching
Language Learning

ROWLEY, MASSACHUSETTS 01969
ROWLEY ● LONDON ● TOKYO

Copyright © 1981 by Newbury House Publishers, Inc. All rights reserved. No part of this book may be reproduced or transmitted in any form or by any means, electronic or mechanical, including photocopying, recording, or by any information storage and retrieval system, without permission in writing from the Publisher.

First printing: May 1981
5   4   3   2   1

Printed in the U.S.A.

Louis Trimble and Mary Todd Trimble
Paipa, Colombia—1977

Biographical Introduction

Louis Trimble has moved from place to place and from one type of work to another, but old homes and old pursuits have a way of recurring. He was born in Seattle, where he now teaches in the Engineering College of the University of Washington, and in the course of developing courses for foreign students of English for the Pacific American Institute he frequently visits the University of Redlands, not far from the area in California where he once ran a hog ranch.

Hog ranching is a pursuit he is quite sure he will not return to, but his earliest interests—science, languages, and writing fiction—are permanent. As a child in Hollywood he built himself a telescope from a kit in order to study the stars, and in the course of more recent studies in Maltese he built his own oscilloscope to investigate some details of pronunciation.

His early studies of chemistry were interrupted by the depression and the war, and over the following years he took a random assortment of jobs to provide bread and butter while he wrote. The jobs included house painting, ditch digging, accounting, and, rather more congenial than hog ranching but quite as demanding of time and energy, stump ranching in northern Idaho. The first books he wrote were mystery novels (about thirty), and he hopes to write more of these when he has time to work out the intricacies of the plots. These were followed by about thirty westerns, some of which are still being republished in translation in various languages. A few years ago he turned to science fiction, where he finds that a writer can be freer of stereotypes in creating character and situation, and in choosing themes and incorporating personal interests. (*Editors' Note*: See the Trimble bibliography in Part Three of this volume.)

When he was able to return to the university again it was to study English at Eastern Washington University. His graduate work—at Eastern Washington, Mexico City College, the University of Washington, and the University of Pennsylvania—was in Comparative Literature, Higher Education, and Romance Linguistics. The interest in education and in linguistics is apparent in his science fiction novels.

In the course of studying he was gradually drawn into teaching, and his present work in the teaching of scientific English to foreign and native learners draws together many of the threads in this varied career—the interests in education, in science, in other cultures, in language, and in the effective organization of writing to serve its specific purpose, whether to inform and explain or to interest and amuse. At the suggestion of Larry Selinker and in cooperation with him, and with Jack Lackstrom and Robert Vroman and, more recently, Mary Todd Trimble, he has done research into the nature of the grammar and the rhetoric of scientific English and the relation between them. The publication of these joint papers has led to correspondence with teachers and researchers in over forty-five countries, and has sent Louis Trimble on working visits to, among other places, Yugoslavia, Colombia, and Morocco. We hope that this volume will renew contacts with old friends and colleagues and be the means of meeting new ones.

Mary Todd Trimble
Devon, England
August, 1978

Acknowledgments

We would like to thank the following people for helpful comments on earlier drafts of some of these papers: Ann Borkin, Kenneth Hill, Richard Rhodes, and Frederick Newmeyer. We have presented these earlier drafts to students in graduate seminars at the Universities of Washington, Michigan, and Minnesota and would like to thank them for their helpful comments as well (particularly Sandra Oster, Ana Sierra, and Johanna Wilson). In the final preparation of the manuscript, we have had invaluable help from William E. Longenecker of the English Language Institute, Oregon State University, and Eleanor Foster and Mekdese Yifru of the English Language Institute, University of Michigan; we thank them. Spirited discussions on the thrust and content of the Editorial Comments were held with J. Charles Alderson, Ann Borkin, and Devon Woods, none of whom is responsible for the final product. Our thanks go also to Susan Gillette, who helped with final proofreading. Finally, we wish to thank Russ Tomlin of the University of Oregon, for bringing his rich background in theoretical linguistics and his growing background in applied linguistics to the task of helping us get the final draft in readable, and especially, in logical form. If the level of argumentation in these pieces reaches the aesthetic goal of "quality," the individual authors and editors have Russ to thank, in addition to themselves.

Editors' Preface

As the field of English for Specific Purposes (ESP) develops, there is increasing demand around the world for access to theoretical and applied papers in the areas of English for Science and Technology (EST) and English for Academic Purposes (EAP). Teacher-training programs, as well as practicing EST/EAP people, have evidenced the need for published collections of readings—both theoretical and applied—in this field.

We believe that all of us working in these areas value the enormous contribution Louis Trimble has made, and continues to make, to our field through his descriptions of the rhetorical structure of EST discourse and through numerous practical applications. Accordingly, it is fitting for us to offer this volume in Trimble's honor. We have gathered together here a collection of papers in the two areas in which Trimble has worked: (1) theoretical and descriptive papers on the rhetoric and grammar of EST/EAP discourse—and papers discussing theoretical notions brought in from overlapping academic disciplines—and (2) papers on practical applications, including descriptions of programs, innovative methodology, and teaching materials. Since some papers clearly overlap these categories, readers may at times wonder why this or that paper is classified the way it is. What we have tried to do is focus on what seems to us as the main point of the paper in terms of the themes running through the volume.

Following each chapter, we present Editorial Comments by Larry Selinker and Elaine Tarone; these comments are presented with the following purposes in mind: (1) to attempt to draw attention to the unifying themes in the volume and (2) to present (hopefully) helpful discussion points for teachers planning to use this volume in graduate and teacher-training courses. Of course, the individual authors are not responsible for our observations.

Why present these papers in this Festschrift? In our view, Louis Trimble has had a major personal influence on a whole generation of applied linguistics scholars with his many publications and lecture tours. He is famous for his kindnesses to young scholars. But more than this, it is our view that Professor Trimble has made a major intellectual contribution to "knowledge," and for that we honor him here. It is hard to document this claim in a short space, but it goes something like this: Louis Trimble some twenty or so years ago took the classical rhetoric of Aristotle et al. (e.g., "definition," "classification" functions), applied these notions to a description of EST texts *where they fit*, modified these notions where they didn't fit, and created an original rhetoric based on the notion of those "organizational choices" the technical writer makes at various levels of "the rhetorical-process hierarchy" in attempting to transmit technical information.

We have every expectation that this major contribution will continue to be developed as Louis continues to mature in his scholarship.

We are pleased to offer these readings in his honor as part of the ongoing development of the field.

Larry Selinker
Elaine Tarone
Victor Hanzeli

Ann Arbor and Seattle
August, 1979

Affiliations of Editors and Authors

Editors

    Larry Selinker   Professor of Linguistics
Director, English Language Institute
University of Michigan

    Elaine Tarone   Assistant Professor of Linguistics
University of Minnesota

    Victor Hanzeli   Associate Professor of Romance Linguistics
University of Washington

Authors

Biographical Introduction:

    Mary Todd Trimble   Director of Curriculum Development
Pacific American Institute, Inc.

Part One

    H. G. Widdowson   Professor of Applied Linguistics
Institute of Education
University of London

John E. Lackstrom	Associate Professor Languages and Philosophy Utah State University
A. Godman	Hon. Research Fellow, Eliot College, University of Kent at Canterbury Sondes House Patrixbourne Canterbury, Kent CT4 5DD
E. M. F. Payne, O. B. E.	Director of Education, Malaya (Retired) 9 Homefield Road Ware Herts.
John Swales	Senior Lecturer/Language Studies Unit University of Aston at Birmingham
Peter Wingard	Senior Lecturer in the Teaching of English Overseas. Division of Curriculum and Educational Methods Department of Education University of Manchester
Deborah Tyma	Graduate Student in Linguistics Teaching Assistant, English Language Institute University of Michigan
Sandra Oster	Graduate Student in Linguistics Teaching Assistant, English Language Institute University of Michigan
Thomas Mage	Fulbright Lecturer Yemen-American Language Institute Sa'ana, North Yemen

Part Two

Christopher N. Candlin	Senior Lecturer, Department of Linguistics and Modern English Language Director, Institute for English Language Education University of Lancaster
Clive J. Bruton	Supervisor, English Language Unit Faculty of Science University of Kuwait
Jonathan H. Leather	Postgraduate Student Department of Linguistics and Phonetics University College, London

Edward G. Woods	Lektor Language Center Free University of Berlin
Ronald Mackay	Assistant Professor of Applied Linguistics TESL Center Concordia University
J. N. Crofts	Director English Language Servicing Unit University of Khartoum
M. L. Tickoo	Professor of Research Coordination and Materials Production Head, Department of Materials Production Central Institute of English and Foreign Languages Hyderabad
Thomas Huckin	Assistant Professor Humanities Department, College of Engineering University of Michigan
Leslie Olsen	Associate Professor Humanities Department, College of Engineering University of Michigan
Ljerka Bartolić	Senior Lecturer in Technical English Faculty of Mechanical Engineering and Naval Architecture University of Zagreb
Maxine F. Schmidt	Graduate Student in Applied Linguistics University of Washington
A. H. Urquhart	Director of Courses English Language Institute University of Michigan

A Note on Terminology

Although there have been contributions from colleagues in other parts of the world, we believe that the two major trends in areas of concern to readers of this volume have, over the last two decades, been either British or American. One of the strengths of the present volume in our view is that it appears to be the first volume on the market to consciously attempt to integrate British and American applied linguistics* in the area of "English for academic and technical purposes". Even though the three editors are American, we have all spent substantial time in Britain, especially at Edinburgh where several of the British authors represented here have also spent considerable amounts of time. And several of the British authors represented here have by now made a pilgrimage to the Trimble estate in Kirkland, Washington.

In working through this developing volume over the past two years, we have come to realize that the old separations and many of the old arguments between representatives of the two traditions just do not seem to fit any more. Here, we believe, there has been an effort, sometimes conscious, sometimes not, made by the editors and most authors to integrate their perspectives and this integration is reflected in the seeming ease with which the American authors represented here use terminology originally developed in British applied linguistics and vice versa. We think this is an important and healthy development.

L.S.
E.T.

---

* The current affiliation of the authors does *not* correspond on a one-to-one basis to British (or to British-trained) or to American (or to American-trained). *We challenge the reader to determine the original home base of each author by the work presented here.*

Contents

	Biographical Introduction—MARY TODD TRIMBLE	v
	Acknowledgments	vii
	Editors' Preface	ix
	Affiliations of Editors and Authors	xi
	A Note on Terminology	xv

PART ONE: Theoretical and Descriptive Papers

1	English for Specific Purposes: Criteria for Course Design—H. G. WIDDOWSON	1
2	Logical Argumentation: The Answer to the Discussion-Problem in EST—JOHN E. LACKSTROM	12
3	A Taxonomic Approach to the Lexis of Science—A. GODMAN and E. M. F. PAYNE	23
4	The Function of One Type of Particle in a Chemistry Textbook—JOHN SWALES	40
5	Some Verb Forms and Functions in Six Medical Texts—PETER WINGARD	53
6	Anaphoric Functions of Some Demonstrative Noun Phrases in EST—DEBORAH TYMA	65
7	The Use of Tenses in "Reporting Past Literature" in EST—SANDRA OSTER	76
8	Scientific and Technical Discourse: A Comparative Analysis of English and Romanian—THOMAS MAGE	91

PART TWO: Papers on Practical Applications

9 Designing Modular Materials for Communicative Language Learning; An Example: Doctor-Patient Communication Skills—CHRISTOPER N. CANDLIN, CLIVE J. BRUTON, JONATHAN H. LEATHER, and EDWARD G. WOODS — 105

10 Developing a Reading Curriculum for ESP—RONALD MACKAY — 134

11 Subjects and Objects in ESP Teaching Materials—J. N. CROFTS — 146

12 ESP Materials in Use: Some Thoughts from the Classroom—M. L. TICKOO — 154

13 Teaching the Use of the Article in EST—THOMAS HUCKIN and LESLIE OLSEN — 165

14 Interpretation of "Information Transfer" from a Diagram—LJERKA BARTOLIĆ — 193

15 Needs Assessment in English for Specific Purposes: The Case Study—MAXINE F. SCHMIDT — 199

16 Operating on Learning Texts—A. H. URQUHART — 211

PART THREE: Bibliography of Louis Trimble's Works: Fiction Books and Academic Studies — 225

PART ONE

Theoretical and Descriptive Papers

1
English for Specific Purposes:
Criteria for Course Design

H. G. Widdowson

The work that has been done to date on the teaching of English for Special or Specific Purposes (ESP) has generally been predicated on the following assumption: If a group of learners' needs for the language can be accurately specified, then this specification can be used to determine the content of a language program that will meet these needs. Thus, if, for example, we can specify what students of economics need to be able to do with English by analyzing their textbooks or what waiters need to be able to do with English by analyzing their interaction with patrons, we can devise custom-made courses of English that incorporate the results of the analysis.

This assumption of the necessary determination of course content by the learner's requirement for the language seems to underlie remarks in Halliday, McIntosh, and Strevens (1964), where mention is made here of "English for civil servants; for policemen; for officials of the law; for dispensers and nurses; for specialists in agriculture; for engineers and fitters." The authors go on to say: "Every one of these specialized needs requires, before it can be met by appropriate teaching materials, detailed studies of restricted languages and special registers carried out on the basis of large samples of the language used by the particular persons concerned. It is perfectly possible to find out just what English is used in the operation of power stations in India: once this has been observed, recorded and analyzed, a teaching course to impart such language behavior can at last be devised with confidence and certainty" (Halliday et al. 1964:190).

A more recent expression of this assumption, illustrated by a detailed demonstration of how it might be put into practice in ESP course design, appears in Munby (1978). The epilogue to that work contains the following statement: "This book has been concerned with language syllabus design. More specifically, the contention has been that, when the purpose for which the target language is required can be identified, the *syllabus specification is directly derivable from the prior identification of the communication needs* of that particular participant or participant stereotype" (Munby 1978:218 [italics added]).

It seems reasonable enough to assume that a specification of language needs should define the language content of a course designed to meet such needs. My purpose in this chapter, however, is to argue that such an assumption is mistaken, at least as far as English for Academic Purposes (EAP) is concerned, and to suggest alternative criteria for course design.

The first point to be noted, perhaps, is that the expression "learner needs" is open to two interpretations. On the one hand it can refer to what the learner needs to do with the language once he or she has learned it. This is a *goal-oriented* definition of needs and relates to terminal behavior, the ends of learning. On the other hand, the expression can refer to what the learner needs to do to actually acquire the language. This is a *process-oriented* definition of needs and relates to transitional behavior, the means of learning. It is the first of these interpretations which is favored in current ESP work. The basic belief is that which seems to be expressed in the quotation from Halliday et al. just cited: Once the language the learners will have to deal with is described, then teaching courses can be devised (with confidence and certainty) by directly applying this description. Thus it is the ends that determine course design. The means, apparently, must shift for themselves.

This goal-oriented approach follows a well-established tradition. Its most familiar manifestation is in the early work on vocabulary selection that served as the basis for the structural syllabus. Here the basic procedure was to delimit the content of the syllabus in terms of linguistic items by reference to primary criteria like frequency, range, and coverage, all of which served to define what it was supposed the learner ultimately ought to acquire as terminal behavior. Factors like learnability and teachability, which relate to means, were only adduced as contingent considerations for making minor modifications to the basic course design. This procedure has been subject to much critical discussion (e.g., Mackay 1965, Widdowson 1968) and more recently Wilkins has pointed out their limitations as a preliminary to his own proposals for what he claims to be a radically different approach. The aproach he proposes however is, with respect to the two kinds of orientation I have mentioned, not really different at all. It is important for my argument here to demonstrate why not.

Having given an outline of the principles of vocabulary control, Wilkins reports, with approval, an observation made in Reibel (1969) to the effect that ". . . what is happening here is that we are taking the language behaviour and the language knowledge that we aim to produce in our learners, we are analyzing the linguistic components of the desired performance and isolating its units. We are then teaching the units piece by piece so as to get back to the very position from which we started. . ." (Wilkins 1976:5).

Now it emerges from subsequent discussion that Wilkins's objection to this procedure is not that it allows goal-oriented needs to determine course design but that the kind of linguistic components that are specified represent only a part of the language knowledge and behavior that the learner needs to acquire eventually. His criticism of these criteria for defining course content is essentially that they operate on the wrong kind of unit: They isolate forms rather than functions and so develop grammatical rather than communicative competence. But the principle of allowing goal-oriented needs to determine the content of a course is retained as fundamental to the approach. This principle is stated quite explicitly in the following passage:

> The process of deciding what to teach is based on considerations of what the learners should most usefully be able to communicate in the foreign language. When this is established, we can decide what are the most appropriate forms for each type of communication. The labelling for the learning units is not primarily semantic, although there is no reason why the structural realization should not also be indicated. A general language course will concern itself with those concepts and functions that are likely to be of widest value. In the same way, in the provision of a course for a more specialized language learner, the limitation is on the types of content that he needs to express and not on the number of structures he needs to know or the situations in which he will find himself. In short, the linguistic content is planned according to the semantic demands of the learner (Wilkins 1976;19).

The innovation here lies in the redefinition of learning units as "concepts and functions" rather than as structures, but the units themselves are still seen as derivable from desired terminal behavior. It is still assumed that syllabus content must be determined by the goals rather than the process of learning.[1] Wilkins's reference to specialized language learners returns us to the main theme of ESP. The point he makes here is much the same as that made by Halliday et al.: With ESP one can be more precise than one can be with "general" language courses in the specification of what language the learner will eventually have to cope with. The difference again lies in how this language is to be characterized. Halliday et al. think in terms of *what* English is used and speak of "restricted languages" and "special registers." Their attention, therefore, is focused on linguistic forms whose incidence can serve to identify different varieties of English usage. Wilkins, on the other hand, thinks in terms of *how* English is used for the expression of concepts and the performance of functions whose incidence can serve to identify different varieties of English *use*. With reference to distinctions I have suggested elsewhere (e.g., Widdowson 1977) the view taken by Halliday et al. (and those of similar persuasion, like Crystal and Davy 1969) leads to a description of language variety as *text* defined as the way a particular language is manifested when it is put to particular purposes. Thus statements about the frequency of the passive or certain modal verbs in written scientific English are statements about text. The view taken by Wilkins, (and those of similar persuasion) leads to a description of language variety as *textualization* defined as the way a particular language realizes the concepts and functions of a particular type of discourse. Thus statements about how the passive or certain modal verbs in English are used to conduct scientific analysis and exposition are statements about the textualization in English of scientific discourse.

There are, then, two ways of describing a particular variety of English identified as the terminal goal of a particular group of learners. One way is to describe it as register: This involves making statements about its formal properties as a type of English text. The other way is to describe it as rhetoric: This involves making statements about the English textualization of a type of discourse, of a mode of communicating. It is in adopting this second mode of description that Louis Trimble and his associates have made their very considerable contribution (e.g., Lackstrom, Selinker, and Trimble 1970,1972; see also Swales, chap. 4) and there seems little doubt that this is the more profitable line to take, accounting as it does for the communicative functioning of language. Furthermore, such a description can be used to adduce aspects of the methodology of academic subjects and so can be made relevant to a process-oriented approach. More of this later. For the present, the point I wish to make is that whether we describe text or textualization, register or rhetoric, if we assume that our language description must directly *determine* course content then in both cases we adopt a goal-oriented approach to course design and focus attention on ends rather than means. I have said that this is a mistaken thing to do. It is time to give some substance to this assertion.

If one allows the description of the language-to-be-acquired to determine course content, whether this is done in terms of linguistic forms or communicative functions, then one assumes an equation between teaching and learning. By this I mean that one assumes that what is to be learned must be expressly and explicitly taught. Yet we all know that learners have an irritating tendency towards independent action and will frequently follow their own patterns of learning behavior in spite of the teaching patterns imposed upon them. These expressions of self assertion are commonly characterized as errors. The term itself indicates that we interpret these expressions as evidence that learners learn *less* than they are taught, and our usual reaction is to try to restore the equation by more teaching. But of course we can equally well take these expressions as evidence that learners learn *more* than they are taught. As is now widely recognized, although these peculiarities of learner language may indicate a failure in teaching in that they deviate from the present norm, they are also evidence of the learner's capacity for developing creative learning processes of his or her own.

It seems to me that the pedagogic equation, upon which the goal-oriented approach to syllabus design depends, must be wrong because the two sides of the equation are essentially different in kind. The teaching side can be expressed as a kind of product, a collection of formal or functional units to be stored away in the mind as knowledge. The learning side can be expressed as a kind of process, a set of strategies for making sense. In the classroom what commonly happens is that the teacher busily tries to change the learner's process into a product and the learner busily tries to change the teacher's product into a process. The teacher attempts to get the learner to put the language data in store and the learner keeps on converting it into energy to drive his or her own acquisition strategies.

Thus a fundamental conflict is created between what the learner needs to do in learning on the one hand and what the learner needs to have acquired after learning on the other. A goal-oriented approach focuses on the latter and makes what I believe to be the mistaken assumption that what the learner has to acquire necessarily has to be taught directly. The irony of the situation is that in trying to place his or her product the teacher inhibits the very process that would enable the learner to eventually acquire it. What, then, is the alternative? I want now to consider what I have called a process-oriented approach, one concerned with transitional behavior and the means of learning.

To begin with, such an approach rejects the pedagogic equation and accepts from the outset that the language data given to the learner will not be preserved in store intact but will be used as grist to the mental mill. Hence the language content of the course is selected not because it is representative of what the learner will have to deal with after the course is over but because it is likely to activate strategies for learning while the course is in progress. In principle, therefore, it is possible to conceive of an ESP course containing very little of the language associated with the special purpose so long as the language that it *does* contain is effective in developing the ability to achieve the special purpose after the teaching is over. In practice, of course, this facilitating language will often correspond quite closely in some respects to that of the special purpose because of the likely correspondence between what the learners need the language for and the ways in which they will acquire it. This point is closely related to the observation I made earlier about the potential relevance of a rhetorical description of language variety. I shall return to it presently. For the moment it is enough to note that if one avoids presenting *The Grapes of Wrath* and *The Mayor of Casterbridge* to students whose goal is to read engineering textbooks it is not because these novels are unrepresentative of engineering English but because we judge that they are not likely to engage the interest and to activate the learning strategies of such students and so would not have the necessary facilitating function.

Whereas the goal-oriented approach, then, focuses on the selection of language by reference to the ends of learning, allowing the means to be devised ad hoc, the process-oriented approach focuses on the presentation of language by reference to the means of learning and allows the ends to be achieved by the learner by exercising the ability he or she has acquired. The first approach assumes that the completion of a course of instruction marks the completion of learning and that all that is left for the student to do is to apply this ready-made knowledge. The second approach assumes that learning will continue beyond the completion of instruction since the aim of such instruction precisely is to develop a capacity to learn: It does not itself realize any special purpose but provides the learner with the potential for its realization.

If one follows a goal-oriented approach one needs to take one's bearing from models of linguistic description since these will define the units of course content. A process-oriented approach, on the other hand, can only be pursued by reference to some idea about how people learn. There is, of course, a vast literature on this subject and this is not the place to review it, even if I felt competent to do so. What I would like to do, however, is to direct attention to certain recent work on different cognitive styles that, tentative though it is, promises to have some relevance to ESP course design.[2]

I want to consider first a distinction made in Pask and Scott (1972) between two types of learners: the serialist and the holist. The strategy adopted by the first of these is to follow a direct route, proceeding step by step, and avoiding digression and irrelevance. The holist's strategy, on the other hand, is to advance on a broad front allowing access to all manner of information that might help him or her to find the way. Pask and Scott express the difference in rather more technical terms: "Serialists learn, remember and recapitulate a body of information in terms of string-like cognitive structures where items are related by simple data links: formally, by 'low order relations.' Since serialists habitually assimilate lengthy sequences of data, they are intolerant of irrelevant information unless, as individuals, they are equipped with an unusually large memory capacity. Holists, on the other hand, learn, remember and recapitulate as a whole: formally, in terms of 'high order relations' " (Pask and Scott 1972:218).

One might suppose that the terms *serialist* and *holist* could refer to alternative learning strategies within an individual's repertoire that are freely selected as appropriate to a particular learning task. But this is apparently not the case: Pask and Scott produce experimental evidence that indicates that there is a distinct difference in individual ability to deal with holist and serialist tasks. We are led to the conclusion that what we have here are two different kinds of competence. The pedagogic significance of this seems clear. If a teacher uses serialist methods he or she will inhibit the learning of holist pupils and vice versa. One might suppose that a solution to this dilemma would be to develop a methodology that combines serialist and holist procedures, thereby providing pupils with an equal opportunity to learn according to their natural cognitive tendencies. The difficulty with such a proposal is that one thereby imposes an unnatural program on the teacher since he or she will be inclined to teach according to his or her particular cognitive style and the lessons are unlikely to be very effective if forced to do otherwise.

We appear to have arrived at an impasse. I have said, approvingly, that a process-oriented approach to course design uses language data as a means of activating learning strategies. Clearly this activation can only occur if the manner in which the language is presented is in accord with the cognitive style of the learners. But how can it be in accord with different cognitive styles, which may indeed be mutually incompatible? As far as I can see, there are only two ways round this problem. One is to design language programs that will in some way provide for parallel development corresponding to the different styles. Here one runs up against the problem of the teacher's style, which I referred to earlier. The alternative is to separate the holists from the serialists and provide them with different programs altogether. This latter looks to be a hopelessly impracticable proposition particularly if it turns out (as seems likely on the face of it) that a much more delicate distinction between styles will be needed. However, in the ESP context, especially where the purposes refer to academic study, it may be that this is a natural and necessary course to take.

The grounds for this belief lie in the likelihood of different types of learner separating of their own accord to follow distinct lines of academic inquiry. There is some evidence to suggest that this does indeed happen and that there is a correspondence between disciplines and cognitive styles. Such evidence is to be found, for example, in the research recorded in Hudson (1966). Hudson also makes a broad distinction between two types of learner: He calls them convergers and divergers, and he defines them with reference to types of intelligence test. A typical question in a conventional intelligence test requires the subject to select from a restricted range of alternatives. Hudson gives the following example:

> Brick is to house as plank is to. . .orange, grass, egg, boat, ostrich.

And he comments: "The victim knows that there is one solution which is correct, and his task is to ferret it out. His reasoning is said to *converge* on to the right answer."

Instead of restricting the subject to a choice from a closed system, however, one can set an open-ended task and so invite a "creative" response, as in the following example:

> How many uses can you think of for a brick?

Hudson comments: "Here, the individual is invited to *diverge,* to think fluently and tangentially, without examining any one line of reasoning in detail" (Hudson 1967:50).

Now it seems to be the case that, as with the case of serialist and holist strategies, these two modes of mental operation are not equally accessible to all individuals. Some perform well on conventional tests and badly on creative tests and are naturally convergent in cognitive style, while others do the opposite and are naturally divergent.

What is of particular significance for the present discussion, however, is that convergers and divergers appear not to be evenly distributed throughout the student population but tend to cluster according to subject. Floyd, in an admirably clear exposition of research on cognitive styles, summarizes the findings of Hudson's work with open-ended tests as follows:

> ... Hudson had hoped that these open-ended tests would cut across the arts/science distinction and give some reflection of the boys' brightness. In fact, the opposite occurred. Scores on open-ended tests provided a very good measure of the arts/science split. Arts specialists tended to be divergers, weaker on intelligence tests than open-ended tests,

whilst the scientists went the other way. In Hudson's sample between three and four divergers went into history, English literature and modern languages for every one that went into physical science; and between three and four convergers did mathematics, physical science, while biology, geography, economics and general arts were studied by convergers and divergers in roughly equal proportions. (Floyd 1976:46) with physical science, while biology, geography, economics and general arts were studied physics and chemistry for every one that studied arts subjects. Classics appeared to belong

It is not clear how far the cognitive styles distinguished by Pask and Scott can be set into correspondence with those of Hudson. It does seem however that serialists and convergers are alike in preferring precision and rational control and in their inclination towards the exact sciences, whereas holists and divergers share a common preference for wider networks of association and for imaginative excursion and incline towards the arts and the social sciences. At all events, the possibility emerges that the methodologies of different disciplines can themselves be characterized in terms of cognitive styles, being formalizations of different ways of resolving problems and of conceptualizing and controlling reality. If this is so, then it becomes feasible in principle to design programs of English for academic study to accord with the learners' cognitive bias because the learners have already grouped themselves by the process of a kind of natural selection in their choice of subject specialization. Thus, a process-oriented approach to the teaching of English to, let us say, physical science students would adopt predominantly serialist/convergent type procedures of presentation. A course for social science students, on the other hand, would adopt procedures of a predominantly holist/divergent kind. All this sounds plausible enough. But how, the opposition might ask, does one set about discovering such procedures? For it must be recognized, (and is recognized by the scholars I have referred to) that a good deal of research has yet to be done before different cognitive styles can be isolated and defined with confidence. And it would seem unlikely that such definite distinctions between serialists/holists and convergers/divergers can be maintained. In these circumstances the best one can do, I think, is to design EAP programs by direct reference to the methodologies of subjects concerned on the grounds that these must of their nature incorporate the cognitive styles associated with their particular areas of inquiry.

Returning to the observation I made earlier, we can now see why it is that in respect to English for academic study what the learners need the language for may closely correspond to the ways in which they will acquire it. Both relate to the particular combination of cognitive styles that define the methodology of the subject of their specialization. So if one allows this methodology to determine the methodology of the language teaching, then one will necessarily be developing strategies in learning that will be applicable to later study. One can also see, I think, why it is that a description of the language to be learned as textualization is to be preferred to one that characterizes that language as text. It is because the discourse that is textualized must, as a particular mode of communicating, also correspond to the cognitive styles that characterize the subject. The difference between a goal-oriented and process-oriented approach lies in the way such a rhetorical description is used. The former uses it directly as a determinant of course content, an area of language to be selected and expressly taught. The latter uses it as evidence of ways of thinking that might indicate how language is to be presented so as to engage the appropriate cognitive styles. Of course, it may turn out in particular cases that the content of a course draws quite extensively on the description but with process orientation it will do so not because it represents the language to be learned but because it is effective in activating the process of learning.

There is, I think, some reason to suppose that a process-oriented approach based on the principles I have tried to outline here would, by satisfying the cognitive needs of the learners, guarantee the eventual attainment of the desired terminal behavior. The means imply the ends and transitional and terminal behavior are simply different points on the same learning continuum. Whereas, as I have suggested, a goal-oriented approach creates a conflict between what the learner needs to do in learning and what he or she needs to have acquired *after* learning, a process-oriented approach based on subject methodologies contains no such conflict because these needs converge in the learning process itself.

All this may sound reasonable enough, but of course no problem has been solved. Things are never as neat as a turn of phrase can make them seem to be. For one thing we clearly need to know more about varieties of cognition: On the one hand, pedagogy, and indeed the very possibility of social life, depends on establishing styles of thinking across individual differences: On the other hand, people are unlikely to fall into neat binary divisions. We need to know more, too, about the cognitive style constitution of different methodologies and to investigate particular ways in which they can be exploited by language teaching procedures. All I wish to suggest here is that we should consider academic purposes in terms of learning processes reflected in specific methodologies rather than as static goals defined as language knowledge. To do this is not to solve an old problem but to restate it in different terms so that it can be approached from another direction.

Notes

1. It could be argued (a point made by Devon Woods) that the structural syllabus in fact focuses on process rather than goal since its proponents did not really suppose that the language presented constituted terminal behavior but only the basis for its ultimate acquisition. I am not so sure about that. Why, if this is so, did frequency, range, and coverage figure so prominently as criteria for course content? And why was success generally assessed by reference to achievement as a measure of knowledge rather than by reference to proficiency as a measure of ability. The truth of the matter is, I think, that the structuralists never really got their criteria clear and so their kind of syllabus contains a basic contradiction (discussed in Widdowson 1968): It was designed by reference to goals but is essentially only justified by reference to process. In both structural and notional syllabuses, at any rate, the assumption is that whatever later learning might take place after the course, it can do so automatically from accumulated knowledge, either of structures or notions.

2. My attention was first directed to this work by Althea Ryan, who is currently conducting research in the Department of Linguistics, University of Edinburgh, on the relevance of cognitive styles to language teaching. This work is supported by the Hornby Trust and Oxford University Press.

References

Crystal, D., and D. Davy. 1969. *Investigating English Style.* Longmans.
Floyd, A. 1976. *Cognitive Styles: Personality and Learning, Block 5.* Milton Keynes: The Open University Press.
Halliday, M. A. K., A. McIntosh, and P. Strevens. 1964. *The Linguistic Sciences and Language Teaching.* Longmans.
Hudson, L. 1967. *Contrary Imaginations.* Penguin.
Lackstrom, J. E., L. Selinker, and L. Trimble. 1970. "Grammar and Technical English: English as a Second Language." *Current Issues,* ed. R. C. Lugton, pp. 101-33. Centre for Curriculum Development.
———. 1972. "Technical Rhetorical Principles and Grammatical Choice." *TESOL Quarterly* 7.127-36.
Mackay, W. F. 1965. *Language Teaching Analysis.* Longmans.
Munby, J. 1978. *Communicative Syllabus Design.* Cambridge Univ. Press.
Pask, G., and B. C. E. Scott. 1972. "Learning Strategies and Individual Competence." *International Journal of Man-Machine Studies* 4.217-53.
Reibel, D. A. 1969. "Language Learning Analysis." *IRAL* 7.283-94.
Swales, J. 1974. "The Function of One Type of Particle in a Chemistry Textbook." (chap. 4, this vol.).
Widdowson, H. G. 1968. "The Teaching of English through Science." *Language in Education,* ed. J. Dakin, B. Tiffen, and H. G. Widdowson, pp. 115-75. Oxford Univ. Press.
———. 1977. "Description du langage scientifique." *Le Francais Dans le Monde,* no. 129.15-21.
Wilkins, D. 1976. *Notional Syllabuses.* Oxford Univ. Press.

Editorial Comments*

We begin this volume with a particularly interesting paper by Prof. Henry Widdowson. In attempting to develop criteria and principles for ESP course design, Widdowson has produced several distinctions of great importance. The division of ESP instruction into "goal-oriented" versus "process-oriented" instruction has implications for everyday practical teaching since ESP materials and teaching to date appear to have been mostly goal-oriented, although, as Widdowson points out, in practice, there may be a close correspondence.

Widdowson's discussion of "divergent" and "convergent" learner types shows once again his ability to see the relevance for our field of distinctions made in an entirely different field of study, although Widdowson would be the first to point out that this dichotomy will most probably not hold strictly in real life. In a graduate seminar one of the editors conducted, the divergent-convergent distinction proved to be one of the most thought-provoking aspects of this paper. In a practical case being studied at the University of Washington, conflict between learning styles of the type suggested by Widdowson seems to be able to account for some aspects of learning problems in a suggestive way. In the case under study, nursing students are sometimes asked to participate in open-ended problem-solving seminars or to answer essay exam questions where there are no "correct" answers, a seemingly "divergent" task in Widdowson's terms. Some non-native speakers of English seem to have an unusually difficult

---

* The editoral comments in this volume were produced by Larry Selinker and Elaine Tarone; the individual authors have not seen these comments before publication of the volume and, hence, bear no responsibility for them.

time with these tasks—*apparently* because of this learning-style conflict. Schmidt (chap. 15) provides a case study that one might wish to compare here.

Widdowson in this chapter has once again made the valuable distinction between "text" and "textualization" studies. It is interesting to note that this chapter seems to mark a clearer (at least to us) commitment by Widdowson to the study of language as textualization, with rhetorical analysis playing a central role in looking at particular genres of EST discourse. What seems extremely valuable here is the linking of this distinction with the two distinctions mentioned in the previous paragraph around the practical considerations of syllabus design.

L.S.
E.T.

Logical Argumentation:

The Answer to the Discussion-Problem in EST

John E. Lackstrom

A great deal of research in English for Science and Technology (EST) has gone into analyzing the vocabulary, sentence structure, and discourse forms of scientific and technical writing. This research has taken as its objective a better understanding of both the comprehension and composition of EST prose. In relation to the discourse forms of EST, the body of research has dealt with the structure of EST technical reports, definitions, descriptions of apparatus, and such. As the research effort in EST discourse expands, it becomes appropriate to look at an increasingly broader range of discourse types. Accordingly, this chapter examines two discourse structures[1] that, to the knowledge of this author, have received heretofore little attention: the *logical argument* and the *discussion problem*. Here we will characterize the internal structure of each of these forms as they appear in introductory textbooks in EST and then relate them to each other in a fashion that has significance for materials preparation.

    The logical argument is a form of discourse in EST in which the author applies a recognized or established principle to a set of facts in an effort to supply a solution to a problem associated with those facts. The EST passage appearing in Table 2-1 attempts, for example, to justify to the reader the assertion that our solar system is moving in a direction toward the constellation Hercules. Initially, the author presents the assertion as the conclusion he is aiming at (1n. 1-3). Next

TABLE 2-1.   EST TEXT A

1	The solar system appears to be moving toward the con-
2	stellation Hercules at about 12 mi/sec relative to the stars
3	that are nearest us in space. ... Proof of this conclusion is
4	based on a familiar phenomenon. As one drives toward a group
5	of houses they seem to spread apart, and as one drives away
6	the houses appear to come together again. Stars in the
7	vicinity of Hercules appear to be diverging, whereas stars
8	on the opposite side of the sky seem to be converging.
9	Therefore, the sun and its family must be moving through
10	space toward Hercules.

Source: Ordway (1966), pp. 311-392

(ln. 3-6), he states a principle in terms of an analogy to familiar experience: Groups of objects appear to spread apart when you approach them and come together when you move away. This principle is what we may call the *governing* principle of the argument and is considered to be established and known to the reader. In lines 6 through 8, he observes that stars in different parts of the heavens behave differently in relation to the principle. In one part of the sky the stars seem to diverge and in the opposite part of the sky them seem to converge. It happens that they diverge if they are in that part of the sky facing the constellation Hercules. This observation of the author is, in terms of discourse structure, the statement of a relevant fact. Finally, the author reaches a conclusion concerning the solution to the original problem: Our sun and its family must be moving toward Hercules (ln. 9-10).

The logical development of the discourse in Table 2-1 matches closely the structure of a deductive syllogism. The statement of the governing principle in the logical argument corresponds to the major premise of the syllogism. The statement of the relevant facts corresponds to the minor premises and the conclusion of the argument, of course, corresponds to the conclusion of the deductive syllogism. We can suggest Table 2-2 as a preliminary outline of the discourse of a logical argument.

TABLE 2-2.   PRELIMINARY OUTLINE OF THE DISCOURSE OF A LOGICAL ARGUMENT

I. GOVERNING PRINCIPLE
II. RELEVANT FACTS
III. CONCLUSION

It is not particularly surprising that the discourse structure of the logical argument of EST should correspond to the structure of a syllogism. The syllogism is the formal expression of the mode of thought the author is presumably engaging in to develop his solution to the problem. It would be only natural for him to pattern his discourse along the lines of the method he intends to follow. The patterning of logical arguments after syllogisms fits in nicely, as well, with observations made in Lackstrom (forthcoming) that empirical EST arguments follow closely the generally accepted descriptions of the scientific method, the method such arguments intend to report. Likewise, formal definitions found in EST discourse follow closely the generally accepted notions of what a formal definition ought to be, as described in pedagogical rhetorics (see Marder 1960). In other words, it seems that authors of EST do *not* diverge much from what we expect from them in the way in which they develop logical arguments.

Table 2-2 presents us then with the rudiments of a logical argument in EST: a Governing Principle, a statement of the Relevant Facts, and a Conclusion. While these are the three essentials, they do not exhaust the discourse-structural elements that may be present as well in the development of the logical argument. In this regard, consider the passage given in Table 2-3. Table 2-3 presents a logical argument over a content area similar to that in Table 2-1. Like Table 2-1, Table 2-3 possesses the essential elements of a logical argument. There is a statement of the Governing Principle of the argument in lines 6 through 12. Like Table 2-1, the Governing Principle in Table 2-3 is stated in the form of an analogy to what the author takes to be a familiar concept to the reader—the escape velocity of rockets shot from the earth's surface. Note, again, that the Governing Principle is assumed

TABLE 2-3.   EST TEXT B

```
 1        The question whether our universe is actually "pulsating"
 2    or "hyperbolic" should be decidable from the present rate
 3    of its expansion.
 4                    The situation is analogous to the case of
 5    a rocket shot from the surface of the earth.
 6                                              If the velocity
 7    of the rocket is less than seven miles per second—the "es-
 8    cape velocity"—the rocket will climb only to a certain
 9    height and then fall back to the earth. . . . On the other hand,
10    a rocket shot with a velocity of more than seven miles per
11    second will escape from the earth's gravitational field and
12    disappear in space.
13                    The case of the receding system of galaxies
14    is very similar to that of an escape rocket, except that
15    instead of just two interacting bodies (the rocket and the
16    earth) we have an unlimited number of them escaping from one
17    another.
18        We find that the galaxies are fleeing from one
19    another at seven times the velocity necessary for mutual
20    escape.
21        Thus we may conclude that our universe corresponds to
22    the "hyperbolic" model, so that its present expansion will
23    never stop.
```

Source: Gamow (1977), pp. 16-17

to be accepted or acceptable to the reader. Table 2-3 also contains a statement of the Relevant Facts in lines 18 through 20. On the basis of the facts and the Governing Principle, the Conclusion—that we are part of an expanding universe—is reached in lines 21 through 23. Governing Principles, Relevant Facts, and Conclusions, however, do not account for all of the discourse elements found in Table 2-3.

There is, first of all, the material found in lines 1 through 3. Here the author is making reference to the question his logical argument intends to resolve—whether our universe is "pulsating" or "hyperbolic." A pulsating universe is one that is forever expanding and contracting. A hyperbolic universe is one that goes on expanding indefinitely. The logical argument found in Table 2-3, then, has the additional discourse-structural element of the statement of the Problem.

We are now left with the statement found in lines 4 and 5: "The situation is analogous to the case of a rocket shot from the surface of the earth," as well as the statement found in lines 13 through 17: "The case of the receding system of galaxies is very similar to that of an escape rocket . . . ."

Both statements express the applicability of the analogy, which is the Governing Principle, to the development of the argument. In the case of the first statement, the situation described in the Problem is asserted to come under the domain of the analogy given as the Governing Principle. In the case of the second statement, the Governing Principle is being related to the Relevant Facts that are to follow in the development of the argument. That is, the author will subsequently present facts that show what the statement concerning applicability suggests: The galaxies are fleeing from each other, like the escape rocket of the analogy. The discourse function of the first statement is to establish the applicability of the Governing Principle to the Problem. The second statement establishes the applicability of the Relevant Facts to the Governing Principle. Thus, the discourse structure of Table 2-3 can be outlined as in Table 2-4.

The passages in Tables 2-1 and 2-3 both employ analogies as a means of expressing the governing principles of their arguments. Both figures, as well, show a similarity in the order in which the discourse structures are presented. Neither of these similarities is a necessary aspect of the logical argument. The Governing Principle need not be expressed in the form of an analogy, and indeed, typically is not. Nor is it necessary that the Governing Principle, Relevant Facts, and Conclusion follow in a fixed order. Table 2-5 is a case in point; it has a discourse

TABLE 2-4.   DISCOURSE STRUCTURE OF EST TEXT B

I.   PROBLEM
II. STATEMENT OF APPLICABILITY (of the Governing Principle to the Problem)
III. GOVERNING PRINCIPLE
IV. STATEMENT OF APPLICABILITY (of the Relevant Facts to the Governing Principle)
V.   RELEVANT FACTS
VI. CONCLUSION

TABLE 2-5. EST TEXT C

1 Consider the diver in Fig. 11-11. Let us assume that as he
2 leaves the diving board he has a certain angular speed ω_o
3 about a horizontal axis through the center of mass, such that
4 he would rotate through half a turn before he strikes water.
5 If he wishes to make a one and one-half turn somersault
6 instead, in the same time, he must triple his angular speed.

7 [How must he change his rotational inertia (I)?]

8 Now there are no external forces acting on him except gravity,
9 and gravity exerts no torque about his center of mass. His
10 angular momentum therefore remains constant, and

11 $\quad I_o \omega_o = I \omega.$

12 Since $\omega = 3\omega_o$, the diver must change his rotational inertia
13 about the horizontal axis through the center of mass from
14 the initial value I_o to a value I such that I equals $1/3\ I_o$.

Source: Halliday & Resnick (1974), p. 200

structure given as Table 2-6. The order is, first, the Relevant Facts (ln. 1-6); then, the Governing Principle expressed as an equation (ln. 11); and, finally, the Conclusion (ln. 16).

There are other differences of note. Observe first that the Statement of Applicability (ln. 9-10) is a Statement of Applicability of the Principle to the Facts—*not* the Facts to the Principle, as in the previous cases. The question of what is being applied to what in a Statement of Applicability is determined by the order of presentation. If the Facts precede the Principle, for example, and there is a Statement of Applicability intervening, the Applicability statement applies the latter to the former. Notice also the form of the Applicability statements in Table 2-5. Whereas the Applicability statements in Table 2-3 were assertions, the Statements of Applicability in Table 2-5 take the form of deductions that are, in effect, *since . . . therefore . . .* statements. The first Statement of Applicability (ln. 8-10) embeds one *since . . . therefore . . .* statement within another and says that "Since there are no external forces acting on the diver except for gravity and since gravity exerts no torque and since, therefore the diver's angular momentum remains constant, therefore . . . . (the Principle given in the equation) applies to the Facts." The second Statement of Applicability in lines 12 through 14 applies the Relevant Fact of the problem that the diver wishes to triple his angular speed, where it states "since $\omega = 3\omega o$," and concludes, in effect, "therefore, he must change I." Here we find an application of the Facts to the Principle. Both Statements of Applicability are embodied in *since . . . therefore . . .* deductions.

Table 2-5 differs as well from Tables 2-1 and 2-3 in that the statement of the Governing Principle has the form of an equation (ln. 11). This form is altogether typical of statements of Governing Principles found in more highly technical logical arguments.

TABLE 2-6.   DISCOURSE STRUCTURE OF EST TEXT C

I. RELEVANT FACTS
II. STATEMENT OF APPLICABILITY (of the Governing Principle to the Relevant Facts)
III. GOVERNING PRINCIPLE
IV. STATEMENT OF APPLICABILITY (of the Relevant Facts to the Governing Principle)
V. CONCLUSION

TABLE 2-7.   DISCOURSE STRUCTURE OF AN IDEALIZED LOGICAL
               ARGUMENT

I. PROBLEM (optional)
II. GOVERNING PRINCIPLE
III. RELEVANT FACTS
IV. CONCLUSION

+ STATEMENTS OF APPLICABILITY (optional)

Finally, Table 2-5 presents us with a case of the author failing to state the Problem. Such ellipsis of steps in the development of arguments appears to be common in EST discourse (Lackstrom 1977). The problem that Table 2-5 is addressing is "How must the diver change his rotational inertia (I)?" The question has been interpolated as line 7 of Table 2-5.

We are able at this point to suggest an outline of the structure of an idealized logical argument replacing Table 2-2 with Table 2-7. The logical argument may (though it need not) contain a statement that there exists a problem concerning a certain set of facts. To this problem, an established and recognized principle is applied, the Governing Principle. The Governing Principle then functions as if it were the major premise of a syllogism. To this principle a set of Relevant Facts are applied in the capacity of minor premises. Finally, a Conclusion is reached solving the initial problem. This Conclusion is the logical consequence of the Principle plus the Facts brought to bear in the course of the argument. Interspersed between the Problem and the Principle, or the Principle and the Facts, may be found Statements of Applicability in which a succeeding stage of the discourse is simply asserted or asserted by virtue of a deductive *since . . . therefore . . . .* expression to be applicable to a former stage of the discourse.

There are departures from the "idealized" logical arguments discussed above. Specifically, elements within the logical argument appear in differing orders, and certain elements may or may not be present. Relevant Facts may initiate the argument. Statements of the Problem and of Applicability may or may not be present for reasons we cannot yet make fully explicit.

We turn now to a discussion of a distinct form of EST discourse: *the discussion problem*. We will show that though the discussion problem is formally distinct from the logical argument, a relationship exists between them of significance to the student of EST.

TABLE 2-8. DISCUSSION PROBLEM A

As a yo-yo is let fall, its angular speed increases steadily with an angular acceleration of 40 rad/sec^2. Through what angle has it turned when its final angular speed is 50 rad/sec?

Source: Miller (1972), p. 183

TABLE 2-9. DISCUSSION PROBLEM B

A snail traveling at a snail's pace (12 ft/day) decides to slow down to only 5 ft/day and allows himself 2 min in which to make the change. (a) Express his initial velocity in mi/hr; in in./year; in ft/s. (b) Compute the acceleration in ft/day · min; in ft/sec^2.

Source: Miller (1972), p. 48

TABLE 2-10. DISCUSSION PROBLEM C

In a detective story a body is found 15 ft from the base of a building and beneath an open window 80 ft above. Would you guess the death to be accidental or not? Why?

Source: Halliday and Resnick (1974), p. 56

The discussion problem is commonly found at introductory levels of instruction in EST in course examinations and at the end of chapters in introductory textbooks. The discussion problem presents a situation and the facts associated with that situation and asks the student to respond to the facts with an appropriate solution to a problem that the facts suggest. In some cases the solution to the problem involves the application of the appropriate formula and the presentation of a concise, nonverbal answer. In other cases, an extended prose response is called for by the questioner. In either case there are difficulties associated with the discussion problem.

In the first place, discussion problems are often couched in language that is filled with culture-bound reference. Consider the discussion problem in Table 2-8. Here, the use of the term *yo-yo* makes the problem fully accessible to only a restricted number of English speakers. It is, nevertheless, the sort of problem that speakers of many cultures will find when studying physics in the United States.

In the second place, discussion problems often make use of idiomatic forms. Such is the case in the problem found in Table 2-9. Here, the term *snail's pace* illustrates the idiomaticity of many discussion problems. Clearly, the *yo-yo* and the *snail's pace* of the two examples need not hinder the comprehension or solution of the problems if the reader, though uncomprehending of the references, is able to apply the appropriate formulas or principles from the text. It has been the experience of this writer, however, that such usages, when uncomprehended, can serve to effectively block comprehension by many non-native speakers of English.

TABLE 2-11. DISCOURSE STRUCTURE OF DISCUSSION PROBLEMS

I. RELEVANT FACTS
II. PROBLEM

TABLE 2-12. RESPONSE TO DISCUSSION PROBLEM C

1	Taking the horizontal distance as x and the vertical
2	distance as y, the death is not accidental if the victim's
3	velocity along the x-axis is significantly greater than
4	zero.
5	Thus for $V_x = \frac{x}{t}$, if V_x is greater than zero, the death
6	will be deliberate.
7	Knowing y to be 80 ft, we can determine
8	t by the equation,
9	$t = \sqrt{-\frac{2y}{g}} = \sqrt{-\frac{2(-80 \text{ ft})}{32 \text{ ft/sec}^2}} = 3.16 \text{ sec}$
10	Thus, knowing $x = 15$ ft,
11	$V_x = \frac{15 \text{ ft}}{3.16 \text{ sec}} = 4.75 \text{ ft/sec}$
12	Since the victim's velocity was significantly greater than
13	zero, the death must have been deliberate.

Note: Response created by Lackstrom

Besides culture-bound language and idiomatic usage, the student of EST is confronted in textbooks and examinations with discussion problems that are deliberately obscure. In point of fact, nearly all such problems will be obscure to some extent. Consider as an example the problem given as Table 2-10. There is nothing particularly idiomatic nor culture-bound in this problem. Nevertheless, discussion problems like that in Table 2-10 present enormous comprehension problems for students of EST. Often students will say, "I know the material of the course but I didn't understand the question he asked." This comprehension problem would be eased if there were a way to characterize the discourse structure and content of discussion problems and, likewise a way of characterizing in a definitive fashion the appropriate discourse response to such a problem. Given these two characterizations, materials could be developed to train students of EST to expect certain structures and content in the discussion problem and respond with appropriate discourse structures containing the content they would already have at their disposal for the answer.

The discourse structure and content of discussion problems appears straightforward in Tables 2-8, 2-9, and 2-10. There is a presentation of Facts and a statement of the Problem in the form of a question or questions (Table 2-11). The discourse-structure of the appropriate response will be evident from a consideration of Table 2-12.

From an examination of Table 2-12, in which the problem in Table 2-10 is answered, it will be evident that the answer to the problem is in the discourse

TABLE 2-13.   DISCUSSION PROBLEM AND RESPONSE: A TEXTBOOK'S ILLUSTRATIVE EXAMPLE

1	As shown in Fig. 9-3.2, a stone is thrown vertically
2	into the air from a tower 100 ft high at the same instant
3	that a second stone is thrown upward from the ground. The
4	initial velocity of the first stone is 50 fps and that of the
5	second stone is 75 fps.
6	When and where will the stones be
7	at the same height from the ground?
	SOLUTION:
8	The initial direction of motion for each stone is upward which
9	we therefore take as the positive sense for s, v, and a.
10	Applying Equ. (9-3.5) and noting that the acceleration
11	for freely falling bodies is $g = 32.2$ fps^2 directed downward
12	and therefore negative,
13	$[s = v_o t + \frac{1}{2} at^2]$
14	we obtain
15	For stone 1: $s_1 = 50t - 16.1t^2$ (a)
16	For stone 2: $s_2 = 75t - 16.1t^2$ (b)
17	From Fig. 9-3.2, $s_2 - s_1 = 100 = 25t$ or $t = 4$ sec
18	Substituting this value of t in Equs. (a) and (b), we have
19	$s_1 = -57.6$ ft $s_2 = +42.4$ ft
20	Hence, the stones pass each other 57.6 ft below the top of
21	the tower, or 42.4 ft from the ground.

Source: Singer (1975), p. 337

form of a logical argument. The argument begins with statements applying the Principle to the Facts (ln. 1-4) as given in the problem. Next (ln. 5-6), there is a statement of the Governing Principle in the form of an equation. What follows (ln. 7-11) is an application of the Facts to the Principle by means of a further equation, in which the values have been inserted. The argument ends with the Conclusions and solution to the problem in lines 12 and 13. This is just the structure of the logical argument found in Table 2-5. It appears that a discussion problem calls not simply for an answer but an answer given in a specific manner—an answer given as a logical argument. Logical arguments are the appropriate discourse forms through which to respond to discussion problems.

Confirmation of this observation comes from an examination of the way in which textbook authors answer their own discussion problems in the illustrative examples that they provide to students in the body of their texts. Here, we provide as an example, Table 2-13. The presentation of the problem in lines 1 through 7 contains the presentation of the Relevant Facts (ln. 1-5) and the Statement of the Problem (ln. 6-7). In the section headed Solution, we find Statements of Applicability of the Principle to the Facts in lines 8 through 12. The Principle is given as an equation in line 13. Subsequently, there is an

TABLE 2-14. DISCOURSE STRUCTURE OF THE DISCUSSION PROBLEM AND RESPONSE

I. DISCUSSION PROBLEM
   A. PRESENTATION OF THE RELEVANT FACTS
   B. STATEMENT OF THE PROBLEM/QUESTION

II. LOGICAL ARGUMENT
   A. STATEMENT OF APPLICABILITY (of the Governing Principle to the Relevant Facts)
   B. GOVERNING PRINCIPLE
   C. STATEMENT OF APPLICABILITY (of the Relevant Facts to the Governing Principle)
   D. CONCLUSION

application of the Facts to the Principle in lines 14 through 19. Finally the Conclusion, or solution, is reached in lines 20 and 21.

We find, then, that EST discourse includes two related and complementary forms: the logical argument and the discussion problem. The structure of the discussion problem has been given in Table 2-11. The structure of the logical argument has been summarized in Table 2-7. Further, we find that the logical argument is the discourse employed to respond to discussion problems. When the logical argument serves in this capacity we can expect the structure of the combined discourse to be that of Table 2-14. In this case the discussion problem takes over the role of presenting the Relevant Facts and the Problem. The logical argument begins with a Statement of Applicability of the Governing Principle to the Facts (cf. Tables 2-12 and 2-13). Again, note that, although there appears to be a preferred ordering of the structures within each of these discourse forms along the lines suggested by their presentations here, we are not yet at a point where we can make definitive or conclusive claims concerning the significance of the ordering or the ways in which it may appropriately deviate from the idealized form.

The significance of our findings thus far is that there appears to be a basis upon which to carefully define and characterize the structure and content of discussion problem and their answers, logical arguments. The work that remains to be done must focus upon those structures within the logical argument that appear to be most crucial for both the comprehension and composition of the arguments themselves, namely, the Statements of Applicability. Making statements of facts, principles, and conclusions is relatively straightforward. Composing appropriate statements of applicability linking facts to principles or principles to facts is a more demanding conceptual and linguistic task. It is perhaps this task more than any of the others that makes responses to discussion problems so difficult and challenges and intimidates students. If a precise description of the nature of applicability statements is forthcoming, it would go a long way to aid in the development of adequate EST materials.

Note

1. Henceforth *discourse structure* will be taken to be the outline of the steps employed by the author in the development of the argument. The steps are described broadly here in terms of their content and their role in contributing to the purpose of the whole argument.

References

Gamow, G. 1977. *The Evolutionary Universe. Cosmology +1: Readings from Scientific American,* pp. 12-19. W. H. Freeman.
Halliday, D. and R. Resnick. 1974. *Fundamentals of Physics.* John Wiley & Sons.
Lackstrom, J. E. 1977. "The Comprehension of EST: Arguments and Definitions." *Studies in Language Learning: Special Issue on LSP* 2.1, pp. 49-66.
Marder, D. 1960. *The Craft of Technical Writing.* Macmillan.
Miller, F., Jr. 1972. *College Physics.* 3rd ed. Harcourt, Brace, Jovanovich.
Ordway, R. J. 1966. *Earth Science.* D. Van Nostrand.
Singer, F. L. 1975. *Engineering Mechanics: Statics and Dynamics.* 3rd ed. Harper & Row.

Editorial Comments

This chapter discusses and relates for the first time to our knowledge two "discourse structures": the logical argument and the discussion-problem. It is part of a larger piece of research that aims to show "that empirical EST arguments follow closely the generally accepted descriptions of the scientific method." Lackstrom's analytical approach to discourse structures is of the "textualization" type mentioned by Widdowson in the previous chapter, with rhetorical notions playing a central role in the description of EST texts.

There is much to discuss in this chapter, but one aspect that caught our eye was the notion that a Governing Principle seems to be a kind of presupposition in that "the Governing Principle is assumed to be accepted or acceptable to the reader." Further, Lackstrom here introduces the idea that in EST texts a mathematical equation can serve as such a Governing Principle. We hope that scholars begin a careful study of the rhetorical functioning of mathematical equations in various EST genres.

Though there are important practical suggestions here, we include this chapter in this section because its main emphasis is to contribute new tools to EST descriptive analysis. For example, we have Lackstrom's perception that the discourse structure of the deductive logical syllogism corresponds to that of both the logical argument and the discussion problem and can be used to analyze both. At the University of Minnesota, this tool has been applied to the discourse of multiple choice tests, following Lackstrom's model (Hanges, in prep.). (We refer the reader to Urquhart (chap. 16) for a discussion of the way in which the deductive logical syllogism may relate to one type of "operation" used by a reader in interpreting an EST text.)

Another tool presented here is the use of the textbook author's sample answer as data for the analysis of discourse structures. This link may provide a model for the EST student to anticipate what sorts of discourse structures may be expected in a typical science course; thus the EST rhetorical analysis appears directly applicable in this case.

Finally, in this chapter Lackstrom mentions the potential necessity of (U.S.) cultural information in understanding introductory textbook materials.

3

A Taxonomic Approach to the Lexis of Science[1]

A. Godman, E. M. F. Payne

There are three levels that must be considered in the study of the language of science: *morphology, syntax,* and *lexis*. These three nonhierarchical but related levels function in the production of scientific statements. Linguistic analysis may operate at any of the levels but the production of statements in discourse requires all to function together. This chapter deals only with part of the lexis of science, with a passing reference to the other levels of language.

Grammar in scientific statements does not appear to differ from that in the general language, although the interpretation of some grammatical structures is different from, and in some cases more precise than, the interpretation considered normal in the general language. Apart from the biological sciences, the morphological process of affixation is the same in the sciences and in the general language. In the biological sciences, bound morphemes are extremely common in the derivation of many terms, with the majority of these morphemes being Greek in origin and a lesser number being of Latin origin. These morphemes are additional to the normal repertoire of morphemes of the language.

Examples of bound morphemes in the biological sciences are *HAEM* (blood); *CYT* (cell); *LYS* (destroy by dissolution); *SIS* (a process); *PATH* (causes harm). Hence we find the terms *haemocytolysis*—the process of destruction of (red) blood cells by dissolution— and *haemopathic*—adversely affecting the circulatory system.

A careful selection of the available affixes leads to an enhanced precision of statement. For example: *-IVE* (denotes an agent), *-OUS* (describes possessing) and *-AL* (is a general adjectival suffix). These suffixes can be applied thus: A chicken's liver is a *nutritive* organ to the chicken, a *nutritious* food to a carnivore, and in both animals the liver takes part in a *nutritional* process. Similarly, an experience can be percept*ual*, but the observer is percep*tive*. Table 3-1 gives further illustrations of morphemes. Additionally, syntax appears to be identical in both general and scientific contexts although scientific writing may use some syntactic structures more frequently than others.

The term *concept* describes those elements, or related elements, (i.e., a proposition) in the realm of thought that are expressed as a statement in language and that form in the mind of the reader an identical set of related elements. If the statement does not produce a congruity of concept in the reader's mind, (i.e., store of knowledge) then there is not a full understanding of the proposition. A lack of congruity may arise in two ways. Firstly, there may be a failure on the part of the author to produce unamibiguous and clear statements. Secondly, there may be, on the part of the reader, a failure to recognize (a) the function of the lexis or (b) the various functions of the grammatical categories.

THE LEXIS OF SCIENCE

Scientific statements contain *technical terms* and *common language terms used technically* (cf. Selinker (1979) section 3.2.)[2], both of which will be discussed in more detail below. Hitherto, teachers have concentrated on explanations of technical terms, while nontechnical terms have generally been neglected, as it has been assumed that they were understood. We hope to demonstrate here that this attitude leads to serious inadequacies of understanding, and hence, because of the relation between lexis, grammar, and concept, the other levels of the language of science are also affected.

Technical terms are those for which there is a congruity of concept between all scientists, whatever the language used. For example, *resistor* describes a specific component of an electrical circuit. The term *electron* describes a hypothetical entity with detailed properties, different aspects of which may be emphasized in the definition depending on whether one's context is physics or chemistry. A *polymer* is a type of chemical substance formed in a particular way and possessing well-defined properties. A *mammal* is an animal with certain specific characteristics. In each case, the properties or characteristics can be enumerated to define the object in an unambiguous manner. Word classes, other than nouns, can also be so defined in a similar way. Nontechnical terms in scientific statements consist of all other terms occurring in the language of science.

TABLE 3-1. EXAMPLES OF BOUND AND AFFIXED MORPHEMES IN SCIENCE

Morpheme	Meaning	Example	Meaning
ptera	a wing or winglike	*exopterygotous*	wings starting from folds on the outside of the body
pinna	a feather or featherlike; or a fin	*pinnatiped*	having webbed feet, as do some aquatic birds
dactyl	a digit or appendage, e.g., finger, toe	*pentadactylism*	the state of having five digits on a limb
caud	a tail	*acaudate*	without a tail as a characteristic feature
hetero-	other, different	*heteromorphic*	having different forms at different times
homo-	the same, alike	*homomorphic*	having the same form
xero-	dry	*xerophobous*	not tolerating drought
halo-	common salt, salty, saline	*haloplankton*	organisms drifting in the sea
-meter	an instrument that measures accurately	*galvanometer*	an instrument for accurately measuring electric current
-scope	an instrument for qualitative observation	*galvanoscope*	an instrument for detecting electric current
-clast	a destroyer, agent for breaking down materials	*osteoclast*	a cell that absorbs or breaks down bone matrix
-icide	a killer of a named animal	*molluscicide*	a chemical for killing snails or other molluscs

THE VOCABULARY OF TECHNICAL TERMS

Every technical term is related to other terms concerned with the same phenomenon, or related phenomena, or to terms concerned with hypotheses or theoretical concepts. In a group of related terms, any one term is defined completely only when all the other terms are defined. Hence the terms of a group are part of the meaning of any one particular term of the group. For example, the phenomenon of the flow of electric current is associated with a group of terms that can be conveniently divided into subgroups (e.g., *resistor, resistance, resistivity,* and *conductor, conductance, conductivity, superconductivity,* etc.). The meaning of any one of these terms involves the meaning of all the terms in the group. For this reason it is advantageous to group technical terms for meaning and thus build up a hierarchy of groups. This leads to the display of technical vocabularies in a taxonomic fashion. Table 3-2 is such a display of technical vocabulary with terms arranged in groups. Group A contains terms from physics, groups B and C contain terms from biology, and group D contains terms from chemistry. It should be noted that all terms in a particular group belong to the same word class. The groups also represent different principles of grouping.

Group A contains the terms that spring readily to mind when a physicist contemplates a moving object approaching another object that may be in motion or may be stationary. The moving object possesses *momentum*. It makes an *impact* with a second object and gives the second object an *impulse*. The overall result is a *collision,* which, depending on the material of the two objects, can be considered *elastic* or *inelastic* (at an elementary level). The *impulse* of force on a body is measured by the change in *momentum* of the body. During a *collision* between two bodies *momentum* is *conserved*. *Impact* gives rise to *impulse*, hence the *point* of *impact* can be of importance in a *collision*.

Group B contains the adjectives used to describe circumstances, conditions, or factors that affect the growth and life of an organism. The list displays a gradation in change from the most to the least suitable circumstances, and such for the organism. Contrast this with group A, which displays concepts of equal importance.

Group C contains adjectives that describe different types of environment for an animal. Terms from this group can be used to demonstrate the precision of meaning of a scientific term. For instance, *amphibian* describes an animal of the class *Amphibia,* who is adapted for life on land and in water but must become temporarily *aquatic* for the purpose of reproduction. There are also structural and morphological characteristics of this class: *amphibiotic* describes an animal that has part of its life in water and part on land (e.g., one with larvae living in water and adults living on land); *amphibious* describes an animal adapted for living both on land and in water. A duck is an *amphibious* animal but is not *amphibiotic* or *amphibian*. A frog is *amphibiotic, amphibian,* and *amphibious*. A dragonfly is *amphibiotic* but is not *amphibious* or *amphibian*.

TABLE 3-2. TAXONOMIC DISPLAY OF SOME TECHNICAL TERMS

Physics	Biology		Chemistry
A	*B*	*C*	*D*
(Related by the event of collision between two bodies)	(Gradation)	(Habit and mode of life)	(Processes and descriptive terms in separation of two solids)
MOMENTUM	ADVANTAGEOUS	AQUATIC	FILTRATION
IMPACT	BENEFICIAL	MARINE	FILTRATE
IMPULSE	FAVORABLE	FRESHWATER	RESIDUE
COLLISION	ECCRITIC	ESTUARINE	DECANTATION
ELASTIC COLLISION	TOLERABLE	RIPARIAN	SUPERNATANT LIQUID
INELASTIC COLLISION	ADVERSE	TERRESTRIAL	CRYSTALLIZATION
CONSERVATION OF MOMENTUM	HARSH	TERRICOLOUS	FRACTIONAL CRYSTALLIZATION
		AMPHIBIAN	MOTHER LIQUOR
		AMPHIBIOUS	SUBLIMATION
		AMPHIBIOTIC	
		ARBOREAL	
		AERIAL	

Group D contains terms that apply to processes, all connected with purification and separation and so to related terms. *Filtration* is a subprocess in *crystallization* and may be in its own right a purification process. *Filtrate* and *residue* are the closely related results of *filtration*. *Decantation* is a method of making a coarse separation of liquid and solid and may precede *filtration*.

THE VOCABULARY OF NONTECHNICAL TERMS

These terms may be divided into two broad categories: There are (1) terms of the general language; for example, logical terms such as *coordinators, subordinators, determiners, quantifiers, adjuncts,* and (2) terms that can be described as a basic list for usage in science. The functions of the logical terms of the general language remain unaltered in scientific statements, while the functions of the terms of the basic list are described below. In this chapter we only discuss type (2).

The terms of the basic list include terms that appear on first sight to belong to the general language, but have, in fact, more limiting definition in their use in scientific statements. The terms are given a precise meaning and are thus "purged of the ambiguity and vagueness of their meaning" (Caws 1964). Scientific information is provided by this limiting definition. As with technical terms, terms of the basic list can be related and consequently listed in "clusters."[3] Within the cluster, each of the terms is part of the meaning of any one particular term, and thus terms of the basic list can be assembled in a taxonomic fashion.

Table 3-3 is a display of six groups of terms from a basic list of usage in science. Each group, it should be noted, contains terms of the same word class, so in group D, the term *study* is a noun and not a verb. The terms themselves are used in the general language, as is evident, but in scientific statements, the use is restricted as described below.

In group A, *occupy* and *establish* differ from the remaining verbs. All the verbs are concerned with matter associated with a place, the first two verbs being concerned with putting the matter in the place and the remaining five with taking the matter away. In each case the verb "focuses" on the place and the result of the process. In brief, *vacate* focuses on the place after an object has been removed (e.g. a position *vacated* by an electron); *evacuate* focuses on the place after all matter has been removed and emphasizes that nothing remains; *exhaust* focuses on the matter in the place and its removal; *dislocate* focuses on an object that is previously fixed or bound to a place and is subsequently displaced; *empty* is also the verb to use with liquids, whereas *exhaust* is particularly used with gases. Other groups of verbs will focus on the object, or matter, leaving a place (e.g., *extract, eject, emanate,* with their associated groups). Within group A, the terms exhibit a "cognate relationship" with definite characteristics. Each term is dependent for a full appreciation of its meaning on the meaning of the other terms in the group. In a particular scientific context, only one term is normally applicable.

TABLE 3-3. TAXONOMIC DISPLAY OF SOME TERMS FROM THE VOCABULARY OF THE BASIC LIST

A	B	C
OCCUPY	HAPPEN	REPLACE
ESTABLISH	OCCUR	DISPLACE
EMPTY	TAKE PLACE	SUBSTITUTE
VACATE	RECUR	EXCHANGE
EVACUATE	BRING ABOUT	INTERCHANGE
EXHAUST	INFLUENCE	
DISLOCATE	INDUCE	
	ENCOURAGE	
	FAVOR	
	EVOKE	

D	E	F
STUDY	FUNDAMENTAL	LIKENESS
ASSUMPTION	BASIC	SIMILARITY
POSTULATE	DISTINCTIVE	CORRESPONDENCE
DISTINCTION	SPECIAL	AGREEMENT
INFERENCE	PARTICULAR	ACCORDANCE
EVIDENCE	GENERAL	CONFORMITY
DEDUCTION	COMMON	CONGRUITY
INDUCTION	ANOMOLOUS	CONGRUENCE
CONCLUSION		

Group C contains verbs that describe the processes by which an object is moved from a position, with descriptions as follows. *Replace*: another object is put in its position, the focus is on the action. *Displace*: an object is forcibly removed from its position, the focus is on the removal of the object. *Substitute*: an object is replaced by another object, which is less suitable, the focus is on the object substituted. *Exchange*: two objects are moved to occupy each other's place. *Interchange*: to exchange similar or identical objects. For example, a fused electric light bulb is *exchanged* for a new one, but two working bulbs of the same wattage are *interchanged*.

The descriptions of terms given in the two previous paragraphs indicate there would appear to be greater precision of meaning of such terms when used in scientific statements. It also indicates that, although the terms are concerned with the same process or type of process, they are distinguished by focusing attention on a particular aspect of the process. Thus for a group of terms, certain parameters can be abstracted that give a guide to the use of the term. The parameters associated with a group of terms are illustrated in Table 3-4.

The diffuse term *change* can be used in place of any of the other terms, but there is an apparent loss of precision of meaning in the process. The parameters illustrate the way in which the meaning of one term is defined clearly only when all the remaining terms of the set are defined. It is not possible to give full details of a definition by setting out a table such as shown in Table 3-4, only the important differences are detailed. The table can be used, for example, to elucidate the following statement: "The voltage of the electricity mains in

TABLE 3-4. SEMANTIC-FIELD CHART SHOWING PARAMETERS OF MEANING

DIFFUSE TERM		change (v.t.)					
ESSENTIALS		transform	transmute	convert	convert		
DETAILS	Different Purpose				adapt		
	Several Changes						vary (v.t.)
	One Change			adjust		alter	
	Same Purpose					modify	
		PROPERTY	ELEMENT	SUBSTANCE	DEVICE	CONFIGUR-ATION	QUANTITY QUALITY
						PROCESS	CIRCUM-STANCE
				OBJECT			

Note: The word *convert* appears twice because it belongs to two clusters.

England is 240V and it is unlikely to be *altered* to 110V. The voltage can be altered by using a transformer, so a transformer can be used to *adapt* an English electric shaver for use on a 110V-system. A radio set has a control for tuning. When turning into a station the control is *adjusted* to receive the signal without distortion. The volume of sound can be *varied* by a further control. A radio designed for use in temperate climates is preferably *modified* for use in tropical regions for humidity changes" (Godman, forthcoming).

THE VERB IN THE BASIC LIST

There are many scientific contexts where only one verb is suitable for linking subject and object or stating a dynamic situation. Such verbs are contextually determined in many cases. For example, the change of position of an object from one place to the other can be discribed by the following verbs: *transfer, transport, translocate, carry, convey, conduct, transmit*. The choice of verb depends on the context and hence on the scientific knowledge of the author of a statement. For instance, from our experience as scientists, it is only correct to say: (a) an electron *carries* a negative charge; (b) oxygen is *transported* by red blood cells; (c) glass *transmits* light waves; (d) a copper wire *conducts* an electric current. Each verb describes unambiguously the action connecting the subject and the object.

A lack of understanding of the verb in a scientific statement may lead to a failure to form a correct concept, the verb in the language of the statement not arousing the correct elements of thought in the reader's mind. Hence when the reader wishes to think about, or to remember, the statement to use the elements for his or her own expression of a new statement the result is quite likely to be incorrect. This is best illustrated by the statements displayed in Table 3-5. The correct answer uses the verb *conduct* because that is the action of a pipe taking fluid from the gall bladder to the duodenum. The term *convey* can also be used, but is less precise in biological sciences, although commonly used in medical sciences. The elements of thought erroneously aroused in the reader's mind from the incorrect statements, are shown in the right-hand column. These answers taken from an elementary situation show lack of understanding of the verbs cited above.

The level of knowledge involved in Table 3-5 is elementary and the examples exhibit looseness of vocabulary. When each one of a set of verbs in a lengthy scientific statement is misunderstood, or imperfectly understood, the final elements in the realm of thought produce a vague final proposition. Incorrect or imperfect understanding of the function of the verbs in a piece of text is, in our experience, possibly one of the greatest obstacles to the comprehension of scientific statements.

32 / ENGLISH FOR ACADEMIC AND TECHNICAL PURPOSES

TABLE 3-5. TYPICAL ERRORS IN SCIENTIFIC STATEMENTS CULLED FROM EXAMINATION PAPERS

Q. STATE ONE FUNCTION OF THE BILE DUCT
A. TO CONDUCT BILE FROM THE GALL BLADDER TO THE DUODENUM
(A biological structure has four possible characteristics: structure, position, function, and mechanism.)

Mistaken Answer	Possible Erroneous Inference
1. Transports bile to the duodenum.	Bile duct would move to the duodenum taking bile with it.
2. To carry bile from the liver to the duodenum.	Bile duct would need a receptacle for bile and would move from the liver to the duodenum.
3. Directs the flow of bile from the liver to the duodenum.	Bile duct could be a channel, and not a pipe; ignorance of structure.
4. Takes bile from the liver to the duodenum.	Diffuse statement implying complete ignorance of structure.
5. Brings bile from the liver to the duodenum.	Observer situated in duodenum; ignorance of structure and function.
6. Bile is gotten rid of by the bile duct.	Ambiguous, diffuse, and definitely erroneous.
7. Is to get rid of waste material to the outside that is not needed by the body from tubes.	Misunderstanding of term *function* (a well-muddled answer).

THE DEFINITION AND MEANING OF TERMS

The grouping of terms into clusters on the basis of a cognate relationship displays their similarity. The precision of definition is then given by examining the differences between the terms. The similarity of the terms arises from the same basic concept, or concepts, they share. This method of definition is hidden by an alphabetical arrangement of terms in a dictionary.

The cognate relationship can be of a variety of kinds. One kind is cause and effect. For example, in the terms below:

Stress (n.)   A force applied to a solid body.
Strain (n.)   The deformation or distortion produced by a stress.
Tension (n.)   A stress that tends to extend a body.
Compression (n.)   A stress that tends to reduce the length of a body.
Shear stress (n.)   Two forces, of equal magnitude but opposite direction, applied to opposite faces of a solid body.
Shear (n.)   The strain produced by a shear stress.

The meanings of the terms, not their full definitions, are given above, but there is enough information to see that the entries, which would be separated in an alphabetical arrangement, reinforce each other in explanation.

Cognate relations can also indicate a gradation in a concept. For example, the following terms relate to the reaction of an organism to prevailing conditions:

Tolerate (v.t.)   To react to conditions that are not beneficial and not adverse but could become adverse if the variation is too great; for example, an estuarine organism *tolerates* a wide variation in salinity of the water, but if the salinity becomes too great, the conditions become adverse.

Withstand (v.t.)   To react to adverse conditions in such a way as to continue existence; for example, certain plants *withstand* a lack of water.

Survive (v.t.)   To withstand adverse conditions until the conditions cease; for example, a plant *survived* a drought lasting for two months.

Persist (v.i.)   To survive several adverse conditions; for example, certain shrubs *persist* in their growth despite several dry seasons.

As will be realized, one situation merges into another, and the divisions are not clear cut. However, with meanings as given above, which are not full definitions, it is possible to pick the correct term to describe a situation needed in a statement.

COGNATE RELATIONSHIPS

Groups of terms have been illustrated in Tables 3-2, 3-3, and 3-4. Each of these groups contains terms exhibiting a close cognate relationship with each other. The principle of cognate relationship can be extended to relationships that are less close and eventually distant. The fewer the similarities in relationship, the greater the number of terms that can be included in the group. By using such principles of close and distant cognate relationship, a taxonomic tree can be devised. Many relationships will be connected in a hierarchical fashion, especially when presented in the two dimensions to which a diagram confines them. The true arrangement of cognate relationships must, however, be polydimensional, as groups of terms separated on branches may recombine and reseparate, and semantic relations, such as antonymy and converseness, may provide further links. An arrangement could thus exhibit *anastomosis* (see figure 3-1).

Figure 3-2 is a taxonomic arrangement of terms related to the most primitive term, *change*. All terms are verbs. Each head term is the most diffuse of a group of terms. The arrangement encourages a search for semantic and conceptual relations. This figure shows the complexity of the total structure.

34 / ENGLISH FOR ACADEMIC AND TECHNICAL PURPOSES

Bifurcate: To form two branches so that the distal end of a structure is V-shaped.

Branch: To form branches from a main structure and to repeat the process several times.

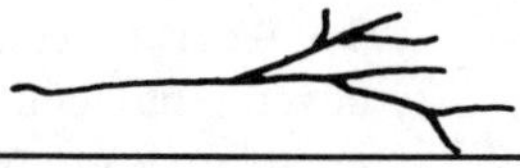

Arborize: To branch repeatedly, similar to the branching of a tree, so that the main structure forms very many small terminal structures, like the twigs on a tree.

Anastomose: Of tubes, ducts, vessels, fibers, to branch and rejoin to form a network of connecting vessels, and such, so that various alternative pathways exist, allowing a fluid, nervous impulse, and so forth, to find an alternative path if any one particular path becomes blocked (e.g., blood capillaries, nerves, the veins in a leaf, all anastomose).
ANASTOMISIS: the formation of a network, the structures of which anastomose.

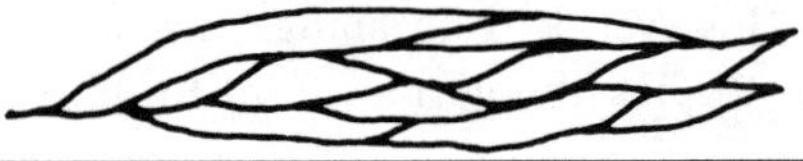

Ramify: To branch repeatedly, or to anastomose, forming a network that covers a defined area or space (e.g., from the solar plexus, nerves ramify to the various viscera; the mycelium of a fungus ramifies over the surface of a plant tissue). The focus is on the covering of the defined area or space. Contrast the previous four terms in which the focus is on the formation of the structure. The term can be used when more than one structure ramifies over a specified area or space.

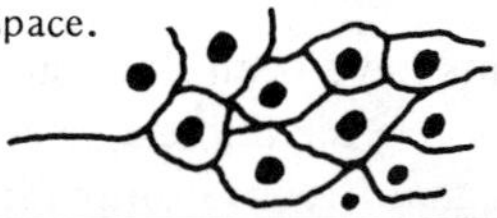

Interdigitate: Of two structures, to grow towards each other, and to branch or put out projections, so that the branches of one structure lie between the branches of the other structure, and the two structures become linked but not connected (e.g., the villi of the placenta and the villi of the uterus interdigitate so that the constituents of blood plasma are interchanged between the placenta and the uterus, although the circulatory systems of mother and fetus are completely separate).

FIGURE 3-1.   A DEFINITION OF ANASTOMOSIS, WITH MEMBERS OF ITS CLUSTER

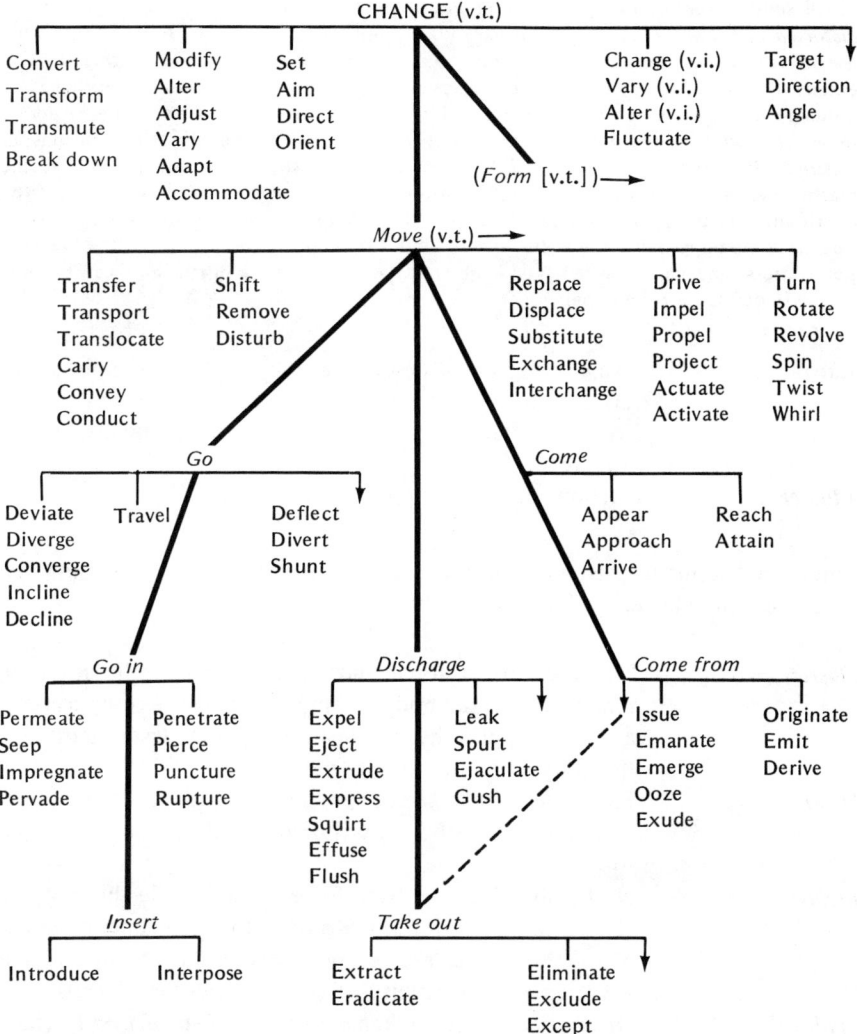

FIGURE 3-2.   A TAXONOMIC ARRANGEMENT OF TERMS

*ADVANTAGES OF A TAXONOMICAL
TREATMENT OF VOCABULARY*

Apart from the precision in meaning and the gradation of meaning that can be obtained from taxonomic grouping, such an arrangement could provide a firm basis for units of teaching in the language of science. As an example of this, the vocabulary necessary for considering the phenomenon of elasticity is now discussed:

All solids either exhibit *elasticity* or *plasticity*. On applying *stress* an *elastic* solid is *distorted* and a *plastic* solid is *deformed*. Plastic and elastic are incompatible terms, as the use of one denies the use of the other. An *inelastic* solid under stress is *distorted* to an extent that is negligible for practical purposes (e.g., concrete can be considered inelastic, although its elasticity becomes apparent in high-rise buildings). An elastic solid is *extended* under *tension*, and the extension is *directly proportional* to the stress. A solid has an *elastic limit*; if the limit is *exceeded* the solid becomes plastic. Metals under stress become plastic (i.e., *malleable* and *ductile*). The stress on a metal can be increased *beyond* the elastic limit to the *yield point* and finally to the *breaking point*. A *brittle* solid is elastic, but has a breaking point *below* the elastic limit. *Compressing* the solid *raises* the breaking point stress, and can raise it beyond the elastic limit, so that a brittle solid can become plastic (Godman, forthcoming).

Cluster A	Adjectival terms describing the reaction of a body to stress.
Cluster B	Terms of state for the effect of stress and the disposition to stress.
Cluster C	Actions of a body under stress.

The individual terms in cluster A will now be given meanings, and in so doing the terms in the other clusters will also be mentioned.

Elastic	Extended by a force and contracts when the force is removed (i.e., the body is temporarily distorted by a force and the original shape is restored by the elastic nature of the body when the force is removed).
Plastic	Extended by a force and remains extended when the force is removed (i.e., the body is permanently deformed by the force).
Inelastic	Negligibly extended by a force so that while the body is elastic, the distortion is insignificant (e.g., a concrete pillar is normally considered to be inelastic, but at the top of a skyscraper the elasticity of concrete can be appreciated).
Malleable	Of an elastic body taken past the limit of elasticity (i.e., the elastic limit is exceeded) and hence becoming plastic, deformable by hitting.
Ductile	Of an elastic body taken past the limit of elasticity, and hence becoming plastic, deformable by tension or by compression.

From the statement above, relevant clusters of terms emerge. For example (a) *elastic, plastic, inelastic, malleable, ductile*; (b) *distortion, deformation, deformity, deformability*; (c) *extend, contract, restore, exceed*. It can also be noted that some of these terms are more apt in other contexts and can thus be included in other groups of terms.

Delicacy in definition arises from considering the term, or associated terms, in different parts of the taxonomy. For example, *light* can be considered at four stages of delicacy: (1) ray optics, with associated terms or mirrors, lenses, and optical instruments; (2) light as a wave motion with prisms, dispersion, interference, and diffraction; (3) light as an electro-magnetic wave, and the place of the visible spectrum in the electromagnetic spectrum, together with the associated quantum theory; and (4) light and the part it plays in the theory of relativity.

Finally, the advantages of a taxonomic approach are also seen in translation from one language to another. Equivalent clusters in the two languages can be compared. It is not likely that there will be a one-to-one correspondence in terms from the basic list. A comparison of the clusters will enable the most appropriate term to be selected; the necessary additional information needed to obtain as near a congruity of concept in translation as is possible will then be brought into focus.

SUMMARY AND CONCLUSION

A term is dependent for a full appreciation of its meaning on the meaning of the other terms in the cluster of which it is a member. Terms in a cluster (e.g., *tolerate, withstand, survive, persist*) may be difficult to define when in isolation and may also exhibit circularity in their definitions. Such difficulties are met in the conventional alphabetical treatment of terms but can be avoided by a taxonomic arrangement.

Clusters were originally assembled on the bases of our own intuitive knowledge of scientific language. From this beginning, an analysis of the bases of clusters was formulated; time has been insufficient and a full analysis has yet to be made. The following bases of cognate relationships have been identified, and further analysis, it is hoped, will extend the list: (1) terms associated with a process, a simple action, or an event; (2) descriptive terms of equal importance concerning a phenomenon or related phenomena; (3) terms exhibiting a gradation of quality, quantity, property, or characteristic; (4) terms of cause and effect; and (5) terms of related states.

GLOSSARY

Cluster: A collection of terms that exhibit a close cognate relationship.

Cognate relationship: (a) Terms whose concepts have much in common are cognate, also (b) terms developed from the original concept are cognate. An example of (a) is given in Table 3-2, clusters B and C. Terms in Cluster B have in common a description of the conditions under which an organism can live. Terms in Cluster C have in common a description of the environment in which an organism can live. An example of (b) is given in Table 2-3, cluster C, in which the terms have the same conceptual basis of an object being moved from its place. Clusters can be grouped together on the basis of a more distant cognate relationship. For example, cluster C, Table 2-3 can be grouped with verbs describing ways of moving an object. These clusters in turn can form part of a group whose common conceptual basis is that of *move*. The taxonomic arrangement thus exhibits a hierarchical system similar to that used in the biological sciences; that is, the greater the number of characteristics the fewer the members of the set, and vice versa.

Focus[4]: The direction of a person's attention to a particular part of a process or to a state of affairs. In a process there is generally an agent carrying out the process and a recipient in whom or on which the process operates. Focus can direct attention to the agent, or the recipient, or the process. For example, the flow of water in a pipe can be stopped by an object in the pipe. When the term *block* is used, the focus is on the pipe, and the pipe is the agent in the process. When the term *observer* is used the focus is on the flow of water, which is the recipient of the process. Saying that a pipe is *obstructed* directs attention to the stopping of the flow of water and no mention is made of the object; saying that the pipe is blocked directs attention to the pipe, and there need be no flow to be stopped. Verbs thus may occur in pairs, focusing attention on the agent or the recipient of the focus, as for example:

Focus

Agent	*Recipient*
Block	Obstruct
Constrict	Impede
Conduct	Flow
Restrict	Hinder

The aspects of focus in relation to verbs have, to date, been examined only in specific cases and a generality seen in that focus can be directed to agent, recipient, or process. Other aspects have been noted concerning place, object, or action, but no particular pattern has emerged as yet.

Diffuse: Describes a term the meaning of which is not restricted; for example, from Figure 3-1, the term *move* is diffuse as it can be applied to many situations with no restriction in its meaning. On the other hand, the term *extract* is not diffuse as its meaning is restricted.

Definition: A clear description that is exclusive and which allows a term to be discussed without misunderstanding.

Meaning: A clear description that is not necessarily exclusive.

Explanation: A statement or a set of statements that give reasons for each assertion.

Congruity: A relationship of a one-to-one correspondence in the essential characteristics, properties, qualities, or features with an object or concept under discussion; it is not a correspondence in all such detail; for example, two triangles of identical shape can be congruent, but if one is red and one is blue, they are not identical.

Precision: Results from the availability of the essential items of correspondence that lead to congruity. A gradation of precision can thus exist from the availability of such items. The greater the availability of these items, the greater is the restriction on the definition on the meaning of a term.

Notes

1. We are indebted to Prof. L. Selinker of the University of Michigan for valuable comments in the preparation of this manuscript.

2. *Editors' note*: "Common language terms used technically" are hereafter referred to as "nontechnical terms." For an explanation of other terms used in this chapter, the reader should refer to the Glossary.

3. See Glossary for terms used in this chapter.

4. *Editors' note*: For more on the concept of *focus* in scientific lexis, see A. Godman, "The Language of Science from the View Point of the Writer of Science Textbooks" in *"Teaching English for Science and Technology,* ed. J. Richards, Singapore: RELC, 1975, 71-78.

References

Caws, P. 1964, *Philosophy of Science,* D. Van Nostrand.
Godman, A. In prep. *A Course on EST.*
Selinker, L. 1979. "On the Use of Informants in Discourse Analysis and 'Language for Specialized Purposes'." *IRAL* 17.3, pp. 189-215.

Editorial Comments

This chapter provides a framework for semantic analysis of EST lexis, as background to a learner's dictionary currently being compiled by the authors for Longmans. The latter is a long-awaited "taxonomic" dictionary of lexis in basic physics, chemistry, and biology.

It has been suggested that Godman and Payne's approach lies in the componential-analysis tradition of semantic theory, with the addition of presuppositional notions such as "focus." Their presentation of specific taxonomic displays of terms in "clusters" is interesting and should prove of practical value. In a cluster technical terms are shown to be related in various ways to other technical terms concerned with the same phenomenon. A central claim of the authors is that one cannot define a technical term completely without serious reference to the other terms in the same domain. This is obviously a very strong claim and one that, we feel, should lead to considerable discussion and research among EST scholars. Perhaps, the next stage of research should be devoted to developing *theoretical criteria* as to how one determines what composes a cluster. Some potential applications of such an approach to the classroom are to be seen in the section entitled, "Advantages of a Taxonomical Treatment of Vocabulary."

We believe also that Godman and Payne have proposed in their work a new type of error analysis (see table 3-5), one where a sentence may be "deviant" *both* in terms of language *and* subject-matter context. Data such as these may add some evidence to the view that grammatical description cannot be successfully separated from concerns of discourse and context—genre-based subject-matter concerns, in this case.

L.S.
E.T.

4 The Function of One Type of Particle in a Chemistry Textbook[1]

John Swales

It has become fashionable in academic discussion and description of English for Specific Purposes (ESP) work to lay strong emphasis on the need to study types of English from the viewpoint of rhetorical function and subsequently to prepare learning and teaching materials that are "rhetorically focused." However, sensitivity to the structure of discourse does not necessarily mean sensitivity to the use of language, just as identification of the forms of language exhibited in a text does not necessarily indicate appreciation of why such forms have been chosen. The importance of considering rhetorical function was recognized early by "The Washington School," as most prominently represented by Louis Trimble and Larry Selinker, but neither has ever been persuaded—unlike some recent converts to the specialism—that adequate categorization of discoursal functions in a text is itself a sufficient basis for the creation of quality ESP programs. Rather, the work with which Louis Trimble is associated has long been concerned with establishing the existence of "grammatical-rhetorical dependencies," and with elucidating such relationships as those between choice of articles and tenses and the communicative intent of scientific and technical writers. This type of study, recently described by Widdowson (1977 and chapter 1, this volume) as "textualization," typically begins from observing that some of the ways in which language is being used in a piece of technical writing are not fully explicable in terms of the statements and explanations found in traditional grammars or modern linguistic descriptions and will only be understood after paying attention to the purpose of the particular text and the structure and function of its various components. An example of this approach is the discussion of *may* and the inconsistent ellipsis of the definite article in Todd Trimble and Trimble (1977); this study on the role of a restricted class of participials in a chemistry text purports to be another.

Studies of scientific and technical English consistently show that writers in this field typically make greater use of attributive *-en* participles[2] than is the case in most other varieties of the language (e.g., Barber 1962). A proportion of these participles are "bare"; that is, they do not have any clause, phrase, or modifying adverb attached to them at the surface-structure level. Here are two examples of such participles from the prescribed chemistry text for Preliminary, Faculty of Science, University of Khartoum,[3] the first being a postmodifier, the second a premodifier:

1. The curve *shown* is a heating curve corresponding to a uniform addition of heat (p. 191).
2. The fact that the *emitted* light is intermittent hints that the electricity flows through the tube as a beam of discrete particles (p. 36).

The aim here is to examine the factors that affect a scientist's choice of pre- or postmodifying position for these bare participles and at the same time to investigate factors affecting a decision to use such a participle as against, on the one hand, its omission, and, on the other, against a decision to include more information by using a participial phrase, prepositional or otherwise. In this way it may be possible to throw light on a noteworthy feature of scientific English that largely has been ignored in published EST courses. Ultimately, of course, the hope is to be able to offer scientists, who are not native speakers of English but who either need or wish to write in that language, useful guidelines for "when to use a bare participle" and "where to place it."

It would seem that the only detailed discussion of the factors affecting the position of these single or bare participles in recent linguistic literature is that by Bolinger (1967). Huddleston (1971) does not deal with it in his extensive study of the sentence in scientific English, nor is there any extended treatment in any of the well-known teaching grammars. However, inevitably enough, Jesperson (1949) does have a number of pertinent observations to make. Jesperson claimed that the position tends to be determined by the essentially adjectival or verbal character of the participle. "When participles have become completely adjectives, they are generally placed before the substantive ... when the verbal character of the participle is present to the mind of the speaker or writer, especially when the time of the action and (or) the agent is thought of, there is a greater inclination to place it after the substantive" (Jesperson 1928, vol. 2, p. 382). Of course, a criterion based on an assessment of how fully a participle is deverbalized raises as many problems as it purports to solve, but the suggestion by Jesperson that postposition may be favored when the writer does not wish to fully neutralize the agent may be of particular relevance to scientific English.

Although Quirk et al. (1972) do not deal directly with the question of position (perhaps because of their decision to deal with premodification and postmodification separately under separate chapter headings) they do make the claim that premodification seems to require the semantic feature of "permanence." They contrast *a lost purse* with *a found purse* and go on to say that "*a lost purse* is grammatical, because although a purse is no longer regarded as 'found' after it has been retrieved, a purse will be regarded as 'lost' throughout the period of its disappearance" (Quirk et al. 1972:911). They also note that as the indefinite article favors the habitual and permanent and the definite article the specific and temporary, it is likely that bare participles will premodify in indefinite (and generic) NPs and postmodify in definite NPs. Given that many NPs are definite because the definite determiners have an anaphoric function, a connected point was made in an EST textbook: "It seems that the past participle only follows the nominal when it refers back to something explained more fully in previous sentences" (Swales 1971:139).

The discussion in Quirk et al. probably owes something to Bolinger's earlier article (1967), in which he contrasts "action" postmodifying participles, as in *the jewels stolen,* with "characteristic" premodifying participles, as in *the stolen jewels.* The former he considers to be derived from a passive, the latter not. As far as *-en* participles are concerned, Bolinger takes as the clearest cases of "characteristic" those attributions that describe leaving a mark; that is, *dented bells* but not *rung bells.* "When one scratches one's head the result is not *a scratched head* but when one scores a glass surface the result is *a scratched surface*." With nonmarking verbs "characteristic" is looked on as being a feature recognized as permanent within the culture (cf., *a lost purse* above).

This brief survey of a rather scant literature indicates that the following features appear to be particularly relevant to decisions about *-en* participial position in English as a whole: The prenominal position of a bare participle can be associated with permanent, characterizable and/or general features; the postnominal position with temporary (or indeed temporal), specific, and/or anaphoric features. However, it would not be altogether surprising if not all of these were important factors in determining choice of position in a piece of "special English" such as a chemistry textbook; or indeed if other variables did not emerge as being relevant.

There were 257 bare, attributive *-en* participles occurring in single-noun NPs[4] in the first 350 pages of the Sienko and Plane chemistry text. One hundred twenty-nine of these referred to events and processes that take place independently of a direct human agent; that is, to those scientific phenomena that occur without human mediation at the instant of their occurrence. Of the four examples that follow the first two have pre-posed participles, the last two post-posed.

3. These interatomic spacings can be determined for x-ray and spectral studies of *bound* atoms (p. 69).
4. The tiny bubbles that form when water is heated are due to the fact that *dissolved* air becomes less soluble at high temperature (p. 223).
5. Another convenient method of preparation is the liberation of water by sodium, but the reaction is dangerous because the hydrogen *evolved* frequently catches fire (p. 8).
6. When atoms combine, the bonds *formed* are such that each atom is surrounded by a complete octet of electrons (p. 96).

A second group of about seventy-five participles apparently refers to various mental and physical acts by a "recoverable" chemist (or chemists), although by virtue of the participle being bare there is naturally no surface-structure agent. In the first two examples the participles are again pre-posed.

7. Some of these reactions will lead to products of *known* structure (p. 58).
8. Natural laws describe *observed* phenomena (p. 13).
9. The masses *taken* are of a size that can be handled with the usual laboratory apparatus (pp. 29-30).
10. If the above experiment is repeated using as a light source a flame to which a vaporizable salt is added, the spectrum *obtained* is not continuous (p. 51).

The Bolinger/Quirk distinction between a prenominal participle reflecting a permanent characterizable feature and a postnominal participle reflecting a specific or temporary attribute holds up reasonably well in the majority of cases—it accounts satisfactorily, for example, for the inappropriateness of *natural laws describe phenomena observed*—and individual sentences containing either of these two main groups of participles will not be further discussed. However, there are occasions when these *semantic* criteria do not appear to have any relevance to the selection of participial position; a typical case is when a particular *-en* participle is found in both positions in a clearly defined discourse. In the following passage *added* occurs three times as a bare participle. (Sentence numbers have been inserted for ease of reference.)

11. (S1) At time t_0 the temperature is absolute zero. (S2) As heat is added, each particle vibrates back and forth about a lattice point, which thus represents the center of the motion. (S3) As more heat is added, the vibration becomes greater. (S4) Though no change is visible because the amplitude of the vibration is so small, the crystal progressively becomes slightly less ordered. (S5) The heat *added* increases the kinetic motion of the particles. (S6) Since temperature measures average kinetic energy, temperature rises along position 1 of Figure 9.2. (S7) This continues until the melting point of the substance has been reached. (S8) At the melting point (abbreviated *mp*) the vibration of the particles is so vigorous that any *added* heat serves to loosen binding forces between neighbouring particles. (S9) Consequently, from t_1 to t_2, *added* heat goes not to increase the average kinetic energy but to increase the potential energy of the particles (p. 191).

In the initial stages of this extract the successive character of the experimental additions of heat is brought out by the contrast between the two time-clauses in

(S2) and (S3) (*As heat is added* and *As more heat is added*). *The heat added* in (S5) refers back to the heating stage mentioned in (S3), and the use of *added* as a postmodifier, as opposed to the use at this juncture of a further time-clause such as *When this heat is added,* allows the authors to draw the reader's attention to the general conclusion that they wish to draw; that is, to the increase in kinetic motion. Thus, *the heat added* in (S5) refers to "given" heat and not to "new" heat.[5]

The second use of *added* as a bare participle occurs in (S8), where it immediately follows *any,* which—as is so often the case in expository writing—can be taken as implying conditionality (e.g., *If any heat were to be added, it would serve to.* . . .). This condition is fulfilled in (S9) and not in (S8), which does not refer to the actual data in Figure 9.2. Therefore, we find (S9) to read "Consequently, from t_1 to t_2, *added* heat goes not to increase. . . ." and not *the heat added* or *the added heat.* (S9) gives information about a "new" heating stage, that from t_1 to t_2.

Thus it seems clear that the positions of *added* in this extract cannot be explained by asserting that the premodifiers indicate a different type of addition to the postmodifier; by claiming (as one would, in a sentence-grammar framework, for instance) that they differ in the permanence of the addition. They are only explicable when one looks beyond the individual sentences to larger rhetorical units and then aligns already "given" information with definite contexts and "new" information with indefinite.

There remain 53 participles out of the original 257 to be discussed; 28 of these are instances of *given* and will be considered separately. The other 25 all have the same type of function. They act as "discourse-coherers"; in other words, they bring to the reader's attention that more information about the referent(s) of the rest of the NP they are modifying can be found elsewhere *in the textbook.*

Usually the participles are used to refer back to some earlier part of the discourse, but this is not always so. For example, we find on page 191:

1a. The curve *shown* is a heating curve corresponding to the uniform addition of heat to an initially solid substance. [In fact, the curve is shown at the bottom of page 192.]

It is, of course, necessary to distinguish carefully between the referents of language and the actual form of words used, because the condition of NP linguistic identity may not always be met, although in many cases it will be. In some instances, as in the example just quoted, the referent is nonverbal; indeed, we would expect to find this with "visual" verbs like *show.*

On other occasions the whole NP functions as a device for summarizing previous description or discussion:

12. However, even *the few facts presented* raise many broad questions (p. 14).

Here the reference is to a discourse on the compressibility of gases and other known chemical phenomena, but nothing in the discourse is specifically called "a fact." On still other occasions there may be assumptions of knowledge of chemistry "in the air":

13. All three of the fluorides *mentioned* normally exist as white solids. . . .(p. 93)

In this case again, fluorides as such are not in fact mentioned at all. What we find twenty lines earlier is the following:

14. Consider the compounds that fluorine forms with sodium, calcium, and aluminum. All three of the compounds are believed to be ionic, ... (p. 92)

There are a number of general observations that can be made about these discourse-cohering participles. First, they all have an underlying locative phrase:

1b. The curve *shown* (at the bottom of page 192). . . .

15. Therefore, in examining any table of atomic radii we must remember that the values *listed* may be meaningful only in providing a comparison of sizes (p. 69).

15a. . . . the values *listed* (in Table 3.28) may be meaningful. . . .

Second, the underlying agent is always the author(s) of the text and not, as in the case of the second group of participles discussed in the previous section, other chemists:

15b. . . . the values *listed* (by us) (in Table 3.28). . . .[6]

Thirdly, if the participle is not bare but has a co-occurring adverbial ostensibly of time,[7] such as *already, previously,* or *just,* the adverbial has to be understood as having a locative function. We cannot sensibly ask of:

16. Before going on, we need to clear up one question *raised previously* (p. 56),

　　　　　　How long ago was it raised?
　　　　　　When was it raised?

but only,

　　　　　　How many pages back was it raised?
　　　　　　Where was it raised?

Finally, perhaps the most interesting thing about these participles is that, through their deleted but recoverable locative references and in their function as discourse-cohering elements, they refer to *textual space* rather than to the physical world of chemical experimentation. It would therefore seem to follow that the effective use of such participles reflects only the communicative competence of the textbook writer and not in any way his or her competence as a scientist.

Of course, an analysis such as the foregoing of the function of bare *-en* participles *as they occur* in a representative text is only part of a pedagogically directed applied linguistic study; if the applied linguist is to be provided with an adequate basis on which to construct an advanced writing course, he or she also has to try and come to some conclusion about the reasons *why* such bare participles occur where they do. This is a difficult task and the steps taken have been faltering and few.

Nevertheless, a reading of the chemistry text does suggest that, at least as far as this particular book is concerned, a major role of discourse-cohering elements is the relating of verbal and nonverbal information. In a number of ways the following longish extract is typical. (Cohering elements containing a participle have been italicized; nonparticipial-cohering elements have been placed within parentheses.)

> Boyle's Law can be summarised by a pressure-volume or P-V plot *like that shown in Figure 6.5.* (In this graph) the horizontal axis represents the pressure of a given sample of gas, and the vertical axis the volume occupied. The curve is a hyperbola, the equation for which is PV = constant, or V = constant/P. The size of the constant is fixed and the mass of the sample and its temperature is specified. If at 4 atm the volume is 1 liter, then at 1 atm the volume is 4 liters. (This can be seen from either the graph or the equation.)
>
> The behaviour specified by Boyle's Law is not always observed. For any gas, the law is most nearly followed at lower pressures and at higher temperatures, but as the pressure is increased, or as the temperature is lowered, deviations may occur. (This can be seen by considering) *the experimental data listed in Figure 6.6.* (In each of these experiments) the quantity of gas is fixed at 39.95g and the temperature is fixed at $100^\circ C$ or at $-50^\circ C$. The pressure is measured when the given mass of gas is contained in different volumes. The PV products (in the last column), obtained by multiplying the values (in the second and third columns) should be, according to Boyle's Law, constant at constant temperature. *The data shown* indicate that at high temperature Boyle's Law is closely obeyed. However, at the low temperature, the PV product is not constant and drops off significantly as the pressure increases; Boyle's Law is not obeyed (pp. 138-140).

If the extract is read with all the bracketed or italicized sections omitted, it becomes clear that the purpose of the verbal-visual linkages is to incorporate graph illustrations into the written scientific explanation. In the first paragraph this is done by supporting the almost complete verbalization with a graph; in the second by providing references to tabular data that would not be fully verbalizable easily. Furthermore, the actual forms of language used in this extract would seem to suggest that the first reference to a visual display of some kind, especially where there may be several potential reference points, requires the use of a locative phrase (in Figure 6.5; in Figure 6.6). It is also worth noting that in both instances the authors appear to be further catering to the reader's presumed need for textual reference by including initial locative phrases in the respective following sentences (*In this graph; In each of these experiments*). But a second reference *The data shown* no longer needs a precise reference to the text, and subsequently (However, at low temperature) reference to the data is presupposed.

Most of these cohering participles occur at similar places in discourse to *the data shown*. A simple example is:

> 18. The cause of cooling by unrestricted expansion can be seen by considering the experiment shown in Figure 6.21. The box *shown* is perfectly insulated from its surroundings, ... (p. 161)

A reading of the text also indicates that a broadly comparable pattern of discourse-cohering elements occurs when the authors make reference to other parts of the written text rather than to nonverbal material, although often the need for a precise reference—and hence an overt locative—is somewhat reduced. In a discussion of Kinetic Theory, Sienko and Plane give four assumptions for a perfect gas, but before discussing these assumptions, they consider how the model can be related to certain observable quantities. Several lines later they write:

19. That the first of the four assumptions *listed* is reasonable can be seen. . . . (p. 151)

However, their paragraph-length discussions of assumptions two, three, and four make no further use of discourse-cohering participles.

It only remains to deal with the occurrences of the bare participle *given*.[8] This is the most frequent participle in the data and has at least three different functions, two of which have proved rather elusive. *Given* occurred twenty-eight times in the context of NPs that contained no more than a single noun or a single compound-noun in their surface structure; these occurrences are listed below:

Postmodifying	*Premodifying*
the list given	a given reaction (3)
the voltage given	a given element (3)
the concentration given	a given experiment (3)
the subscripts given	a given substance (2)
the only information given	a given temperature (2)
	a given (sub)-shell (2)
	a given energy level
	a given O atom
	a given oxidization state
	a given compound
	a given nucleus
	a given bottle
	a given oxidising agent
	a given equilibrium

The five postmodifying participles are all of the discourse-cohering[9] type; moreover, they occur where they do according to the general scheme outlined in the previous section:

20. Figure 14.12 lists various half-reactions with their oxidation potentials. A more extensive listing is given in Appendix 7. The double arrows indicate that under appropriate conditions the half-reactions can be made to go in either direction. The voltage *given* applies when the half-reaction proceeds in the forward direction (p. 310).

21. In a series of experiments, all done at the same temperature but differing in initial concentrations of A and B, the results shown in Figure 13.2 are obtained. The concentrations *given*, in moles per liter, are those in the equilibrium state (p. 270).

The function of the pre-posed examples of *given* is quite different. The following sentence and its surrounding text shows this clearly:

22. Figure 9.5 shows how the vapour pressure of a *given* substance changes with temperature (p. 196).

This sentence falls in the middle of a two-page discussion of Vapor Pressure of Solids, at no place in which is there any mention of any particular substances or anaphoric reference to any. Further, Figure 9.5 is a graph that does not include information about or make any reference to any identifiable substance, the axes of the graph being labeled merely *Vapor Pressure* and *Temperature*. Therefore, it is hard to see how *given* in (22) could be taken as having a locative phrase in underlying structure.

At this point it could be noted that pre-posed *given* seems to occur rarely in conversation on everyday topics and hardly ever in literature and that we are most likely to find it used in such subjects as science, mathematics, and philosophy. If this is so, it might seem that a writer is inclined to use this type of *given* only when he or she feels the need to establish in ways more precise than ordinary language permits how a noun phrase that forms part of a proposition the writer is making is to be interpreted. In the *Chemistry* text it would seem that *a given* has two principal functions; one for signaling that the sentence is to be interpreted as an exemplification, the other for specifying the "determiner range" of the NP as a means of qualifying a generalization. Exemplifications will be taken first:

23. For example, suppose *a given* chemical reaction requires 0.1000 mole of Km_nO_4 ... (p. 234).

24. In *a given* experiment it is observed that, when 0.1000 mole of $BaSO_4$ is formed, the temperature changes from $20.123°C$ to $20.316°C$ (p. 124).

25. A *given* bottle contains a compound which upon analysis is shown to contain 0.600 gram-atom of phosphorus and 1.500 gram-atom of oxygen. How many grams of compound are in the bottle? (p. 127)

These three extracts are "examples," the first two being "worked" by the authors, the third to be worked by the students. In such practice material, the function of *given* appears to be to prevent unnecessary and irrelevant inquiries of the nature:

Is this a typical reaction? (S23) Who did the experiment? When was it done? Or is it a made-up experiment? (S24) How large was the bottle? (S25)

In science, "attribution" is an important convention; that is, the sources of experimental work should be acknowledged in each case. The role of *given* in sentences (23), (24), and (25) and other similar ones is, therefore, to signal unmistakably that the convention is being suspended. It may or may not be the case that (S24) describes actual experimental data, but whether there was actually such an experiment or not is shown by *given* to be an inappropriate line of inquiry. In addition, all three sentences contain further clues pointing to an illustrative and exemplifying interpretation—the use of *for example* and *suppose* and the choice of the present rather than the past tense—which operate to counteract the tendency, fostered by the references to very precise temperature readings and so on, to give an experimental reading to the extracts.

All eight examples in the corpus of this use of *a given* premodified the first NP in the surface-structure sentence—thus, seemingly placed early to prevent misinterpretation—and co-occurred with a verb or verbs in the present tense. However, there does not seem anything impossible or improbable about:

24a. In a given experiment, it *was* observed that. . . .

What we would expect to find is:

24b. In an experiment, it *was* observed that. . . .

because (24b) leads us to suppose that this is going to be a description of an actual experiment and, at the same time, breaks the attribution convention. Even more unlikely would be an overt clash of historical attribution and illustrative function, as in:

24c. In a given experiment by Rutherford, it is observed that. . . .

The fact that there were only eight instances of this type of *given* suggests that the authors rarely took up the option of further clarifying the exemplificatory character of examples. Presumably one reason for this is their consistent use of the present tense, which itself functions perfectly well to indicate the exemplifying purpose of a sentence or a set of sentences. There does not, for instance, appear to be any real possibility of misunderstanding:

24d. In an experiment, it is observed that. . . .

However, if the past tense had been chosen then the need for *given* would have been more apparent—as the difference between (24a) and (24c) demonstrates.

Given also occurred fifteen times in general statements, many of them actual generalizations. Again, they all preceded the noun and were found in indefinite NPs; however, their function was different to that of the "exemplifiers." The following text is reasonably representative:

26. The equilibrium constant has a specific value at a *given* temperature. If the temperature is changed, K may change. For reactions which are endothermic, experiments show that raising the temperature causes K to increase. For those reactions which are exothermic, experiments show that raising the temperature causes K to decrease (p. 283).

Whatever the grammatical status of *given* in (26), intuitively it seems to function in a way not dissimilar to that of a determiner, comparable but different in meaning to *a certain*.[10] Here are two further examples:

22. Figure 9.5 shows how the vapor pressure of a *given* substance changes with temperature (p. 196).

27. We have implied that all the electrons in a *given* shell are of the same energy level (p. 56).

This crypto-determiner *a given* appears to have a very precise meaning that is not easily or neatly expressed by any of the well-established members of the determiner class. Examples (26), (22), and (27) would appear to be shorthand versions of:

26a. The equilibrium constant has a specific value at *any one particular temperature (of all the temperatures under consideration)*.

22a. Figure 9.5 shows how the vapor pressure of *any one particular substance (of all the substances under consideration)* changes with temperature.

27a. We have implied that all the electrons in *any one particular shell (of all the shells under consideration)* are of the same energy level.

In all three of these examples, and indeed in the others, *a given* does not have any obvious ordinary-language substitutions. Consider:

22b. Figure 9.5 shows how the vapor pressure of *a certain* substance varies with temperature.

22c. Figure 9.5 shows how the vapor pressure of *a particular* substance varies with temperature.

Both of these readings are insufficiently generalized as they imply that Figure 9.5 only deals with one as yet unspecified substance. Conversely,

22d. ... the vapor pressure of *any* substance varies with temperature.

22e. ... the vapor pressure of *every* substance varies with temperature.

are over-generalized because they imply that the temperature/pressure relationship would hold for any possible substance at any conceivable pressure and temperature rather than for that subset of the conditions selected by the authors. Nor are simple lexical substitutions possible—for example, *chosen* or *selected*—because they undergeneralize in the same way as *a certain*. Thus, there is at least some reason to believe that further research into this function-type of *given* may confirm its membership of the class of determiners, however restricted its use may be to certain academic varieties of English.

It was intimated at the beginning of this chapter that the ESP practitioner, by looking at specific texts for his or her own specific purposes, may come across examples of language use that have not come to the notice of those who look to the "common core" of English for their data. In this particular case, there is nothing opaque about the part bare participles play in the sort of expository writing found in a science textbook; it is there for the unprivileged observer to see. Indeed, the importance for position that arguably can be attributed to whether or not participles clarify that certain information is already "given," or to the apparent existence of a specific *cohering* functional type of post-posed bare participle, or to the academic uses of *given* have emerged from a simple decision to look at the text as a text. For it would seem, at least on the limited evidence presented here, that single-sentence citations illustrating the different uses of pre- and post-posed bare participles are atypical in that they are unusually heavily loaded with *semantic* differences.

This chapter has attempted to examine a small area of grammar in a particular genre of text, albeit a genre of considerable importance in ESP work. It has not been the purpose here to offer any contribution to syntactic theory, but it may not escape the reader's notice that the findings from the narrow field of pedagogical texts in chemistry support Bolinger's criticism of the facile application of Relative Deletion Transformations, for if we accept that *the stolen jewels* and *the jewels stolen* or *added heat* or *heat added* function differently and, thus, may exhibit differences in meaning, it is difficult to accept a transformational process by which the former is derived from the latter.

Notes

1. An earlier version of this chapter appeared in mimeo form as "Notes on the Function of Attributive *-en* Participles in Scientific Discourse," University of Khartoum, 1974. I would like to thank Andreas Lambrou for his help in collecting the data and Dwight Bolinger and Ian Pearson for their useful comments.
2. The use of *-en* avoids the prejudgements that inevitably arise with the traditional labels, *past, perfect,* or *passive.* In fact, nearly all instances studied were passive, one of the few exceptions being *reacted* as in: "Boiling off of water from a *reacted* mixture leaves a white powder."
3. *Chemistry*: M. J. Sienko and R. A. Plane (McGraw-Hill, New York, 3rd ed., 1966). All numbered instances are taken from this text; italicization is my own.
4. This chapter does not consider "bare" participles occurring in NP + prep + NP structures because the factors affecting position in such contexts are much more complex.
5. For the vagaries of the "given/new" distinction, see Prince (1979).
6. The complications that would arise with quoted material have not been considered, because there are hardly any direct quotations in the *Chemistry* text.
7. As bare participles cannot by definition, be themselves modified by adverbs, instances like (16) were not included in the corpus. They were noted, however, and about seventy found, of which nineteen had a discourse-cohering function. There were as many as seven examples of *just mentioned.*
8. The use of *given* in scientific texts is not, as many might expect, a fairly recent phenomenon; for instance, the Oxford English Dictionary gives this citation from 1726: "The Obliquity of the Ecliptic being given, to find by calculation, the right Ascension and Declination of a *given* point in it." (*Editor's note*: This was first pointed out by Kenneth Hill in a 1978 University of Michigan seminar, where an earlier version of this paper was discussed.)
9. Thus giving a final total of thirty discourse-cohering participles.
10. Although this use of *given* did not occur in plural NPs, this is probably incidental for a sentence like the following would seem to be perfectly acceptable: "For given amounts of x we will always find corresponding amounts of y."

References

Barber, C. L. 1962. "Some Measurable Characteristics of Modern Scientific Prose." *Contributions to English Syntax and Philology*, pp. 21-43. Almqvist and Wiksell.
Bolinger, D. L. 1967. *Adjectives in English: Attribution and Predication.* Lingua 18.
Huddleston, R. D. 1971. *The Sentence in Written English: A Syntactic Study Based on an Analysis of Scientific Texts.* Cambridge Univ. Press.
Jesperson, O. 1928. *A Modern English Grammar on Historical Principles.* Vol. 2. Allen and Unwin.
Prince, E. F. 1979. "The Given/New Distinction in Spoken and Written English." Paper presented at San Diego State University Linguistics Colloquium, April 24, 1979.
Quirk, R., S. Greenbaum, G. Leech, and J. Svartvik. 1972. *A Grammar of Contemporary English.* Longmans.
Swales, J. 1971. *Writing Scientific English.* Thomas Nelson.
Todd Trimble, M., and L. Trimble. 1977. "The Development of EFL Materials for Occupational English." *International English for Specific Purposes Seminar, Proceedings,* 52-70. Bogota, Colombia: The British Council.
Widdowson, H. G. 1977. "Description du Langage Scientifique." Le *Francais dans le Monde*, no. 129. 15-21.

Editorial Comments

We believe that this chapter is in the best tradition of applied linguistics in that there is feedback from a descriptive study of goal-oriented language data to more general theoretical concerns about the nature of language. The author himself modestly notes that his piece is a contribution to syntactic theory in that it supports a Bolinger critique of a classical transformational position.

In this chapter (which has aready proven influential as it has been circulated widely in an earlier draft), Swales takes account of the communicative functions of certain crucial morpheme elements, in the specific context of a chemistry textbook. One of the editors used the earlier version of this chapter as basic reading in a graduate seminar, where Swales' material was carefully compared with the relevant passages in the original (i.e., in the introductory chemistry textbook Swales uses as primary data). Using specialist-informant consultation on the chemistry content involved, we found Swales' conclusions—reached through an approach combining grammatical, rhetorical, and subject matter concerns—accurate and very insightful.

In our view, the analysis presented here is a model of careful linguistic description, clearly and articulately presented. One point we particularly like is Swales' lucid description of "textualization" (see also Widdowson, chap. 1), which we reproduce here: "This type of study . . . typically begins from observing that some of the ways in which language is being used in a piece of technical writing are not fully explicable in terms of the statements and explanations found in traditional grammars or modern linguistic descriptions, and will only be understood after paying attention to the purpose of the particular text and the structure and function of its various components."

L.S.
E.T.

5
Some Verb Forms and Functions in Six Medical Texts

Peter Wingard

A good deal of research has been published on the grammar and rhetoric of scientific and technological English. The small studies reported here were carried out while the writer was working in Egypt without the time or facilities for reference to this literature.

FINITE VERBS IN FOUR MEDICAL PAPERS

The immediate situation that called forth this study was a discussion with an Egyptian doctor attending an English course for postgraduate students in the Faculty of Medicine, University of Alexandria. An extremely able person, he was on the staff of the Medical Research Institute of the University.

His class had been doing exercises designed to practice the use of the Simple Present Active verb in descriptive passages, since it was thought that this was an important form/function in much scientific, including medical, English, and also because it had been found that Egyptian doctors made frequent errors in its use. The Egyptian doctor argued, however, that this form/function was little used in research papers in this field, endoscopy, and that the Simple Past Passive was the chief form required.

54 / ENGLISH FOR ACADEMIC AND TECHNICAL PURPOSES

The teacher (the present writer), while agreeing that the Simple Past Passive was important, thought the Simple Present Active was important too. He was prompted to carry out a small study, probably with mixed motives: (a) curiosity as to whether the doctor might be right, (b) the hope of finding out that he was not, and (c) the desire to impress the doctor and the rest of the class by showing them that scientific investigation was not altogether unknown in English teaching.

Four research papers in endoscopy were supplied by the Egyptian doctor:

1. Safrany, L. "Endoscopy and retrograde cholangiopancreatography after Billroth II operation," *Endoscopy* (Stuttgart) vol. 4, no. 4 (1972), 198-202.
2. Kasugai, T., et al. "Endoscopic pancreatocholangiography with special reference to manometric method," *Medical Journal of Australia,* 1973:2, 717-725.
3. Soma, S., et al. "Clinical application of duodendofiberscope," translation from an article in Japanese published in *Gastroenterological Endoscopy* (Tokyo) vol. 12, no. 1 (1970), 97-110.
4. Ogogshi, K., et al. "Endoscopic observation of the duodenum and pancreatocholedochography using duodenal fiberscope under direct vision," translation from an article in Japanese published in *Gastroenterological Endocscopy* (Tokyo) vol. 12, no. 1 (1970) 83-96.

An interesting aspect of the material is that all four papers were almost certainly written by nonnative speakers of English. The first appeared in a journal that, though published in West Germany, appears in English. The one published in Australia may have been written directly in English. The other two are translations of papers originally appearing in Japanese. No information was available about the processes of translation these papers had undergone or the processes of editing any of the four papers had undergone. The English of the first two appeared indistinguishable from that of a native speaker, while the English of the other two seemed to exhibit a certain amount of deviance from native-speaking norms.

Although it was thought that nonfinite verbs were important in these papers and functioned to a considerable degree as alternatives to finite verbs, the limits of time available only permitted a study of the latter.

It was decided to use a scheme of analysis based on traditional grammatical categories, since these seemed adequate and would be most easily understood by most university English teachers in Egypt. An alternative scheme considered, which would have counted only the finite-verb word in each verb group (e.g., only *has* in *has been found*) was rejected on these grounds.

All finite verbs in the texts were listed, including those occurring in captions to the few visual displays (illustrations/diagrams/tables). Very few problem cases occurred. There were twelve instances, out of approximately one thousand counted, where there was doubt whether a form should be counted as an adjective or as a participle. These were counted as participles. There were three cases of marginal modal verbs (e.g., *have to*) that could have been classified as modal or nonmodal. These were counted as modal. Results are given in Table 5-1 below. The individual verb forms are not listed because of limitations of space.

Although Passive verbs preponderate in the first and shortest paper (60%), Active verbs preponderate in the other three and in the total (60%). The most frequent form overall is Simple Present Active if we include *is/are* (17% without *is/are* + 11% *is/are* = 28%), followed by Simple Past Active if we include *was/were* (14% without *was/were* + 8% *was/were* = 22%). The next most frequent is Simple Past Passive and after that Simple Present Passive. As well as in the total, these four forms are the most frequent in each of the four papers taken separately, though the first three differ in their order of frequency in the different papers. Simple Present Passive is always fourth in frequency.

If we separate *is/are* from Simple Present Active and *was/were* from Simple Past Active, the most frequent forms are: Simple Past Passive (18%), Simple

TABLE 5-1. FINITE VERBS IN FOUR MEDICAL PAPERS

	Text 1	Text 2	Text 3	Text 4	Total
All forms	63/100	244/100	346/100	446/100	999/100
All active forms	25/40	139/60	169/68	268/60	601/60
All passive forms	38/60	105/40	77/32	178/40	398/40
Simple present active including *is/are*	11/16	48/19	86/33	130/29	275/28
Simple past active including *was/were*	12/18	78/31	60/24	69/15	219/22
Simple present active excluding *is/are*	4/6	26/10	52/21	80/18	162/16
is/are	7/10	22/9	34/12	50/11	113/11
Simple past active excluding *was/were*	10/15	42/17	38/15	54/12	144/14
was/were	2/3	36/14	22/9	15/3	75/8
Simple present passive	8/12	17/7	25/10	64/14	114/11
Simple past passive	21/30	64/26	27/11	66/15	178/18
Modal active	2/3	5/2	16/6	11/2	34/3
Modal passive	8/12	12/5	19/8	27/6	66/7
Present perfect active	0/0	6/2	1/0	54/12	61/6
Present perfect passive	0/0	12/5	3/1	19/4	34/3
Past perfect active	0/0	1/0	6/2	1/0	8/1
Past perfect passive	1/0	0/0	3/1	2/0	6/1
Modal perfect active	0/0	1/0	0/0	1/0	2/0
Present continuous active	0/0	0/0	0/0	1/0	1/0
Present perfect continuous active	0/0	0/0	0/0	1/0	1/0

Note: Modal includes *will/shall*
Note: Number of forms counted/Percentage to the nearest whole number

Present Active (17%), Simple Past Active (14%), Simple Present Passive (11%), *is/are* (11%), *was/were* (8%). These six forms (or four as previously reckoned) account for 79% of all finite verbs.

The only other consistently important form is Modal Passive (7% in total and not less than 5% in any paper; N.B. Modal includes *will/shall*). The almost total absence of Perfect and Continuous forms is noteworthy. The large number of Present Perfect Active forms in Text 4 is odd, and on inspection quite a number of these would be classed as doubtfully acceptable in the contexts where they occur; that is, they seem to suggest that the translator was neither a native speaker of English nor a non-native speaker with fully native command.

Coming now to the question this small study was designed to answer, it is clear that, in the type of scientific English represented by these research papers, both Active and Passive are important and, in each case, both Present and Past.

A subjective assessment was made, by glancing through the texts, of the main functions carried by each of the four leading forms. It appeared that the Simple Past Passive was used mainly in narrating the sequence of procedures in the actual research that was being reported. The Simple Present Active including *is/are* seemed to be used mainly in describing apparatus, phenomena, and such but also in making statements about the likely significance of results (*shows,* etc.). This form might be expected to be especially frequent in a field like endoscopy, where the research is largely concerned with the effectiveness of particular equipment, which must be described in detail. The Simple Past Active including *was/were* appeared to be chiefly used for making statements about the likely significance of the results (*showed,* etc.). The Simple Present Passive seemed to be used chiefly in describing procedures habitually used, either by the writers of the papers or by other workers in the same field.

FINITE AND NONFINITE VERBS IN TWO MEDICAL TEXTS

This was a smaller follow-up to the small study of finite verbs in four medical papers. Again the motivation was multiple:

(a) First was the continuation of the Egyptian doctor's interest that had called forth the first study. Discussion with him brought out the need for further information, and he at once produced further material for study.

(b) In the previous study time had not permitted investigation of nonfinites, while inspection of the texts had strengthened the impression that they were important.

(c) The papers of the previous study were all probably written by non-native speakers of English. Although this had appeared not to affect the results greatly, it seemed desirable to investigate material written by native speakers.

(d) The previous materials were all research papers in endoscopy. It was now desired to see whether the results could be generalized to other medical material.

It was realized that non-native speakers/native speakers (see (c) above) and endoscopy/other medical material (see (d) above) were independent variables and could not validly be investigated in a single study. The assumption is made here that non-native speakers/native speakers does not seriously affect the results, because the material of the first study only appeared to deviate to a very small extent from standard written English.

Material under study was:

5. Blumgart, L. H., and Salmon, P. R., "Fiberduodenoscopy and transpapillary cholangiopancreatography," *Recent Advances in Surgery*, no. 8 (1974?).

6. Baker, H. W., et al., *Oral Cancer*, American Cancer Society (1972).

The first item is a research paper in endoscopy of a similar kind to those of a previous study. As far as could be discovered, it was written by native speakers of English. The second item is of an entirely different kind. It is a short manual of multiple authorship, consisting of nine chapters by seven different authors, all, as far as could be discovered, native speakers of English. It is intended to help general practitioners and other doctors to achieve early diagnosis of oral cancer. Whereas the endoscopy texts were all written by specialists for specialists, this text was written by specialists for qualified medical readers who were not specialists in the particular field. More important, as regards linguistic function, its aim is not to report a particular piece of research, but to summarize and illustrate up-to-date knowledge in a fairly restricted field. Its contents are as follows:

(a) James, A. G., "Introduction"

(b) Baker, H. W., "Diagnosis of oral cancer"

(c) Baker, H. W., "Benign oral tumours and tumour-like conditions; tumours of the jaw"

(d) Baker, H. W., "Biopsy: definitive diagnosis of oral cancer"

(e) Pickles, H. H., "Oral exfoliative cytology"

(f) Helsper, J. T., "Staining techniques: screening tests for oral cancer"

(g) Jesse, R. H., "The treatment of oral cancer"

(h) Stark, R. B., "Oral cancer: reconstruction and rehabilitation"

(i) Osterkamp, O. and Whitten, J. B., "The etiology and pathogenesis of oral cancer"

There was not enough time available for study of all the finite and nonfinite verbs in the two texts. For each text, a sample containing 100 finites was taken.

As it was desired to know the proportion of finites to nonfinites, the following method of sampling was adopted:

Text 5: On each of the twenty-nine pages of this text, a stretch of text including three finites was taken (29 x 3 = 87). This was done by starting at the top of the page and continuing until three finites had been collected, then continuing to the end of the finite clause in which the third finite occurred. A further thirteen finites (87 + 13 = 100) were sampled at roughly equal intervals of one per two pages through the text. This was done by beginning at the start of a sentence and continuing until one finite had been collected, then continuing to the end of the finite clause in which it occurred. All nonfinites were then collected.

Text 6: This text had fifty-two pages. The procedure used was to take from each of the first forty-eight pages a stretch of text including two finites (48 x 2 = 96), and from each of the last four pages a stretch including one finite (96 + 4 = 100). All nonfinites within these stretches of text were then collected.

In counting nonfinites, all those were excluded that occurred as part of a finite (for example, *been* and *passed* in *has been passed* would be excluded). Similarly, all nonfinites were excluded that occurred after the first nonfinite in a "compound nonfinite" (for example, *been* and *passed* in *having been passed* would be excluded).

There were a good number of visual displays (illustrations/diagrams/tables) in the texts, especially in Text 6, where visual displays, not counting their captions, took up 40% of the page area. Many visual displays had lengthy captions, and captions were included in the sections of text sampled. One would expect a high occurrence of nonfinites in captions, and this may go some way to explain the greater proportion of nonfinites found in Text 6 as compared with Text 5; but quite a lot of finites also occurred in captions.

For the finites, the same scheme of analysis was used as for the previous study, for the reasons given there, and to permit comparison.

For the nonfinites, it was decided not to use traditional grammatical terminology, as this seemed less well-known to Egyptian university English teachers than in the case of the finites. For the group consisting of Stem + *ed* forms and irregulars such as *eaten,* the term Past Participle might have been satisfactory. For the group consisting of Stem + *ing* forms, traditional terms such as Gerund, Gerundive, Present Participle might have caused problems. Likewise for the group consisting of Stem with or without *to,* the term Infinitive might have caused difficulties.

The nonfinites were therefore first listed merely according to their occurrence in one of the above three forms. Next they were divided according to the grammatical unit in which they occurred, using traditional categories found in Quirk and Greenbaum (1973): Noun-phrase, Verb-phrase, Adjective-phrase. Thirdly, they were divided according to their grammatical order and function in the phrase, as Premodifier, Head, Postmodifier. Very few problems occurred in identifying or classifying the forms.

RESULTS

Finites

A comparison will first be made between the texts of the previous study and Text 5, since these are apparently of similar character. Text 6 will then be compared with Text 5 and with the texts of the previous study (Texts 1-4). Full details are given in Table 5-2.

	Texts 1 - 4	Text 5
All Active forms	60%	65%
All Passive forms	40%	35%
Total	100%	100%
Simple Present Active including *is/are*	28%	40%
Simple Past Active including *was/were*	22%	7%
Simple Present Passive	11%	7%
Simple Past Passive	18%	6%
Modal Active	3%	11%
Modal Passive	7%	15%
Present Perfect Active	6%	6%
Present Perfect Passive	3%	7%
	98%	99%

Active forms preponderate as before, in fact slightly more than before. The very high proportion of Simple Present Active including *is/are* would be expected, especially in view of the high frequency in this text of statements about results and descriptions of equipment. The other three forms that stood out in the texts of the previous study (Simple Past Active, including *was/were*; Simple Present Passive; and Simple Past Passive) are also important in Text 5, though to a somewhat reduced extent.

A striking difference is the high frequency of modals, both Active and Passive, in Text 5. Together they amounted to 26% of all finites. Nearly half of the occurrences are *may,* and over one-third *can.* A more thorough analysis in terms of meaning would be profitable. From brief impressionistic analysis it appears that *may* is used most often to make guarded or tentative statements, while *can* is used to indicate more definite possibilities. It is also noteworthy that, both in the texts of the previous study and in Text 5, Modals go against the general tendency, in this data, for Active forms to outnumber Passive ones.

Present Perfect Active had about the same frequency in Text 5 as in the texts of the previous study, but Present Perfect Passive was more than twice as frequent in Text 5 as in the texts of the previous study. It seems to be used mainly in referring to the work of previous researchers (for example, *has been performed, has been described*).

TABLE 5-2. FINITE VERBS IN TWO MEDICAL TEXTS

	Texts 1 to 4	Text 5	Text 6
All Active forms	60%	65%	76%
All Passive forms	40%	35%	24%
Simple Present Active including *is/are*	28%	40%	57%
Simple Past Active including *was/were*	22%	7%	6%
Simple Present Active excluding *is/are*	16%	26%	39%
is/are	11%	14%	18%
Simple Past Active excluding *was/were*	14%	3%	6%
was/were	8%	4%	0%
Simple Present Passive	11%	7%	12%
Simple Past Passive	18%	6%	2%
Modal Active*	3%	11%	9%
Modal Passive*	7%	15%	7%
Present Perfect Active	6%	6%	0%
Present Perfect Passive	3%	7%	2%
Past Perfect Active	1%	1%	0%
Past Perfect Passive	1%	0%	1%
Modal Perfect Active	0%	0%	0%
Present Continuous Active	0%	0%	0%
Present Perfect Continuous Active	0%	0%	0%

Note: *Modal* includes *will/shall*
Note: in percentages to nearest whole number

Overall, then, we find the same eight leading forms in Text 5 as in the texts of the previous study, with a good deal of similarity in their distribution but also some differences.

Text 6 will now be brought into the comparison:

	Texts 1 - 4	Text 5	Text 6
All Active forms	60%	65%	76%
All Passive forms	40%	35%	24%
	100%	100%	100%
Simple Present Active including *is/are*	28%	40%	57%
Simple Past Active including *was/were*	22%	7%	6%
Simple Present Passive	11%	7%	12%
Simple Past Passive	18%	6%	2%
Modal Active	3%	11%	9%
Modal Passive	7%	15%	7%
Present Perfect Active	6%	6%	0%
Present Perfect Passive	3%	7%	2%
	98%	99%	95%

Active forms preponderate still more in Text 6. This increased preponderance of Active forms is concentrated in Simple Present Active including *is/are,* which accounts for well over half of all finites in Text 6. This high level is what, I hypothesize, one would expect from the descriptive nature of the text, summarizing current knowledge in its field. The relatively high proportion of Simple Present Passive that, as was suggested in the previous study, seems to be chiefly used in describing procedures habitually used, fits neatly into this picture. So does the very low proportion of Simple Past Passive, since there is very little narration of procedures followed by the writers or by other workers.

Modals, while less striking in numbers than in Text 5, are more frequent than in the texts of the previous study. Again nearly half of them are *may*. A glance at the meanings of *may* suggests that in Text 6 it is often used in its permissive sense, rather than to make tentative statements. This again is what one would likely expect from the nature of the text, a treatise by specialists for nonspecialists. More than half the Modals in Text 6 are Active, unlike those in Text 5 and the texts of the previous study.

Present Perfect Active was not found at all in the sample of Text 6 studied, and Present Perfect Passive occurred twice.

Overall, however, Text 6 shows a good deal of similarity with Text 5 and the texts of the previous study. Seven of the same eight leading forms are found, though their distribution differs somewhat. On the whole Text 5 resembles the texts of the previous study quite closely, while in certain respects it is intermediate between Text 6 and the texts of the previous study, which are certainly farther apart than Text 5 and the texts of the previous study.

Nonfinites

	Finites	Nonfinites
Text 5	100	64
Text 6	100	78

The results are basically similar for the two texts, showing nonfinites to be fewer but not very greatly fewer than finites. This would seem to confirm the importance of nonfinites, an importance that is not always recognized in teaching materials.

Full details of the analysis of nonfinites are given in Table 5-3. The following are some leading features:

	Stem + *ed*	Stem + *ing*	Stem	Total
Text 5	47%	39%	14%	100%
Text 6	43%	41%	16%	100%

The results are remarkably similar in the two texts and show Stem + *ed* and Stem + *ing* as almost equally frequent across forms, with Stem far behind.

	In Noun-phrase	In Verb-phrase	In Adjective-phrase	Total
Text 5	80%	11%	9%	100%
Text 6	69%	19%	12%	100%

TABLE 5-3. NONFINITE VERBS IN TWO MEDICAL TEXTS

Place in structure	Form									
	Stem + *ed*		Stem + *ing*		Stem		Total			
	Text 5	Text 6	Text 5	Text 6	Text 5	Text 6	Text 5	Text 6		
In Noun Phrase										
Premodifying	15/24	15/20	10/15	9/12	0/0	3/4	25/39	27/35		
Postmodifying	7/11	8/11	3/5	6/8	3/5	1/1	13/21	15/19		
Head	0/0	0/0	11/17	10/13	2/3	2/3	13/20	12/15		
Total in noun phrase	22/35	23/31	24/37	25/33	5/8	6/8	51/80	54/69		
In Verb Phrase										
Head	6/9	4/5	1/2	4/5	0/0	7/10	7/11	15/19		
In Adjective Phrase										
Postmodifying	0/0	0/0	0/0	0/0	2/3	2/3	2/3	2/3		
Head	2/3	5/7	0/0	2/3	2/3	0/0	4/6	7/9		
Total in adjective phrase	2/3	5/7	0/0	2/3	4/6	2/3	6/9	9/12		
Total in All Places	30/47	32/43	25/39	31/41	9/14	15/21	64/100	78/100		

Note: Number of forms counted/Percentage to the nearest whole number

The results are again very similar in the two texts, with the Noun-phrase greatly preponderating, but occurrences in the Verb-phrase and Adjective-phrase rather more frequent in Text 6 than in Text 5.

	Pre-modifying	Post-modifying	Head	Total
Text 5	39%	24%	37%	100%
Text 6	35%	22%	43%	100%

The results are again very similar for the two texts and show all three positions as frequent, but the Postmodifying one least so.

In the Noun-phrase, about half the occurrences counted were Premodifying (Adjectival) and about a quarter each Head-word (Gerund) and Postmodifying (no common traditional label).

In the Adjective-phrase, nonfinites occurred more frequently in Head position than in Postmodifying position.

Looking now at the positions in which the three forms occur: Stem + *ed* has about half its occurrences in Premodifying position, and about a quarter each in the other two positions; Stem + *ing* has about half its occurrences in Head position and one-third in Premodifying position; Stem has more than half its occurrences in Head position and about one-third in Postmodifying position.

It is clear that the dominant function of Stem + *ed* is as Premodifier (Adjective) in a Noun-phrase. For Stem + *ing* the functions of Premodifier (Adjective) and Head (Gerund) are about equally frequent.

CONCLUSIONS

A few major points that seem to deserve special emphasis will be recapitulated here.

Among finite verb-forms, Active occurs far more often than Passive in both Text 5 and Text 6. Simple Present Active including *is/are* occurs with far greater frequency than any other form in both texts. Modals are quite common, the commonest by far being *may*. We find the eight preponderating forms (except Present Perfect Active in Text 6) in both texts as well as in the texts of the previous study. Comparison between Texts 5 and 6 shows differences reflecting, I hypothesize, the more descriptive and less narrative character of the latter. More than half of the finites are Simple Present Active including *is/are,* and there exists a high proportion of Simple Present Passive, reflecting, it seems, the description of procedures habitually used.

Nonfinites are fewer, but not very much so, than finites. Stem + *ed* and Stem + *ing* are equally important, and together account for over five-sixths of nonfinites in each text. More than two-thirds of nonfinites in each text occur in the Noun-phrase. Premodifying and Head position are equally common, and together account for over three-quarters of nonfinites. The three dominant uses of nonfinites are all in the noun phrase: Stem + *ed* as Premodifier (Adjective); Stem + *ing* as Premodifier (Adjective); and Stem + *ing* as Head (Gerund).

Reference

Quirk, R. and S. Greenbaum. 1973. *A University Grammar of English,* Longmans.

Editorial Comments

We believe this chapter to be a useful example of the sort of ESP research that may be done by a teacher in a real teaching context—in fact, this chapter derives from a teacher-student dialogue on the frequency of usage of particular verb forms in medical texts. While this admittedly is a small study (and the statistics are admittedly impressionistic), it is indicative of possible future directions for more rigorous research.

Wingard investigates the degree of relative frequency of some verb forms and their functions as they occur in medical research papers. His results show the way in which verb usage may shift as the overall purpose of the text shifts; see, for example, table 5-2 and the functional hints presented in the discussion. The possibility that grammatical structures may occur with varying frequency from text to text, even within a single field, should make researchers cautious about making sweeping generalizations about "*the* grammar of EST." It is clear that a wide variety of texts will need to be examined and compared before such generalizations can be made safely. Studies of the frequency of rhetorical/grammatical units are needed to address the questions of generalizability and validity that we raise in connection with Oster's paper (see Chapter 7) and, in that regard, we applaud this study.

The second part of Wingard's study is directly related to Swales' paper (see Chapter 4) in its focus on nonfinite verbs as they occur, here, in two medical texts; this study, however, is, on the one hand, more global and, on the other, less detailed in its investigation. Wingard mentions the rhetorical/functional importance of nonfinite verbs in this type of EST text.

L.S.
E.T.

6
Anaphoric Functions of Some Demonstrative Noun Phrases in EST[1]

Deborah Tyma

In *Grammar and Technical English*, Lackstrom, Selinker, and Trimble (1972) conclude that "sentence-oriented grammatical explanations are not sufficient" (p. 13) for non-native speakers of English who need to learn to write acceptable technical papers. With a perspective not limited to the level of the sentence, the authors focus on rhetorical considerations that include judgments on "the order of the presentation of information within the paragraph and within the total piece" (p. 4) as well as on the position of a particular sentence "in its rhetorical relationships to the rest of the paragraph" (p. 14). This higher-level focus leads them to advocate "treating definite noun phrases and pronouns alike as anaphoric units" (p. 8). Considering paragraph-level relationships allows one to recognize the similar anaphoric use in English of Science and Technology (EST) of some *demonstrative noun phrases* (i.e., noun phrases whose determiners are demonstrative adjectives). The purpose of this chapter is to examine some instances of such phrases in EST and the way they function in particular paragraphs. In the examples presented here, demonstrative noun phrases are shown to be involved in the order in which information is presented: as anaphoric references, they appear to provide cohesion in the implicit presentation of definition and classification as well as in the linear expression in EST of nonlinear concepts.

Data considered in this chapter are drawn from two textbooks, one on electrical engineering (Angus 1968) and another on chemical engineering

(Andersen and Wenzel 1961). It is useful to work with texts such as these because general textbooks are likely to be the first technical materials the engineering student encounters in his or her field. However, using data from textbooks alone raises the possibility that a style of writing unique to such texts may be influencing the use of language, so the analyses and conclusions presented here cannot necessarily be extended to other forms of scientific writing.

The examples[2] shown in Table 6-1 represent paragraphs in which demonstrative noun phrases occur. The italics have been added to point out the noun

TABLE 6-1. EST EXAMPLES INCLUDING DEMONSTRATIVE NOUN PHRASES

(1) This particular curve has a peak which is the maximum power transfer point. Although *this point of maximum value* can experimentally be determined rather closely, it is also possible to compute it exactly by means of differential calculus (Angus 1968: 94).

(2) Market research, the first step in new product sales, begins long before the new process is in operation. It answers the fundamental question "Will it sell?" If the proposed product is completely new, market research contacts potential users to determine their needs and thereby establish whether a market exists. If management decides to continue the project on the basis of *this preliminary market survey*, the pilot plant may produce sufficient product to supply samples to potential customers so that they may test the product for their applications (Andersen and Wenzel 1961: 43).

(3) The chemical engineer cannot abandon his attempt to understand a process simply because it cannot be described by a neat, rigorous mathematical expression.... Unfortunately, many systems with which the chemical engineer deals do not fit simple theory. For example, the perfect-gas law fits certain real gases at moderate temperatures and pressures; but many real gases cannot be defined by *this ideal model*, especially at extreme temperatures and pressures (Andersen and Wenzel 1961: 49).

(4) Because the current in the equivalent circuit must be identical to the total current in the general parallel circuit, we equate *these two expressions* as follows: $GE = G_1E + G_2E + G_3E + \ldots + G_nE$ (Angus 1968: 76).

(5) In a very dilute solution, Henry's law may hold for the solute gas, and Raoult's law must then hold for the solvent liquid. For example, in equilibrium between air and liquid water, the solubility of oxygen and nitrogen in water is given by Henry's law. Because *these gases* are so slightly soluble in water, Raoult's law may be used to determine the quantity of water vapor in the air (Andersen and Wenzel 1961: 145).

(6) Using a digital computer to solve a problem requires a succession of steps. First the problem must be reduced to numerical form. The computer can handle only simple arithmetic steps and yes or no decisions; so that integrals, differentials, trigonometric functions, logarithms, etc., must be reduced to *these simple operations* (Andersen and Wenzel 1961: 89).

(7) On the other hand, if the dimension "F" is used for force and "E" for energy, the dimensions of Eq. (3.49) are

$$\frac{E}{M} + \frac{FL^3}{L^2M} + \left(\frac{L}{\Theta}\right)^2 + \frac{L}{\Theta^2}L = \frac{E}{M} - \frac{E}{M}$$

This equation is dimensionally inconsistent. The first, second, and third terms cannot be added in their present form. *This problem* arises because the redundant MFELΘT system of dimensions was used. To achieve dimensional consistency, it is necessary to use dimensional constants relating the redundant dimensions to the fundamental ones (Andersen and Wenzel 1961: 104).

phrases whose functions will be discussed below. In each example in Table 6-1, the italicized phrase consists of a demonstrative adjective, either *this* or *these*, plus a head noun and, in all but (5) and (7), other modifiers.

Quirk, Greenbaum, Leech, and Svartvik (1972) note that *this* and *these*, among other determiners, can be used "to signal that a noun phrase is referentially equivalent to a previous noun phrase" (p. 702); noun phrases with such determiners may therefore function as anaphoric references. Halliday and Hasan (1976)[3] have also noted the anaphoric character of demonstrative noun phrases; they state that the head noun may be an "explicit repetition" of the "presupposed item," or it may be "some form of synonym," such as a "superordinate" (pp. 63-64). In any case, the occurrence of the demonstrative adjective marks the noun phrase as an element whose interpretation depends on an earlier or presupposed[4] item.

Given the anaphoric nature of demonstrative noun phrases, antecedents may be found for the phrases in (1)-(7), as shown in table 6-2. While Quirk et al. deal primarily with demonstrative noun phrases that refer back to other noun phrases, in examples (2) and (7) I have proposed antecedents that are not noun phrases but independent clauses. Selecting clauses as antecedents for noun phrases represents a slight deviation from the treatment of noun phrase coreference found in Quirk et al., but, as will be shown, the rhetorical functions of the anaphoric reference make such an alteration necessary.

TABLE 6-2. DEMONSTRATIVE NOUN PHRASES AND THEIR ANTECEDENTS IN (1) - (7)

Demonstrative noun phrases	Antecedents
(1) this point of maximum value	a peak that is the maximum power transfer point
(2) this preliminary market survey	market research contacts potential users to determine their needs and thereby establish whether a market exists
(3) this ideal model	the perfect-gas law
(4) these two expressions	the current in the equivalent circuit; the total current in the general parallel circuit
(5) these gases	oxygen and nitrogen
(6) these simple operations	simple arithmetic steps and yes or no decisions
(7) this problem	This equation is dimensionally inconsistent. The first, second, and third terms cannot be added in their present form.

ANAPHORA AND IMPLICIT DEFINITION AND CLASSIFICATION

Lackstrom, Selinker, and Trimble (1972) discuss technical definition as a rhetorical device that, when formally expressed, follows the formula *T*erm = *C*lass + *D*ifferentia.[5] A more detailed treatment of definition as well as of classification is offered by Selinker, Todd Trimble, and Trimble (1976), who consider examples that deviate somewhat from the above formula. They note that the specific rhetorical functions of definition and classification, when stated explicitly, include three types of important information: for definition, "(1) the term *naming* the concept being defined; (2) the class (or set) of which the term is a member; and (3) selected essential characterising information about the differences which distinguish the concept being defined from all other concepts which are members of the same set x" (p. 284); for classification, "(1) the name of the class; (2) those members of the class which the writer feels are important to the discussion at hand. . .; and (3) a basis for classification; that is, in what respect the members differ from one another" (p. 285). With the matrix of Table 6-3, I attempt to summarize their descriptions of explicit definition and classification.

Selinker et al. do not state explicitly whether the order in which they list the three kinds of information necessary for explicit classification and definition is the order in which explicit information must be presented. Nonetheless, they suggest that for the purposes of teaching non-native speakers how to read EST more efficiently, implicit information be reordered into explicit form (p. 286); this suggestion indicates the importance of a preferred order in distinguishing implicit from explicit information. Furthermore, in their examples of implicit classification and definition, the three types of information are presented in an order different from that suggested for explicit functions, usually with the information shown in the first horizontal row of Table 6-3 (i.e., *term* or *name*) appearing last. According to Selinker et al., another factor separating implicit from explicit information is that the former rarely functions as a core generalization or as part of one. They claim that implicit classification and definition instead are usually "buried" (p. 285) in paragraphs having a rhetorical function different from that of the implicit information. Recognizing these

TABLE 6-3. ADAPTATION OF SELINKER, TODD TRIMBLE, AND TRIMBLE'S (1972) DESCRIPTION OF EXPLICIT DEFINITION AND OF EXPLICIT CLASSIFICATION

		Rhetorical Functions	
		Definition	Classification
Kinds of Information	1	term	name of class
	2	class	members
	3	differences	basis for classification

characteristics of implicit definition and classification enables Selinker et al. to describe several examples of implicit information and to show how such writing may present difficulties for the non-native reader.

Before using their insights into this problem to analyze the examples shown in Table 6-1, however, I must clarify two necessary assumptions. In an interpretation of their criteria for explicitness, it will be assumed here that, to be termed *explicit*, defining or classifying information must (1) include all three kinds of information listed by Selinker et al. and (2) present the three terms in the order suggested. As a corollary of that assumption, any classifying or defining information presented differently—that is, either with one of the three parts missing or with the parts in a different sequence—is considered to be stated implicitly.[6]

Taken together, the demonstrative noun phrases and their antecedents as shown in Table 6-2 appear to function in (1), (2), and (3) as definitions, while those in (4), (5), and (6) seem to have a classifying function (example (7) will be considered below). In addition to mentioning how the "point of maximum value" can be determined, the writer of (1) in Table 6-1 defines that point as "a peak which is the maximum power transfer point." Applying the Selinker et al. criteria for explicit definition shows that example (1) includes all three kinds of information: the *term* is "this point of maximum value"; the *class* is the class of "peaks"; and the *difference* distinguishing the peak concerned from all other peaks is that it is "the maximum power transfer point." However, the three parts of the definition are not mentioned in the order suggested by Selinker et al. Because the term being defined appears after the class and the difference are noted, the definition in (1), following the second assumption discussed in this section, may be considered implicit. In example (2) the term being defined, "this preliminary market survey," again appears after the rest of the defining information, so the definition is stated implicitly. But in this case an additional factor renders the definition implicit: the *class* to which "preliminary market survey" belongs is not mentioned; only the "selected essential characterizing information" (the *difference*) is given. By omitting one type of information and reversing the order of *term* and *difference*, the authors have defined that *term* implicitly. In example (3), the anaphoric demonstrative noun phrase "this ideal model" provides the defining information for the *term*, represented by the antecedent "the perfect gas law." Since "ideal" is the *difference* and "model" the *class*, this definition follows the order of *term-difference-class*, instead of the "explicit" order of *term-class-difference*. Another feature contributes to the implicit quality of the definition in (3): the purpose of the including paragraph appears to be to describe potential problems rather than to define. Because the defining information is buried, as well as presented in a different order, (3) may also be considered an example of implicit definition.

The demonstrative noun phrase and its antecedent in (4) effect a classification because, taken together, they associate "current in the equivalent circuit" with "total current in the general parallel circuit" in the class represented by the word "expressions." All three kinds of information necessary for an explicit definition are included: The *name* of the class is "expressions"; the *members* of the class are "currrent" and "total current"; and the *basis* for classification is "in the equivalent circuit" and "in the general parallel circuit." With the forms representing the *members* and the *basis* interspersed in the surface structure, and with the *name* of the class mentioned last, the order in which the information is presented makes the classification implicit. Moreover, since the main rhetorical purpose of the including paragraph is not to classify but to discuss theory, the classification is, in the expression used by Selinker et al., buried. As in (4) the *name* of the class in (5), "these gases," is mentioned after the *members*, "oxygen and nitrogen." But the *basis* for distinguishing the members from each other is omitted, contributing a second reason to consider the classification[7] of (5) implicit.

In (6) the anaphoric noun phrase and its antecedent participate in a complex two-level classification, as shown in Figure 6-1. For various reasons, all three classifications found in (6) may be considered implicit. In the first, no *basis* is given for distinguishing "arithmetic steps" from "yes or no decisions," and the *name* of the class appears after the members are listed, violating the order for explicit classification. The second classification again includes no *basis*, and the *name* of the class ("operations that are not simple") must be inferred from the opposition with the first class. Since the only kind of classificatory information explicitly mentioned in the second classification is the *members*, the presentation order is irrelevant. Though it is possible to supply a *name* for the third class ("all the operations that a chemical engineer would want to perform"), the authors do not assign one. A second reason to consider the third classification implicit is that the *basis* for distinguishing the *members*, "simple" or "not simple," appears as part of the name of one *member*, "these simple operations." The presentation order of the information for the third classification is therefore more complex than that suggested by Selinker et al. for the terms of explicit classification.

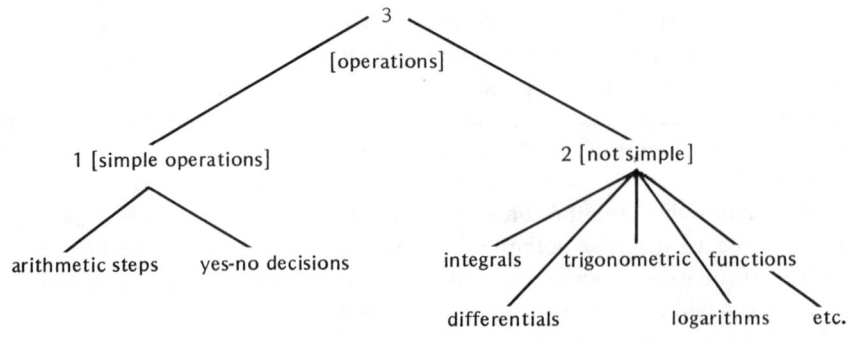

FIGURE 6-1.   COMPLEX TWO-LEVEL CLASSIFICATION OF (6)

According to the criteria for explicitness presented by Selinker et al. and as interpreted in this chapter, then, the first six examples shown in Table 6-1 include implicit rhetorical information. While (2), (5), and (6) lack one of the three necessary kinds of information, all three definitions and all three classifications are buried in paragraphs with rhetorical purposes different from those of classifying or defining. Another characteristic common to these six examples is that in each, the parts are given in an order different from that in which explicit information is presented.

In the six examples, it is the anaphoric nature of the last part of each classification or definition that mediates the reversed or inverted order. As both Halliday and Hasan, and Quirk et al. note, the determiners *this* and *these* act as signals that the reader should look back in the preceding text to find material necessary for the interpretation of the anaphoric item. In the examples of Table 6-1, it is quite clear just how necessary the earlier material is to the reader's understanding of the demonstrative noun phrase: In two of the definitions, the antecedent phrases give the defining information, while in all three of the classifications the members of the general class, which are the details of the classification, are mentioned in the antecedents. Although not all the antecedents are noun phrases, only the clausal antecedent in (2) is sufficient for the interpretation of the demonstrative noun phrase. The evidence from this example may therefore suggest an easing of the condition that the antecedent of an anaphoric noun phrase itself be a noun phrase.

Lackstrom, Selinker, and Trimble (1972) suggest that definite noun phrases (*the* plus a noun) may fulfill an anaphoric function similar to that shown by these demonstrative noun phrases. Indeed, the demonstrative adjectives of (1)-(6) could probably be replaced by the definite article without damage to the defining or classifying functions of the examples. But as a deictic element, a demonstrative adjective is a very clear signal to the reader that he or she must look back in the preceding text to find important information, whereas the definite article connotes no such urgency. As Halliday and Hasan note, "*every* lexical item *may* enter into a cohesive relation, but by itself it carries no indication whether it is functioning cohesively or not" (p. 288). In (1)-(6), the demonstratives *this* and *these* give precisely that indication, so the reader will know that he or she must find an antecedent. Once that antecedent is found, the non-native reader may, in the words of Selinker et al., consciously "extract and reorder" the information into explicit classifying or defining form (p. 286).

ANAPHORA AND THE LINEAR EXPRESSION OF NON-LINEAR CONCEPTS

The description of simultaneous events or perspectives in the linear mode of expository writing involves ordering problems of a kind somewhat different from that encountered in implicit classification and definition. While the implicit

72 / ENGLISH FOR ACADEMIC AND TECHNICAL PURPOSES

presentation of rhetorical functions described in the previous section entails permutation of an expected order of *term-class-difference*, for definition, or of *name-members-basis*, for classification, the linear expression of concurrent events or states appears to require a modification of chronological order. Constrained by the nature of expository discourse, the writer must choose one of two (or more) simultaneous events to mention first. In such a case, the linear expository order imposed on the events or states would not accurately reflect the actual chronological order (or nonorder). Pike and Pike (1976), recognizing this problem, suggest that two events may "merge into one, and then diverge into two again; but . . . the grammatical reporting of that situation must be in a linear form of one word after another" (p. 344). Example (7), given in Table 6-1, describes such a merging of events, which can be graphically represented by a network[8] as in Figure 6-2. At step 1, two events (or rather, for the same event, a narrow perspective, using F and E, and a broader perspective, using MFELΘT) are shown; at step 3 the discovery that the equation is dimensionally inconsistent and that the terms cannot be added happens simultaneously with the appearance of "this problem." The two concurrent chains of events remain separate until they are joined in step 4 when, in order to deal with all three events shown in step 3, the engineer uses dimensional constants.

While it is not difficult to draw a network such as that shown in Figure 6-2, in expository writing some other means of communicating simultaneity of events must be found. Since demonstrative noun phrases, functioning anaphorically, were shown to mediate the problem in implicit classification and definition. It should not be surprising to find such an anaphoric phrase, "this problem,"

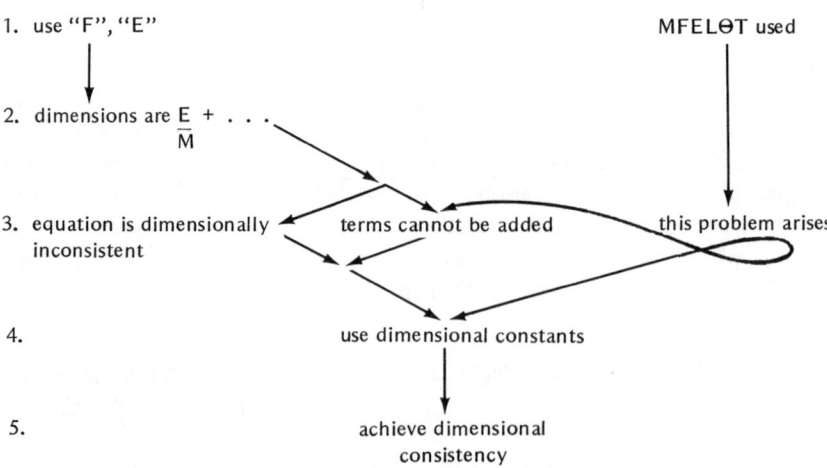

FIGURE 6-2. THE CHRONOLOGICAL NETWORK OF EVENTS IN EXAMPLE (7)

creating cohesion in (7) between the original description of the problems and their assessment in the fourth sentence. In other words, the writers' use of the phrase "this problem" leads the reader to look for an antecedent;[9] the anaphor-antecedent link then ties all three events of step 3 together to reflect the existence of the chronological network. In fitting the nonlinear network into a linear description, some cohesive device is necessary to reflect simultaneity. In Figure 6-2 the cohesive effect is indicated by the arrow connecting "this problem" to the other two events of step 3; in the paragraph of (7) it is the anaphoric use of the demonstrative noun phrase that "points back" to the earlier mentioned but nonetheless simultaneous events.

To understand why anaphoric reference should be useful in confining a nonlinear structure in the linear mode of expository writing, it is helpful to consider the dual function of anaphora. While the anaphoric reference directs the reader's attention back to an element occurring or implied earlier in the text, the rest of the sentence in which the reference item occurs continues. In addition to the cohesive function of pointing back, then, in its own sentence the anaphor has a grammatical function, such as subject or object, which should not be overlooked. As linear structures that look forward as well as backward, anaphora may thus be a solution to the problem of describing a nonlinear concept with the necessarily linear surface grammar of expository English.

CONCLUSION

The seven demonstrative noun phrases considered in this chapter have been shown to function anaphorically to refer the reader back to an element occurring earlier in the text. In (1)-(6), the antecedents, along with the anaphora, were shown to be terms in implicit classifications or definitions (Selinker, Todd Trimble, and Trimble 1976); the interpretation required by the anaphoric reference appears to lessen the effect of the out-of-order presentation of the information. The antecedents of the anaphoric demonstrative noun phrase of (7) were shown to be two earlier sentences describing events simultaneous with that expressed by the demonstrative noun phrase; in this case the cohesion provided by the coreference appeared to reflect the simultaneity of the events, thereby softening the linear effect imposed by the expository mode. In these seven examples, then, anaphoric demonstrative noun phrases appear to mediate ordering problems in three rhetorical functions: implicit definition, implicit classification, and the linear expression of simultaneity. It is important to note that the list of functions is not exclusive: while all three functions apparently may be fulfilled by cohesive devices other than demonstrative noun phrases, such anaphoric noun phrases themselves appear to have functions other than creating cohesion in problems of order. Nonetheless, the data considered here seem to provide additional evidence of the importance of considering "the order of the presentation of information within the paragraph and within the total piece" (Lackstrom, Selinker, and Trimble 1972:4).

Notes

1. An earlier version to this work was presented as a term project in a course entitled "Discourse Structure" offered at the University of Michigan by Professor Ann Borkin, whose comments have been very helpful. I am grateful to Professor Larry Selinker for his most generous assistance and advice regarding revisions. In the development of my thoughts on this subject I have benefited greatly from comments from Professor Kenneth Pike and from discussions with Stephen Tyma.
2. Although these seven examples include two additional demonstrative noun phrases, here I consider the functions of only the seven underscored demonstrative noun phrases.
3. In addition to Halliday and Hasan (1976) and Quirk et al. (1972), several others have dealt with the anaphoric use of demonstratives. The reader may wish to compare R. Lakoff (1974), in which the alternation between *this, that,* and other determiners is discussed. The reader may also find interesting Gensler's (1977) treatment of demonstrative pronouns and "nonsyntactic" anaphora.
4. Halliday and Hasan here appear to use the term "presupposed" synonymously with "earlier mentioned" (p. 314).
5. The authors note that the formula may also be reversed: Class + Differentia = Term. As will be discussed below, I now consider the order $C + D = T$ to be a formula for implicit definition.
6. In this interpretation, then, explicit presentation is seen as the "normal" version, while implicit presentation is any variation from that normal form. The reader may wish to consider Pike and Pike (1977), who have dealt extensively with this problem of variation, using the terms "norm" and "off-norm."
7. The information given by this classification, that oxygen and nitrogen are gases, may appear too trivial to be of interest. But chemical engineers, dealing with extreme temperatures and pressures, may frequently encounter familiar substances in unfamiliar physical states. In this context the information given by the implicit classification is certainly not trivial but necessary to the student's comprehension of the text.
8. Relational network notation as it is used in stratificational theory (see Lockwood 1972) would be very helpful in graphically representing merging and diverging events, as Pike and Pike (1976) suggest.
9. The "antecedent" of "this problem" is the two sentences that directly precede the anaphor in the example; only the information contained in those two sentences specifies the nature of the problem. As noted in the text above, Quirk et al. do not deal with the occurrence of independent clauses and full sentences as antecedents for anaphoric noun phrases. But in (7) it is unmistakably clear that the only possible antecedent for the reference is two complete sentences.

References

Andersen, L. B., and L. A. Wenzel. 1961. *Introduction to Chemical Engineering.* McGraw-Hill.
Angus, R. B., Jr. 1968. *Electrical Engineering Fundamentals.* Addison-Wesley.
Gensler, O. 1977. "Nonsyntactic antecedents and frame semantics." *Papers from the 3rd Meeting, Berkeley Linguistic Society,* 321-35.
Halliday, M. A. K., and R. Hasan. 1976. *Cohesion in English.* Longmans.
Lackstrom, J. E., L. Selinker, and L. P. Trimble. 1972. "Grammar and Technical English." *English Teaching Forum,* September-October, 3-14.
Lakoff, R. 1974. "Remarks on *this* and *that.*" *Papers from the Tenth Regional Meeting, Chicago Linguistic Society,* 345-56.
Lockwood, D. G. 1972. *Introduction to Stratificational Linguistics.* Harcourt, Brace, Jovanovich.

Pike, K. L., and E. G. Pike. 1976. "Referential versus Grammatical Hierarchies." *The Third LACUS Forum,* 343-54. Hornbeam.

———. 1977. *Grammatical analysis.* SIL academic publications.

Quirk, R., S. Greenbaum, G. Leech, and J. Svartvik. 1972. *A Grammar of Contemporary English.* Longmans.

Selinker, L., R. M. Todd Trimble, and L. Trimble. 1972. "Presuppositional rhetorical information in EST discourse." *TESOL Quarterly* 10.281-90.

Editorial Comments

This descriptive chapter, in the textualization framework as well, examines electrical and chemical engineering textbooks to show the way in which demonstrative noun phrases provide anaphoric reference in (1) implicit definition, (2) implicit classification, and (3) "the linear expression in EST of nonlinear concepts." The various influences brought to bear on this study—Halliday and Hasan, Lamb (through Lockwood), Pike and Pike, Selinker and Trimble—show an interesting merging of scholarship.

We feel that one of the contributions of this chapter is the observation that demonstrative NP's may refer back not only to NP's, but also to independent clauses. It is in examining the rhetorical functions of anaphoric reference that this relationship may be most easily seen.

Another contribution is the attempted clarification of the concepts "explicit" versus "implicit" definition and classification; the suggestion is made here that to be *explicit*, definition and classification must each present three kinds of information in a set order and that any variation from this formula must then be termed *implicit*. The author goes on to suggest that where inverted order in implicit definition and classifcation occurs, anaphoric items such as demonstrative adjectives may be used to aid the reader in extracting the necessary implicit information.

Finally, the author presents the suggestion that anaphoric structures are useful for describing nonlinear concepts because they have a "dual function"; that is, the item in question appears to *simultaneously* preserve a cohesive function of "pointing back" while having "a grammatical function . . . which should not be overlooked." Tyma has suggested one major way in which authors carry on the flow of written discourse; the real possibility that this mechanism is *not* limited to written discourse makes research in "implicit anaphora" rather central to linguistic concerns.

L.S.
E.T.

 The Use of Tenses in "Reporting Past Literature" in EST[1]

Sandra Oster

Recent studies by Louis Trimble and his colleagues have postulated certain relationships between grammatical form and rhetorical function in the English of Science and Technology (EST). One rhetorical function of considerable importance to the researcher and the student of technical disciplines is the "reporting of past literature." Recent linguistic work has been focused on the relationship between verb tenses and this rhetorical function.

In Selinker et al. (1972) the present tense has been suggested for expressing "generally accepted facts" in "background material" (p. 5). Lackstrom et al. (1972) proposed a relationship between present tense and the expression of a "core generalization." Lackstrom et al. (1973) suggested that when the technical author wishes "to claim no generality for the facts given in support of a core generalization . . . . then he will present the information in the past tense" (p. 136). In this same article, the authors noted that the past tense is also used "when the past research does not bear directly—in terms of importance—on the work described in the report" (p. 133). In contrast to this proposed use of past tense, the use of the present perfect has been seen as relating to the past literature when it is "directly relating—in terms of importance—to the work described in the report" (p. 133).

These studies are noteworthy for their ground-breaking attempts to relate rhetorical function to grammatical choice in the presentation of conclusions concerning the relationship between verb tenses and reporting of past literature. It is important to attempt to discover the extent to which these claims apply in different types of EST literature; this chapter is a contribution to that effort. Here, two technical articles in the journal *Chemical Engineering Science* have been examined, and I will argue that the uses of verb tenses as they relate to this rhetorical function may be more complex than initially suggested by Trimble and his colleagues.

It is important to note that the concept "reporting of past literature" needs refinement in itself. It appears that this rubric covers *subfunctions* that include (among others): (1) reporting of the conclusions of past literature—both in terms of numerical results and in terms of exposition; (2) reporting of the procedures of past literature; and (3) evaluating the results and procedures of past literature. Though it is beyond the scope of this chapter to enumerate and discuss the subfunctions involved in the cover term "reporting past literature," I introduce the complexity here to define the scope of my discussion in dealing with one of these subfunctions: the examination of verb tenses when reporting the conclusions of past literature.

I wish to propose the following hypotheses concerning the use of verb tenses in reporting the conclusions of past literature in these two technical articles:

Hypothesis I: The Present Perfect Tense
1. *Primary Use*: The present perfect tense is used to indicate *the continued discussion* of some of the information in the sentence in which the present perfect tense occurs as a main tense.
2. *Secondary Use*: The present perfect tense is used to claim *generality* about past literature.

Hypothesis II: The Past Tense
1. *Primary Use-1*: The past tense is used to claim *nongenerality* about past literature.
2. *Primary Use-2*: The past tense is used when it refers to quantitative results of past literature that are *nonsupportive* of some aspects of the work described in the technical article.

Hypothesis III: The Present Tense
1. *Primary Use-1*: The present tense is used when it refers to quantitative results of past literature that are *supportive* of or *nonrelevant* to some aspect of the work described in the technical article.
2. *Primary Use-2*: The present tense is used to *refer* to past literature, rather than to discuss it.

Tables 7-1 and 7-2 (excerpts taken from the two technical articles Pikios and Luss [1977] and Patel and Simpson [1977]) contain passages from the articles in which past literature is reported. I use the following conventions in the figures: the Arabic numerals to the left of each column mark the orthographic paragraphs in which the passage occurs in the text; the Roman numerals indicate titles of sections under which the passages occur; the ellipsis between paragraphs mark texts that do not report past literature and have thus been omitted; main verbs considered in this study are in italics.

TABLE 7-1.   PASSAGES "REPORTING PAST LITERATURE" IN PIKIOS AND LUSS (1977)

I. INTRODUCTION
1. Sustained isothermal, concentration oscillations *have been observed* in recent experimental studies involving the oxidation of either CO or H_2 over metal catalysts [1-9]. Various mechanisms *have been suggested* to explain this interesting phenomenon, which is not caused by an interaction between the chemical and transport rate processes. Hugo and Jakubith [3] *suggested* that the oscillations may be due to a shift during the reaction between two forms of chemisorbed CO, while Eigenberger [10] postulated a shift from an ignited to an extinguished state due to a slow variation in the surface concentration of some unreactive, chemisorbed form of oxygen. Dauchot and Cakenberghe [4] and Carberry *et al.* [5] *assumed* that the oscillations were caused by a change in the reaction mechanism with surface coverage, while Slinko *et al.* [7.9] *claimed* that they were induced by variations of the activation energy with surface coverage.

II. DEVELOPMENT OF THE MATHEMATICAL MODEL
6. Brunauer *et al.* [11] *have pointed out*, that when chemical reactions occur on catalytic surfaces, the activation energy may depend on surface coverage. This may be caused either by intrinsic surface heterogeneity, or interactions between the surface and the adsorbed species, or by a combination of both. Temkin [12] *discussed* in detail the influence of surface heterogeneity on reaction rate constants.

III. STEADY STATE DETERMINATION AND UNIQUENESS ANALYSIS

IV. STABILITY ANALYSIS
16. A linearized stability analysis indicates that a steady state is asymptotically stable to small disturbances if

$$\frac{\partial f_1}{\partial x} \frac{\partial f_2}{\partial y} - \frac{\partial f_1}{\partial y} \frac{\partial f_2}{\partial x} > 0 \qquad (25)$$

$$\frac{\partial f_1}{\partial x} + \frac{\partial f_2}{\partial y} = -(a_1 + a_2 + b_1 + b_2) + (\mu xy - x - y)e^{-\mu y} < 0. \qquad (26)$$

17. It follows from Bendixon's second theorem [13, p. 78], that when a unique steady state is unstable sustained oscillations occur, since all the trajectories are bounded in the region of interest:

$$0 \leq x \leq 1 \qquad (27a)$$
$$0 \leq y \leq 1 \qquad (27b)$$
$$0 \leq x + y \leq 1. \qquad (27c)$$

TABLE 7-1. Continued

Gavalas *has proven* [14] that condition (25) is satisfied for every unique steady state solution. Thus, when uniqueness is assured, violation of (26) is a sufficient condition for the existence of a limit cycle.

Note: The Arabic number before each orthographic paragraph refers to its place in the total text; there are a total of twenty-one orthographic paragraphs in the article. The Roman numerals indicate titles of sections under which these paragraphs occur. Main verbs considered in this study are in italics.

While the hypotheses considered below and their discussion account for all occurrences of the present perfect, past, and present tenses in the data, only representative cases from the data will be discussed in this chapter.

HYPOTHESIS I: THE PRESENT PERFECT TENSE

In Hypothesis I, the functions of the present perfect tense are divided into *Primary Use* and *Secondary Use*. This hypothesis claims that the primary function of the present perfect tense, at least in these EST articles, is to indicate to the reader that some of the information in the sentence in which the present perfect tense occurs will be mentioned to some extent in the discourse following this sentence. Through this tense, there is a promise of continuation of some topic to be pursued in the subsequent discourse. The data presented in Tables 7-1 and 7-2 support Hypothesis I.1 and I.2 for these two articles in the field of chemical engineering.

Hypothesis I.1

In Table 7-1, the first occurrence of the present perfect is at the very beginning of the report. The first two sentences of the report contain *have been observed* and *have been suggested* respectively. If Hypothesis I.1 holds, one would expect an "information item" to be mentioned again in the subsequent discourse. This, indeed, is the case, for in sentence 2 of Table 7-1, the information item that is continued from sentence 1 is expressed as *this interesting phenomenon*. The antecedent to this anaphoric phrase occurs as the subject in sentence 1, namely *sustained isothermal, concentration oscillations*.[2] The next example of the present perfect tense functioning according to Hypothesis I.1 also involves sentence 2. Here *various mechanisms* (the subject of sentence 2) is specified in the rest of the paragraph through the reporting of the mechanisms proposed in the past literature by Hugo and Jakubith, Eigeberger, and others. Another example occurs in paragraph 17 (P-17): *has proven*. The concept of "uniqueness" is the information item continued into the subsequent discourse.

TABLE 7-2. PASSAGES "REPORTING PAST LITERATURE" IN PATEL AND SIMPSON (1977)

I. INTRODUCTION

1. In contrast to the large number of investigations of wall-to-bed heat transfer in gas-fluidized beds, comparatively little [2-7] *has been published* on heat transfer in liquid-fluidized beds. From these studies the following conclusions may be drawn on wall-to-bed heat transfer in such beds:

6. The most thorough investigation to date *has been* that of Wasmund and Smith [6]. In a previous paper [7], these authors *developed* a theoretical model for heat transfer in which the thermal conductivity of the particles played a major role. In their subsequent experimental work [6] they *found* that particle thermal conductivity has only a slight effect for porosities less than 0.75 and essentially no effect for higher porosities. The temperature profiles in the bed *were found* to be parabolic, in contrast with the flat profiles characteristic of gas-fluidized beds. They also *found* that the resistance to heat transfer in a liquid-fluidized bed is divided between the region immediately adjacent to the wall and the interior of the bed. Furthermore, the major portion of the resistance shifts from the region of the wall to the bed interior as the porosity decreases. Wasmund and Smith used several sizes of glass beads and aluminum particles with water as the fluidizing medium. Their bed expansion data for these materials plotted by the method of Richardson and Zaki [19] *show* that these beds fluidized particulately [6].

7. Several correlations and models for wall-to-bed heat transfer *have also appeared* [8-10]. Of these, Hamilton's [9] correlation *fits* the data of Wasmund and our own data for glass particles (see below) quite well. The others generally *predict* low values of the heat transfer coefficients and do not predict the attainment of a maximum in the transfer coefficient versus porosity function [11]. Other works of interest *include* those of Ruckenstein *et al.* [12], Jagannadharaju [13] and Doraisamy [14].

8. It should be noted that most previous workers *have studied* fluid-particle systems that fluidize in the particulate mode, (that is, no "bubbles" are present) as is characteristic of most liquid-solid systems. Gas-fluidized beds, on the other hand, fluidize aggregatively, and above minimum fluidization velocities, bubbles or voids of gas appear and pass upward through the bed. It is generally acknowledged that the magnitude of the density difference between the solid particles and the fluid determines whether or not the bed fluidizes aggregatively. Thus Harrison *et al.* [15] and Reuter [16] *have studied* bubbles in liquid-fluidized beds of water and lead shot, which, because of the density difference between lead and water, exhibit aggregative fluidization.

9. ... Jackson [29] *has reported* that voidage fluctuations grow with height above the distributor; one might therefore expect some effect on wall-to-bed heat transfer with height above the grid. Again, a comparison with gas fluidization is pertinent. Certain correlations (e.g. [27]) of heat transfer in gas-fluidized beds *show* that the height of the heated section influences the heat transfer coefficient. In a later study, Gel'perin *et al.* [28] *have concluded* that this is not the case as long as the heated section is located above the thermal stabilization zone of the bed just above the grid. It appears then, that in gas-fluidized beds, whatever voidage variation exists with height above the grid is not sufficient to affect the heat transfer coefficient. We find this to be true for liquid-fluidized beds as well.

II. EXPERIMENTAL

10. The equipment consisted of an electrically heated once-through flow loop containing a 27.5 in. tall fluidized bed. Water was used as the fluidizing medium. Water flowed from the mains through a pump (used for high flow rates), through rotameters, up the bed and thence to the drains. A complete description *is given* by Simpson [17].

TABLE 7-2. Continued

11. It should be noted that this arrangement allowed measurement of *local* heat transfer coefficients, in contrast to the work of Wasmund and Smith [6] where the coefficient *was calculated* based on heat transfer through their entire heated section which was 18 in. long.

III. RESULTS

Bed expansion

16. Expansion data of the glass and the lead beds were correlated by the method of Richardson and Zaki [19]. The results *showed* that the glass particules fluidized particulately whereas the lead particles exhibited aggregative fluidization [17]. In beds of lead particles small 1/16 to 1/8 in. dia. bubbles were observed at porosities near 0.7 and greater. Glass beds were uniform with no trace of bubbles.

Heat transfer

17. Heat transfer data were obtained for all the particle types shown in Table 1. The data for glass beads are in general agreement with those of Wasmund [6] and other workers [3,20] and are thus not reported in detail here. Full details *are given* by Simpson [17].

Comparison with correlations

20. Various correlations and models for all heat transfer in liquid-fluidized beds are available [6,8–10] as discussed above. Data obtained in this study were compared with the predictions of the correlations. For the glass particles, the equations of Wasmund and Smith [6] and Hamilton [9] *are* in very good agreement with our data. For the two larger sizes of glass their equations slightly *underpredicted* our data. The average deviation *was* -3 to -10%. [Here deviation = (correlation value—expt. value)/expt. value]. For the two smaller sizes the average deviation *was* greater, roughly -30%. This increased deviation may be due to agglomeration of the smaller size glass particles. The overall agreement is quite good considering that our equipment gave coefficients also slightly above those for the open pipe correlation. In marked contrast, the equation of Tripathi and Pandey [8] *showed* an average deviation of 50–70% below our data for glass, depending on particle size, and the turbulent model of Wasan and Ahluwalia [10] *fell* below our data for one size by an average 60%. The latter model also greatly underestimates Wasmund's [6] data—see [17]. For lead particles, the Wasmund and the Hamilton correlations *do not apply*, and were not tested. The Tripathi correlation again *fell* about 40–60% below our data for lead; the Wasan model *showed* about 40% deviation for one size of lead. Further details are give by Simpson [17].

We conclude that the Wasmund and the Hamilton equations *fit* the data for glass particles very well. The other equations *show* large negative deviations.

Bed temperature profiles

22. The radial temperature profiles for glass beds were found to be similar to those reported and discussed by Wasmund [6].

Two-resistance model

24. The shapes of the observed temperature profiles suggest a two-resistance model for heat transfer. Crider and Foss [22] and other workers *have developed* such models for packed beds, and Wasmund and Smith [6] *have also used* it to analyze their fluidized bed data. The two-resistance model envisages the overall resistance to heat transfer to exist in two regions; a hypothetical film at the wall, and the bed region.

Wall Stanton numbers

26. ... As mentioned above, at porosities above 0.55, the bed changes rather abruptly from a more or less quiescent, slightly expanded state to a very turbulent swirling type of flow. Cairns and Prausnitz [24] *have observed* this instability and have related it

82 / ENGLISH FOR ACADEMIC AND TECHNICAL PURPOSES

TABLE 7-2. Continued

qualitatively to particle size, particle density and the ratio of particle-to-tube-diameter. The change in slope in Fig. 5 is very probably linked to this effect.
Bed resistance and Peclet numbers

27. ... Figure 6 shows the bed resistance as a percentage of the total resistance for beds of lead particles. It is clear that at most values of porosity, the bed resistance is very significant, and previous models that neglect this resistance would fail to correlate data for different bed diameters. Corresponding values for glass particles are similar and *are given* by Simpson [17].

28. Figure 7 shows Pe_r^* plotted against particle Reynolds number for our data on glass particles and also data from the dye tracer work of Hanratty *et al.* [25], the salt tracer measurements of Cairns and Prausnitz [24] and the heat transfer measurements of Wasmund and Smith [6]. All these results *are* for glass particles. Fair agreement *is shown* considering the variety of techniques used and the difficulty of these measurements. This agreement *lends* support to the applicability and the usefulness of the eddy diffusivity model of radial mixing in such beds. Note that because of the definition of the modified radial Peclet number Pe_r^*, Fig. 7 is somewhat misleading in that it shows Pe_r^* to be smallest for the smallest particle size thus implying best mixing for these particles. Radial mixing given by the radial eddy diffusivity. E_r is actually greatest for the largest size of glass particles and decreases monotonically with particle size at constant porosity. Simpson [17] *has reported* the actual values of E_r. Our data for E_r for the two smaller sizes of glass are somewhat high (low values of Pe_r^* in Fig. 7) compared to those of Hanratty and of Wasmund, and probably result from particle agglomeration.

29. ... There appears to be only one previous study of radial mixing in beds of lead particles fluidized with liquids, that of Cairns and Prausnitz [24]. These workers measured radial eddy diffusivities by a salt tracer method for 2.96 mm (0.117 in.) lead spheres in a 4 in. column using water as the fluidizing medium. These data plotted as modified radial Peclet numbers *are also shown* in Fig. 8. These authors *have concluded* [24,26] that the fluid-to-solid density difference and the particle diameter to bed diameter ratio, D_p/D are the variables that affect flow patterns and mixing most strongly. Accordingly, in order to compare our results with theirs, this ratio is shown on Figs. 7 and 8. It may be seen that there is fair agreement between their data (D_p/D = 0.0293) and our results for the largest lead particles (D_p/D = 0.259). The discrepancies are greatest at low values of porosity; further Cairns' data *do not show* the rise in Pe_r^* at porosities between 0.6 and 0.7 as exhibited by all sizes of lead used in our study. It should be noted that Cairns' curve reproduced in Fig. 8 *was based* on only three data points between the packed bed and open pipe values of porosity, and consequently the effect we have observed may have been missed in their study.

IV. CONCLUSIONS

36. The correlations of Wasmund [6] and Hamilton [9] *are* reliable for fluidized beds of glass. Other available correlations [8,10] give large negative deviations from the data values.

Note: The Arabic number before each orthographic paragraph refers to its place in the total text; there are a total of thirty-six orthographic paragraphs in the article. The Roman numerals indicate titles of sections under which these paragraphs occur. Main verbs considered in this study are in italics.

In Table 7-2, the technical authors' use of the present perfect tense also supports Hypothesis I.1. The use of this tense in reporting past literature is numerous in the article; its occurrence in P-1, P-6, and P-7 will now be examined.

The first occurrence of the present perfect tense in this article is paper- and paragraph-initial (similar to its first occurrence in Table 7-1). The first sentence in Table 7-2 appears to function to introduce information that will be discussed in the following discourse. The information items discussed further are the publications themselves; though they state that "comparatively little has been published," the technical authors here have reported on what does exist. Thus, the subsequent paragraphs 6, 7, 8, and 9 pursue the discussion of this past literature. In P-6, the presence of the present perfect tense *has been* seems to mark the subsequent literature as dealing with information in the sentence in which this verb tense occurs, and the subsequent text does indeed deal with the examination of the Wasmund and Smith investigation. In P-7, the present perfect tense also functions in accordance with Hypothesis I.1, for the *correlations and models* are discussed in the remainder of the paragraph.

Hypothesis I.2

This hypothesis claims that the present perfect tense is used to generalize about past literature. *Generality* in Hypothesis I.2 refers to information items that include greater semantic domains than related items in the subsequent discourse.[3] This hypothesis does not coincide with Lackstrom et al. (1972) who have suggested, "In technical English the present tense means generalization—and the present tense will occur where technical rhetoric requires the expression of this meaning. One of these places will be in the expression of the core idea" (p. 6). Hypothesis I.2 proposes that this usage is found in the present perfect tense in the two articles examined, not in the present tense as these authors suggest.

In Table 7-1, as mentioned above, the first two instances of the present perfect tense have been noted to indicate that there will be a continuation of certain material in the discourse. The purpose of this indication reflects the secondary nature of the present perfect as found here: to introduce a topic of greater domain of information than that found in the subsequent discourse. The topic within the sentence containing *have been observed* deals with introducing the core idea of oscillations, while the next sentence, with *have been suggested,* deals more specifically with the *various mechanisms* of oscillations. This latter sentence is still general in that it introduces the broader topic of "various mechanisms" that is pursued in the rest of the paragraph. *This* relationship between these two present perfect tenses is examined in the Discussion section at the close of the chapter.

In P-6 of Table 7-1, the present perfect *have pointed out* introduces the information item *surface coverage.* The subject of this sentence is definite, unlike the two previous cases, but nevertheless they both occur in sentences that function to introduce a general topic (cf., Lackstrom et al. 1973 for a discussion of the interaction of tenses and noun phrases related to "degree of generality").

This general topic *surface coverage* is more inclusive in its domain of information than *surface heterogeneity* found in the subsequent discourse.

In Table 7-2, similar uses of the present perfect tense can be found in support of Hypothesis I.2. The first occurrence *has been published* (P-1) occurs in a general statement about the past literature; this statement deals with the quantity of past literature that discusses heat transfer. Paragraphs 6, 7, 8, and 9 identify actual studies that explore this topic. For example, P-6 deals with the Wasmund and Smith study. The occurrence of the present perfect *has been* (P-6) is followed in the subsequent discourse by a series of specific results from the Wasmund and Smith study. The present perfect *has been* indicates an information item (the Wasmund and Smith study) is of a broader information domain than the specific results of the study.

The reader should note that in this discussion I am not suggesting that the absence of the present perfect tense (i.e., the choice of another tense) indicates that the topic of the subsequent passage will not have been mentioned previously and that the absence necessarily indicates lack of generality. What I am suggesting here is that when reporting past literature in these two technical articles, the presence of the present perfect tense indicates that some information item in the sentence in which the present perfect occurs will be pursued in the subsequent discussion and that the information item is of a broader information domain than related items in the subsequent discourse.

HYPOTHESIS II: THE PAST TENSE

Hypothesis II has been divided into two primary and independent functions, the first of which relates to the secondary use of Hypothesis I. Hypothesis II.1 claims that the past tense is used to claim nongenerality. From examining the data in these two technical articles, it appears that in reporting past literature, the past tense occurs when some item within the sentence in which the past tense occurs has been mentioned in the previous text. And this previous mention is usually at a higher level of generality; that is, at a broader domain. Thus, the past tense would predictably occur in a sentence with a lower level of generality, a relatively more limited domain, than the sentence in which the referent first occured. This use of the past tense supports the claim by Trimble and his colleagues that the past tense may be used when the author wishes "to claim no generality for the facts given in support of a core generalization. Then he will present the information in the past tense" (Lackstrom et al. 1973:136). Hypothesis II.1 appears to be supported by the data in Tables 7-1 and 7-2.

Hypothesis II.1

In Table 7-1, P-1, the two general introductions in which the present perfect tense occurs are subsequently supported by a series of sentences with past tense main verbs: *suggested, postulated, assumed, claimed*. In P-6, *discussed* indicates that the sentence beginning with "Temkin" reports about a topic at a lower level of generality than the information in the sentence introducing its generalization (indicated by *have pointed out*). In Table 7-2, though the orthographic paragraph set-up is slightly different, a series of specific information about past literature follows a more general claim about the Wasmund and Smith investigation. The expressions *developed, were found,* and *found* indicate that the sentences function to give information of a more limited domain than the initial sentence of P-6 that establishes a broader domain, that of the Wasmund and Smith investigation.

In both these technical articles, the use of the present perfect and the past tenses in tandem demonstrates the rhetorical relationship of general/specific, respectively. The use of the present perfect here appears to imply to the reader that a topic within that sentence will be pursued in the subsequent discourse and that the use of the past tense indicates that the information about the past literature is given as more limited information for a preceding statement of a larger domain of information.

Hypothesis II.2

The second primary use of the past tense is related to the type of expression of the results of the past literature. In Table 7-2, the past tense occurs in P-20, in which equations are reported from the past literature: ". . . their equations slightly underpredicted our data. The average deviation was -3 to -10%." Other similar uses of the past tense in reporting past literature in which quantitative results do not support the work being described in the report can be found in Table 7-2, and they will be compared to the use of the present tense below (cf., Hypothesis III.2).

HYPOTHESIS III: THE PRESENT TENSE

Hypothesis III has also been divided into two primary and independent functions as well; the first of these relates to Hypothesis II.2. The proposed functions of the present tense appear to have a much more limited function than what Trimble and his colleagues found in their technical literature. Whereas Lackstrom et al. (1972) claim that the present tense is seen to mean "generalization," in the data examined here, this function appears to be carried out by the present perfect tense. The question remains regarding the function of the present tense when reporting past literature.

Hypothesis III.1

This hypothesis proposes that when results of a quantitative nature are reported, and when these results support some of the work described in the report, then the present tense is used. In Table 7-2, the first occurrence of the present tense in P-6 seems to support this hypothesis: "their bed expansion data . . . show." In P-7, the use of the present tense is also supportive of Hypothesis III.1; for example, "Hamilton's correlation . . . fits the data of Wasmund and our own data . . . ." (For use of *include* in P-7, see below.) In P-9, *show* is linked with *correlations of heat transfer*.

A clear example in support of the interweavings of Hypothesis III.1 and also of Hypothesis II.2 is in P-20 of Table 7-2. The data of Wasmund and Smith and Hamilton are in support of the work being described in the report and are expressed in the present tense, while the nonsupportive data of certain past research is in the past tense: "the turbulent model of Wasan and Ahluwalia fell below our data . . . . the Wasmund and Hamilton correlations do not apply . . . . The Tripathi correlation again fell about 40-60% below our data for lead; the Wasan model showed about 40% deviation for one size of lead . . . . We conclude that the Wasmund and the Hamilton equations fit the data for glass particles very well."

In addition to the tenses of the verbs, the forms of the nonsupportive data appear also to be expressed by a negative (e.g., do *not* apply) or by verbs and prepositions that indicate a subordinate position (e.g., *fell* about 40-60% *below* our data), and supportive data appear to be expressed by the absence of the negative and by verbs that do not indicate a subordinate position (e.g., fit the data).

In P-29, *data do not show* at first appears to be an exception to Hypothesis III.1 because, by the presence of the negative, it looks nonsupportive, yet it is in the present tense. However, upon closer examination of the semantics of this phrase and the passage in which it occurs, it appears that the shortcoming of Cairn's data is presented in support of the greater adequacy of the technical author's research data. Because it is in support, though expressed in the negative, the present tense is used. The form and the tense of the verb appear to indicate supportive and nonsupportive data more clearly than the presence or absence of the negative and the verb and preposition choices.

Hypothesis III.2

Another function of present tense in reporting past literature is to make references to past literature. Selinker et al. (1972) have suggested (p. 5) that the present tense is used when reference is made to tables and other illustrations. I would like to expand this claim to include reference made to past literature. Data in support of this are in Table 7-2, P-7, in which *include* refers to the literature of Ruckenstein et al., Jagannadharaju, and Doraisamy. In Patel and Simpson (1977), the reader is frequently referred to past literature by *Simpson*; this referencing occurs in the present tense in P-10, P-17, P-20, and P-27. The one apparent exception to the present tense referencing function is found in P-28: "Simpson has reported." Here, the present perfect is used. If this occurrence follows Hypothesis I rather than Hypothesis III, I would expect that there is a continuation of the discussion of some aspect of the Simpson report, and this aspect would be at a higher level of generality than its handling in the subsequent discourse. In fact, this appears to be the case here where a continuation of the discussion of the "values of E_r" is found in the subsequent sentence.

DISCUSSION

The uses that I have proposed for the three tenses have been discussed as discrete categories with discrete relationships. But I believe the situation is more complex than this. It appears that there are *interrelationships* between the functions, and these functions suggest conditions in which one verb tense may be chosen over another.

In P-1 of Table 7-1, the present perfect *have been suggested* has been discussed as less general relative to the first sentence of the paragraph. Even though the second sentence is less general, it is still *not* "nongeneral"; it functions to claim generality about certain past literature dealing with *various mechanisms*, and the discourse following sentence 2 specifies various technical literature dealing with this topic. Hence, the choice of the present perfect tense over the past indicates that though sentence 2 is less general than sentence 1, it still functions to introduce a topic that will be discussed further in the text. It is because of this function that I adopt the term "nongeneral" in Hypothesis II.1 rather than the term "specific." The information of the present perfect tense is nongeneral relative to its subsequent discourse, though it is of a more limited domain relative to its preceding discourse. Hence, the tense used to specify the literature that introduces the topic of the mechanisms in sentence 2 is the present perfect, and the tense used to specify the literature that specifically identifies the past literature dealing with investigations about the mechanisms is the past tense.[4]

Notice that in Tables 7-1 and 7-2, the sentences in which the past tense occur are actually general statements about the conclusions of the past literature. That the past tense is chosen to express such generality seems at first contrary to Hypothesis II.1. It is not. When the present perfect tense is used in reporting past literature, I believe the reader would expect some sort of continued discussion about the literature at a more limited domain of information, since whenever this tense occurs in the data examined here, there is such a continuation of discussion. When the past tense is used, I believe the reader would not expect some sort of continued discussion, since when examining the data, the sentence containing the past tense is not followed by more specific information. It appears, then, that the choice of verb tense reflects technical writing strategies for including information about past literature in a report, and for signaling to the reader that the information will or will not be pursued in the subsequent discourse.

The notion of "subsequent discourse" has been used throughout this chapter, and I now offer a partial clarification of this concept. It first appears that subsequent discourse means the sentence immediately following a sentence with the salient feature of present perfect tense. However, this is not always the case.

In Table 7-2, there are four paragraphs that intervene between sentence 1 in P-1 and the specific literature that discusses the general topic of the sentence. These intervening paragraphs are concerned with listing generally accepted conclusions about "wall-to-bed heat transfer" in gas-fluidized beds. The reporting of past literature is not presented until after these conclusions. It appears that subsequent discourse here is not the immediately subsequent text.

However, the other extreme is possible. In P-9 of Table 7-2, the subsequent discourse for *has reported* begins with the sentence in which the present perfect verb occurs; it is the second clause of the sentence.

There are obviously problems with and expections to these hypotheses. For example, in Table 7-2, P-21, we find *other equations show*. These equations refer to quantitative results of past literature that do not support the present study. According to Hypothesis II.2, I would expect that the verb tense would be past, but it is not. This might be due to the concluding tone of the passage. Here, the author is drawing conclusions about certain data of past literature rather than presenting the conclusions of the past literature. It may be possible that the rhetorical function of drawing conclusions about past literature is expressed in the present tense. In any case, though, to what extent this conclusion fits the category "reporting conclusions of past literature" as I have defined past literature here is unclear to me at this time.

The reader may be interested in the following passage, where an indeterminacy occurs: "Several attempts *have been made* at finding limit cycles for cases in which nonunique steady states exist. We simulated several cases for which the system has three steady states, two of which were unstable" (Pikios and Luss (1977), P-21) Here it is unclear, at least to me, whether "past literature" or "procedures" are involved. To obtain greater accuracy of description in cases such as these, it is clear that one needs to develop techniques to use with a specialist informant (cf. Selinker, 1979).

CONCLUSION

To examine the relationship between the rhetorical function of "reporting past literature" and the choice of verb tenses, certain distinctions in the concept of "reporting past literature" were made. The hypotheses proposed in this chapter concerning the present perfect, past, and present tenses within the subfunction of "reporting the *conclusions* of past literature," have been supported by the data in the two technical articles examined. However, even though the data bears out certain relationships between rhetorical function and grammatical form, I believe the results cannot as yet be generalized beyond the scope of this study. Perhaps the uses of verb tenses described here reflect individual author styles that are not representative of the writing used in the English of chemical engineering, let alone the whole range of genres of EST texts.

Another reservation concerning generalizing from the results here is that there may be different *sets* of verb choices used in "reporting the conclusions of past literature." Perhaps my study describes only one such set; many other sets (e.g., past perfect, present perfect, and present) may exist. Also, the function of "reporting past literature" needs further refinement, and once more work is done on this topic, perhaps yet other distinctions can be made in the relationship between choice of verb tenses and the rhetorical function of reporting past literature.

I believe the value of this study rests in that it is a contribution to research on which sound *practical* procedures may be developed. It is my guess that both native and non-native speakers/writers need to be aware of the subtle distinctions in tense usage of the kind reported here. One must be cautious in the practical domain and must distinguish between goal-oriented and process-oriented instruction (cf. Widdowson, chap. 1). The value of research of the type described here is that one now has a stronger data base for such important practical decisions.

Notes

1. I wish to thank Larry Selinker for his encouragement in my investigation of verb tenses and their relationship to rhetorical functions. I am grateful to him for his numerous suggestions regarding earlier drafts of this chapter. Of course, he is not responsible for any specific claims made.

2. Of considerable interest is the relationship between anaphoric items and verb tenses in reporting past literature. See Tyma (chap. 6) for a discussion of the relationship between cohesion and the rhetorical functions of definition and classification. A rich area for further investigation is the cohesive relationship between anaphoric items and verb tenses.

3. Hypotheses I.1 and I.2 differ in this respect of generality. Hypothesis I.1 makes no claims about the semantic domains of the information items but deals with the textual location of the information units, independent of their levels of generality. Hypothesis I.2 makes no claims about the textual location of the information units but deals with their semantic domains.

4. See Oster (In Preparation), which investigates verb tenses and relative levels of generality.

References

Lackstrom, J. E., L. Selinker, and L. P. Trimble. 1972. "Grammar and Technical English." *English Teaching Forum,* September-October, 3-14.

———. 1973. "Technical Rhetorical Principles and Grammatical Choice." *TESOL Quarterly* 7. 127-36.

Oster, S. In prep. *Relative Levels of Generality and Verb Tenses in EST.*

Patel, R. D., and J. M. Simpson. 1977. "Heat Transfer in Aggregation and Particulate Liquid-fluidized Beds." *Chemical Eningeering Science* 32.67-74.

Pikios, C. A., and D. Luss. 1977. "Isothermal Concentration Oscillations on Catalytic Surfaces." *Chemical Engineering Science* 32.191-94.

Selinker, L. 1979. "On the Use of Informants in Discourse Analysis and 'Language for Specialized Purposes.'" *IRAL*, August 1979.

Selinker, L., L. P. Trimble, and R. Vroman. 1972. Working papers in English for science and technology. University of Washington, College of Engineering.

Tyma, D. 1979. "Anaphoric functions of some demonstrative noun phrases in EST." (chap. 6, this vol.)

Widdowson, H. G. 1979. "ESP: Criteria for Course Design." (chap. 1, this vol.)

Editorial Comments

To our knowledge, Oster's is the first paper in the EST literature that deals exclusively with tense usage in the rhetorical function area of "reporting past research," though, as she herself points out, this area is a recognized part of Trimble's rhetoric, and he and his colleagues have related this function to tense usage in past work.

One contribution in this chapter is the recognition that reporting past research is *not* just one unitary function but at least three subfunctions. In a textualization case study using as data two chemical engineering technical articles (a genre of data not previously reported on in the EST literature), Oster studies one of these subfunctions in depth and its relation to tense choice. She proposes testable hypotheses (some of which go counter to earlier work) as to the rhetorical functioning of the past, present perfect, and present tenses in reporting the *conclusions* of past literature in an EST discipline. It just may be that some grammatical choices are more genre-based than had been earlier thought.

Oster's paper brings up the problem of "reasonable sizes of sample." Oster is very careful to limit her claims to the case study and the data presented, but the problems of generalizability and validity remain. How much data is enough? And for what purpose? Any one who has tried to rummage for data in a transportation library, say, and has seen the vast amount of technical material available in one engineering discipline alone, is bound to realize that validity in the area of EST goal-oriented textualization research will be hard to come by.

Finally, an interesting area suggested for future research (note 2) is the cohesive relationship between anaphora, as discussed by Tyma, and one use of verb tense in reporting the conclusions of past literature.

L.S.
E.T.

8
Scientific and Technical Discourse:
A Comparative Analysis of English and Romanian

Thomas Mage

Until recently, linguistics has concerned itself mainly with language facts found at the word or sentence level and most teaching methods based on linguistic findings are derived from sentence-oriented grammars. As a result, one might expect that the facility for reading and comprehending individual sentences does not necessarily lead to a facility for reading and comprehending passages of continuous prose.

This fact became readily obvious to me while tutoring foreign students enrolled in the science and engineering programs at the University of Washington. My involvement in a program designed by Louis Trimble and his colleagues—a sequence of courses in the College of Engineering set up specifically for foreign learners of English studying theoretical and applied sciences—made me aware of the fact that although students had little difficulty understanding the individual sentences in a paragraph, the meaning of the entire paragraph was often unclear to them.

If this is the case then, that understanding individual sentences does not necessarily lead to an understanding of continuous passages of writing, we should be just as careful in examining language at the discourse or suprasentential level as we are at the word or sentence level. When we deal with language at the discourse level, it would also seem more appropriate to examine language function and use rather than only language structure.

In examining the various functions and uses of language at the discourse level, especially in relation to scientific discourse, it appears that certain kinds of well-ordered sequences of language are connected with certain reasoning processes that are given expression through basic rhetorical patterns of definition, classification, generalization, and such. When confronted with these rhetorical patterns, it is the reader's task to decipher a code; to break this code he or she has to recognize how the rhetorical patterns are used in the language of a text to structure and interpret that text correctly.

Thus far the terms *use* and *function* have been rather vague, and a more precise statement of how the language of a text is to be characterized is needed. H. G. Widdowson provides a working description of the structure of a piece of discourse.

DISCOURSE ANALYSIS

Widdowson (1974:30) points out that when one is confronted with a sample of language, a chapter from a chemistry textbook, for example, the description of that sample might proceed along two different lines. First, "...we may treat it as an exemplification of the language system and point out the incidence of certain linguistic structures and items of vocabulary: in other words, we can describe its formal properties as an instance of linguistic usage." He adds, however, that we fail to account for a number of things if we treat linguistic usage strictly as a sample of language: "In the first place it clearly does not just exist as usage, as an exemplification of the language system: It is also an instance of use; it communicates something and does so in a certain manner. If we were to ask the author or the reader to describe the sample, the likelihood is that he would characterize it as a description or a report of a set of instructions, or an account of an experiment."

These latter terms, *description, report, set of instructions*, and *account of an experiment*, do not refer to the linguistic properties of the sample "but to the communicative function of the sample as discourse." Elsewhere Allen and Widdowson (1974:3) suggest that we shift our attention from the grammatical to the communicative properties of language. They would develop in the language student a capacity to recognize "how sentences are used in the performance of acts of communication, the ability to understand the rhetorical functioning of language in use" and to develop a like capacity in recognizing and manipulating "the formal devices which are used to combine sentences to create continuous passages of prose." The use of sentences is roughly defined as discourse, and the investigation into the way sentences are put to communicative use in the performance of social actions is discourse analysis.

Further, Widdowson (1973:9) claims that irrespective of the language used in composing technical discourse, whether it is English, French, Indonesian, or Chinese, the writer is compelled by the basic cognitive and methodological process of scientific investigation to use similar rhetorical patterns in the writing of science and technology. He suggests that the way English is used in science and for other special purposes may be more aptly described "not as formally defined varieties of English, but as realizations of universal sets of concepts and methods or procedures which define disciplines or areas of enquiry independently of any particular language."

Widdowson's last statement sets forth an interesting hypothesis; it initially served as the departure point for my study contrasting the discourse of technical English and Spanish (Mage 1977). It again provides the reason for further investigation into the possible existence of universal tendencies in the languages of science and technology. This chapter will investigate what similarities can be found, at the discourse level, between the writing of English and Romanian for Science and Technology (EST and RST, respectively).

More specifically, this chapter will compare specific rhetorical functions in RST with equivalent areas in EST in which research has already been done. These areas are: (1) the notion of the conceptual paragraph as the basic rhetorical unit; (2) the rhetorical function of direct definition; and (3) the rhetorical function of direct classification. Particular attention will be given to the type, amount, and organization of rhetorical information presented in a piece of discourse.

RESEARCH IN EST

Since 1967, several researchers, for example, Lackstrom, Selinker, and Trimble, have dealt with the notion of *rhetoric* in scientific and technical English. They claim that in EST, rhetoric is concerned with organizing information and relating concepts such that the concepts are the most functional for the purpose of the discourse and for a particular kind of reader. When rhetorical function is talked about, it is in terms of what the paragraph does; for example, the paragraph may function to define, classify, present an hypothesis, draw a conclusion, and so forth. This is perhaps what Widdowson means when he says that the language student must develop a capacity to recognize how sentences are used in the performance of acts of communication and to understand the rhetorical functioning of language in use.

Lackstrom, Selinker, and Trimble (1973:129) establish the paragraph as the basic rhetorical unit and define it as "a unit of discourse which presents a selected amount of information on a given subject for a given purpose." However, their notion of *paragraph* is not often found in traditional textbooks; traditionally the paragraph has been defined as a group of sentences forming a complete unit of thought and marked on a page of text by spacing or indentation.

Upon close examination we notice that the traditional definition involves two separate ideas; first it mentions "content" and then talks about "form." If we isolate these two parts of the definition and look at each separately, we find that the result is two different meanings for the term *paragraph*. The first half of the definition, "forming a complete unit of thought," describes what is called the *conceptual paragraph,* while the second half of the definition, "marked on a page of text by spacing or indentation," describes what is referred to as the *physical paragraph* (Selinker and Trimble 1967).

The traditional definition of paragraph appears to be the cause of varying degrees of student misunderstanding; years of direct classroom observation and testing by Trimble and associates, suggest that many non-native readers of EST tend to assume that a new physical paragraph signals the presentation of a new subject. The student is "misled in respect to the relationships of the information given in consecutive physical paragraphs when, often, they represent simply parts of a larger whole" (Lackstrom et al. 1973).

This distinction between physical and conceptual paragraph is important both on the theoretical level and on the applied level. On the theoretical level we are interested in how speakers of different languages organize their written information and on the applied level our interest concerns matters of second language teaching methodology.

In EST it is the conceptual paragraph that functions as the basic unit of discourse, and "the writer makes rhetorical decisions and organizational choices which he incorporates within the framework of the EST paragraph" (Lackstrom et al. 1973). This paragraph is fairly simple in basic concept and develops in a straightforward manner. It either contains, or its content clearly implies, a generalization called the *core*. This core develops, not out of grammatical considerations, but "out of the organization required for technical prose. This organization is fairly rigid in form, with the core of each conceptual paragraph being a generalization in relation to the specificity of the supporting facts contained within the paragraph" (Lackstrom et al. 1973).

If this core is overtly specified, it is either stated in the first sentence of the paragraph, stated as a separate sentence, or (as pointed out in Lackstrom, Selinker, and Trimble 1973, Figure 2) "rhetorically embedded" in adjoining sentences. That the domain of the conceptual paragraph extends across the boundaries of more than one physical paragraph holds true as long as the core is supported by succeeding information. In subsequent physical paragraphs the support is often initially indicated through the use of lower level generalizations or subcores. Example 1 (Lackstrom et al. 1973) illustrates the EST paragraph.

1. *The components composing the urban system* can be categorized into two major categories. These *are the land use configuration and the transportation system*. These two categories interact with each other as well as with themselves.

    Land use refers to the spatial configuration of the supply and demand of opportunities: for instance, the demand for interaction of opportunities is located in institutional, commercial, and industrial areas. The supply side of opportunities is measured in terms of the intensity of attractiveness, which may be expressed by the number of jobs in the specific zone. The spatial location and quantities of these entities (supply and demand of opportunities) in relation to the others are the major attributes of the land use components of the urban system.

    The transportation system determines the ease of interaction between the supply and demand configurations. The transportation system has two attributes. One is the transportation network, which determines the spatial coverage of its service, and the other is the level of service or quality of the transportation system. Both factors have an effect on the interaction between activities.

(Extracted from "The Achievement of Opportunity Objectives Through Transportation and Land-Use Planning," *The Trend In Engineering*, 22.2:29-30, 1970.)

Note that the first physical paragraph contains the following core idea: "The two major components of the urban system—the land use configuration and the transportation system—interact with each other and interact internally." The author subsequently develops each of these parts in a separate physical paragraph. Notice that each of the physical paragraphs has a core of its own which, as previously stated, is called a subcore. These subcores are generalizations of a lower level than the one stated in the first physical paragraph. In the example they are first, "the land use components in the urban system," and second, "the transportation system interaction." This example, of one conceptual paragraph composed of three physical paragraphs, illustrates a one-to-more-than-one correspondence that has already been found in the writing of technical Spanish (Mage 1977) and that we hope to find in RST.

The first step in our analysis is to determine whether or not the conceptual paragraph operates as the basic unit of discourse in the writing of RST as it does for the writing of EST, and if core and subcore generalizations can be similarly isolated. Example 2 shows that the conceptual paragraph in RST is equivalent in form and development to that of the EST example.

2. *Ungerea motoarelor se face prin barbotaj, prin presiune sau, de obicei, print-o combinare a acestor sisteme.*

   Ungerea prin barbotaj se obține prin răspîndirea uleiului din carter sub formă fin pulverizată (ceață) cu ajutorul unor proeminențe ale bielelor. Picăturile de ulei se depun pe suprafețele care trebuie unse, în special pe fața interioară a cămășilor de cilindru, sau se adună în scobituri care comunică cu orificiile de ungere ale organelor. Este necesar deci ca nivelul uleiului . . . .

   Ungerea sub presiune se obține cu una sau mai multe pompe de ungere care trimit uleiul in cantitatea dorită și cu presiunea necesară la toate punctele care au nevoie de ungere. In același timp, uleiul este trimis și prin filtre care îndepărtează particulele mecanice fine ce s-au desprins din fusurile unse și care ar putea provoca o sporire a uzurilor.

   Ungerea mixtă se obține folosind pentru organele principale, și anume pentru fusurile arborelui cotit și manetoane, ungerea sub presiune, iar pentru rest ungerea prin barbotaj. Dezavantajele barbotajului se mențin și la ungerea mixtă.

   (Extracted from Banărescu, M., "Motoare cu ardere internă"[1] II, *Editura Tehnică*, București, 1959, pp. 504-506.)

This RST example presents a conceptual paragraph formed of four physical paragraphs; that is, a one-to-more-than-one correspondence. The three subcores "ungerea prin barbotaj," "ungerea sub presiune," and "ungerea mixtă" support the core idea of "ungerea motoarelor." The second, third, and fourth physical paragraphs expand upon the three ways in which lubrication takes place within an internal combustion engine.

Now that we have hypothesized that there are conceptual paragraphs in RST that function like the basic rhetorical units in EST and that core and subcore ideas can similarly be isolated, let us examine another basic rhetorical notion in EST—that of the rhetorical function of the conceptual paragraph.

In the following comparisons we are concerned with the basic rhetorical functions of paragraphs that define and classify. It seems important to compare definition and classification because they are two of the basic manners in which scientists provide their reader-audience with information. In comparing the role of definition and classification, as it functions in EST and RST, we want to determine whether the same amount and type of information is given in EST as it is in RST.

DIRECT DEFINITION

In EST there are two types of definition that the writer can employ in developing a piece of discourse, *direct* and *indirect*.[2] Within the category of direct definition there are various types of definition the writer can choose, depending upon the amount of information he or she wishes to provide the reader. If concerned with giving the reader a maximum amount of information in as precise a manner as possible, the writer uses a *formal definition*.

A definition is said to be formal when it has a form consisting of three parts. The first part is the *term*—the word or object, idea or concept, to be defined. The second is the *class* (or set)—the genus, group, or category in which the term belongs. The third part deals with the *differences*—the distinctive characteristics that distinguish the term from other members of the class. Example 3 is an illustration of a formal definition in EST:

> 3. A triode is a vacuum tube which contains 3 elements: a cathode, an anode, and a grid. The triode is used where signal to noise ratio is not critical and signal amplification from 0 to 100 is desired. Other standard vacuum tubes are .... (Extracted from a student paper.)

What the author considers important about whatever is being defined is indicated by the nature of the differences. If, for example, the writer is defining an electronic device (a transistor, a tube, a circuit, etc.), he or she may choose to stress the physical structure of that device; therefore the differences will be statements about the physical nature of the device. Notice that this is what is happening in example 3; the term being defined is *triode*, and it belongs to the class of *vacuum tubes*. The basic differences that distinguish it from all other vacuum tubes are elements of its physical structure (i.e., a cathode, an anode, and a grid).

The writer may, however, want to consider how the device operates; in this case he or she will stress the function—either the function of the whole or of the parts or both. The writer can also present the differences of both the physical and functional nature of the device, although this much information is seldom presented in a single sentence.

Let us compare the following definition in RST with the EST example just given to determine: (1) if the same amount and type of information is given and (2) if this equals a formal definition:

> 4. Dioda este un tub electronic cu doi electrozi: anodul și catodul. Catodul este realizat dintre-un corp metalic ca are proprietatea de a emite electroni in condițiile arătate anterior. Anodul captează electronii emiși de catod.
>
> (Extracted from Millea, A., Popovici, Al., "Initiere în Electronića," *Editura Tehnică*, București, 1964, p. 112.)

The *term* to be defined in this example is "dioda," the *class* is "un tub electronic" and the *differences* are "anodul si catodul," in effect, the differences that distinguish it from other possible members of the same class.

As in the case of the EST example, the RST example can be characterized as a formal definition because it also gives the same type and amount of information. This formal definition is stated in terms of physical traits and purpose of a "dioda"; by referring the reader to a graph, picture, or schematization, he wishes to make his core idea clear, here again, in terms of the physical characteristics of *diodes*.

In comparing the basic rhetorical functions of formal definition, we have seen that the EST and RST paragraphs manifest striking similarities. These similarities demonstrate that the EST and RST paragraphs do indeed give the same type and amount of information and that in both cases this information is definable as a formal definition. Let us now turn to classification.

DIRECT CLASSIFICATION

Classification is the process of relating a concept to that segment of knowledge of which it is a part: it provides information concerning what segment of the universe the concept fits into and what other concepts are related and in what manner, and how these other concepts differ from it (Weisman 1962: 194-96). Like definition, classification appears to be an essential part of organized thinking.

Writers often use the rhetorical function of classification as the basic organizational structure of an entire piece of writing, of a series of paragraphs, or a single paragraph. The importance to the reader in classification is the type of information given: the class, the items listed, and the criterion of differences and similarities.

Classification can be divided into two types: direct and indirect. Direct classification is easy for the reader to detect; the author tells the reader, in the first sentence, that he or she is going to classify. Such words as *classify, group, categorize* leave no doubt in the reader's mind as to what is going on. Example 1 illustrates direct classification in EST.

The first thing that signals the reader's attention in example 1 is the phrase, "can be categorized into . . . ." Notice that in the first paragraph "urban systems" are classified into "land use" and "transportation system."

RST example 5 shows that an identical process takes place in Romanian:

5. *Circuitele basculante pot fi clasificate după numarul starilor stabile distincte,* în care se pot gasi, astfel: circuite basculante bistabile, circuite basculante monostabile și circuite basculante astabile.

Circuitele basculante bistabile pot ramîne un timp oricît de îndelungat într-una din cele două stări stabile distincte pe care le pot avea. Trecerea dintr-o stare în alta se face la aplicarea unui impuls scurt de comandă din exterior.

Circuitele basculante monostabile au o singură stare stabila, în care pot ramîne un timp oricît de îndelungat. La aplicarea unui impuls din exterior, aceste circuite trec într-o stare nouă care dureaza un interval de timp bine determinat, dupa care revin în starea stabila anteriara.

Circuitele basculante astabile trec automat cintr-o stare în alta, stări care durează intervale de timp bine determinate. Trecerea dintr-o stare în alta nu este provocată de impulsuri aplicate din exterior.

(Extracted from Millea, A., Popovici, Al., "Inițiere în Electronică," Editura Tehnica, București, 1964, pp. 297-298.)

This example provides the reader with a classification; "circuitele basculante" have been classified into three groups: "circuite basculante bistabile," "circuite basculante monostabile," and "circuite basculante astabile." Here it is obvious that classification is taking place since the author expresses it directly: "pot fi clasificate."

Up to this point my research has dealt only with direct EST and RST definition and classification—in my paper on English and Spanish (Mage 1977) examples of both direct and indirect definition and classification were found. Although comparisons in the area of indirect definition and classification will not be drawn in this chapter, a brief idea of how it works in English should prove valuable.

INDIRECT DEFINITION AND CLASSIFICATION IN EST

When definition and classification are not stated but are given by implication, they are considered to be indirect. This type of information is frequently found in EST writing; it is often mixed throughout the paragraph with other kinds of information and it is often difficult for the reader to realize he or she *is* being given indirect definition and classification (henceforth *"indirect* D and C").

When the writer uses indirect definition and classification, he or she may intend that particular information to be relevant and important to the subject matter. If this is so, it is incumbent on the reader to abstract this information and he or she usually is not able to until he or she has learned to recognize what kinds of information make up direct D & C. Once the reader has learned the manner in which direct D & C operate, he or she should be better equipped to convert the information given in indirect D & C; thus the reader would grasp a more precise idea of the information being presented. Example 6 shows how indirect definition functions in EST:

> 6. Underground water reserves are much larger than those in the surface, but as they are unseen we tend to underestimate them. It is vitally important that we make use of these underground reserves, but never haphazardly. For example, where does the water come from which we find in one or another of the underground water-bearing layers (aquifers") . . . .
> (Extracted from "Courier," UNESCO, Batisse, M., July 1964.)

The definition to be abstracted here is, "Underground water reserves are those types of water reserves which lie beneath the surface and are unseen."

Example 6 also contains classificatory information. As we saw with indirect definition, if the reader can take information and arrange it into a formal statement of classification, then there is reason to believe there exists classificatory information in the writing. The reader should recognize this type of information when reading and be able to put it into a framework. The framework into which we would put this information is: class equals "water reserves"; members of the class are "underground reserves" and "surface reserves"; and the basis for difference are "location" and "visibility." (See Selinker, Todd Trimble, and Trimble [1976] for further discussion of this and other examples.)

SUMMARY

Our major premise has been that in become aware of the rhetorical functions that the writer employs to express information, the reader is better able to locate indirect definition and classification and translate it into the kind of information that direct definition and classification provide.

The same situation prevails when the reader recognizes how a paragraph is structured; that is, how the paragraph develops a generalization (stated or implied); and also, which statements are lower level generalizations that provide an organized hierarchical structure of information. To recognize that a series of "paragraphs" might actually share one generalization and, therefore, be all one "conceptual" paragraph also lends to recognition of organization and through it the relationship of the ideas presented.

Although this chapter has treated a small area of discourse and the data base is admittedly small, we can, on the basis of the similarities found in the type, amount, and manner in which information is presented in the discourse of EST and RST, suggest that this is a productive manner in which to proceed toward providing a basis for the establishment of universals of scientific and technical discourse. This in turn might well suggest "universals of reading strategy which would clearly be relevant to the development of teaching materials" (Trimble, Todd Trimble, and Widdowson, MS.).

The establishment of universals of scientific and technical discourse seems entirely possible in view of the fact that scientific investigation and reporting impose a considerable restraint on an author's style in writing. As stated at the outset, there appears to be a connection between certain well-ordered sequences of language and certain reasoning processes. These well-ordered sequences of language have to be observed if one is to provide objective and accurate accounts of facts to be recorded, experiments to be performed, accounts of processes to be followed, and reasoned exposition of hypotheses and theories to be considered.

Although linguistic theory is not yet rich enough to write complete rules for discourse, there is an increasing recognition that we must pay as much attention to "rules of use, the speaker's communicative competence, as to rules of grammar, his grammatical competence and that an adequate linguistic description must account for both" (Trimble et al.). Also, there seems to be no reason why "rhetoric as the description of communicative competence should not achieve similar standards of precision as grammar has in the description of grammatical competence" (Widdowson 1971).

The fact that we do not, at present, possess a totally precise manner in which to describe communicative competence does not obviate an inquiry into the pedagogical implications of our research. In fact, Widdowson insists that we make a clear distinction between linguistic and pedagogic grammars. A linguistic grammar, he indicates, "is concerned with a specification of the formal properties of a language, while the purpose of a pedagogic grammar is to help a learner acquire a practical mastery of language" (Widdowson 1971).

Trimble, Selinker, and Lackstrom (passim) have suggested that once we describe discourse, even partially, we may be able to decide on effective materials derived from our description. These materials provide a way of bridging the gap between a learner's grammatical competence and his or her communicative competence by concentrating on rhetorical functions instead of on linguistic elements and vocabulary items. Teaching rhetorical functions such as definition, classification, generalization, and so forth, *involve* the teaching of linguistic elements and vocabulary items, and these are taught much more meaningfully because they are given a definite communicative import.

APPENDIX

Translation of Romanian Examples

Example 2:

The oiling of motors is done by "pan", by pressure, or normally, by means of a combination of these systems. Oiling by "pan" works by spreading of the oil from the crankcase in a finely atomized form (a mist) with the help of prominences on the piston rods.

Drops of oil are spread on the surface to be oiled, especially on the interior of the cylinder sleeves, or it collects in grooves which lead to the oiling orifices of the mechanism. It is necessary then that the level of the oil . . . .

Oiling by pressure with one or more oil pumps provides the desired quantity of oil under the right pressure to all the oil points. At the same time the oil is sent through filters which separate out the fine metallic particles that break loose from the oiled shafts and which can cause an accumulation of wear.

Mixed oiling is done by pressure for the principle mechanisms, for the drive shafts, and for the piston rods, and for the rest by pan oiling. The disadvantages of pan oiling remain even in the mixed oiling system.

Example 4:

A diode is an electronic tube with two electrodes: the anode and the cathode. The cathode is made of a metallic body and has the property of emitting electrons under the conditions mentioned above. The anode receives the electrons emitted by the cathode.

Example 5:

Bascule circuits may be classifed according to the distinct stable states, in which they may be found: bistable circuits, monostable bascule circuits, and nonstable bascule circuits.

Bistable bascule circuits can remain for any length of time in one of the two distinct stable states available. The transition from one state to the other takes place with the application of a short impulse triggered from without.

Monostable bascule circuits have a single stable state in which they may remain for any length of time. At the command by an impulse from without, these circuits pass into a new state which lasts a well-determined interval of time and after which they return to the previous stable state.

Nonstable bascule circuits pass automatically from one state to another at determined intervals. The passage from one state to another is not triggered by exterior impulses.

Notes

1. *Editors' Note:* See Appendix for translation of these RST examples. The Editors thank James Augerot, Associate Professor, Slavic Languages and Literature, University of Washington, who translated these examples.

2. *Editor's Note:* These are earlier terms in the Trimble rhetoric and have been replaced by the terms *explicit* and *implicit* definition and classification. See, for example, Selinker, Todd Trimble, and Trimble (1976).

References

Allen, J. P. B., and H. Widdowson. 1974. "Teaching the Communicative Use of English." *IRAL* 12.1, pp. 1-21.

Lackstrom, J., L. Selinker, and L. Trimble. 1973. "Technical Rhetorical Principles and Grammatical Choices." *TESOL Quarterly* 7.2, pp. 127-36.

Mage, T. L. 1977. "Contrastive Discourse Analysis: EST and SST." *Proceedings of the IV International Congress of Applied Linguistics,* Vol. 1, pp. 237-48. Hochschulverlag.

Selinker, L., and L. Trimble. 1967. Technical Communication for Foreign Engineering Students, Unpublished Ms.

Selinker, L., M. Todd Trimble and L. Trimble. 1976. "Presuppositional Rhetorical Information in EST Discourse." *TESOL Quarterly* 10.3, pp. 281-290.

Trimble, L., M. Todd Trimble, and H. Widdowson. 1974 Ms. A Proposal for Research in Scientific and Rhetorical Universals.

Weisman, H. M. 1962. *Basic Technical Writing.* Merrill Books.

Widdowson, H. G. 1971. "The Teaching of Rhetoric to Students of Science and Technology." *Science and Technology in a Second Language,* ed. G. Perren, pp. 31-40. (*CILT Reports and Papers* 7) Centre for Information on Language Teaching and Research.

―――. 1973. "Directions in the Teaching of Discourse." *Theoretical Linguistic Models in Applied Linguistics: 3rd AIMAV Seminar, Neuchâtel.* pp. 65-76. AIMAV.

―――. 1974. "An Approach to the Teaching of Scientific English Discourse." *RELC Journal* 5.1, 27-40.

Editorial Comments

This chapter ties in with Lackstrom's feeling (chap. 2) that the "scientific method" affects EST discourse structures in predictable ways, ways Lackstrom describes for introductory textbook material. One could look at this theme, a theme underlying Mage's research as well, as predicting that texts in other languages when expressing scientific concepts will show highly similar discourse structures as EST no matter what the shape of the "basic" discourse structures in that particular language. This is clearly one of the major themes of EST research and we expect it to keep reappearing in various forms. Mage goes on to investigate the claim that where the discourse itself functions to transmit scientific information in diverse languages, the rhetorical patterns used in those languages may then be similar.

In exploring a conceptual framework common to EST and RST, Mage provides a summary of some of the main ideas of classical Trimble rhetoric. This should prove useful to readers of this volume since this material has been previously available only in highly technical articles or classes taught by Louis Trimble himself. Mage's research has been influenced by Trimble personally; his master's thesis, which compared some of the rhetoric of EST and SST (Spanish for Science and Technology) was done under Trimble's supervision.

Mage focuses here on the Trimble-defined notions of the conceptual paragraph, direct and indirect definition, and direct and indirect classification, showing that these patterns appear to exist in RST as they do in EST. (As mentioned in note 2, *direct* and *indirect* are earlier Trimble terms for *explicit* and *implicit,* respectively.)

We find this comparative approach to EST rhetoric to be valuable and wish to encourage it. We hope this and other studies will go on to examine the interesting question of whether similar rhetorical patterns exist in the scientific writing of languages that do *not* share such close linguistic roots and rhetorical traditions as the three (English, Spanish, and Romanian) looked at to date.

L.S.
E.T.

# PART TWO

Papers on Practical Applications

9. Designing Modular Materials for Communicative Language Learning; An Example: Doctor-Patient Communication Skills

Christopher N. Candlin, Clive J. Bruton,
Jonathan H. Leather, Edward G. Woods

In the United Kingdom and the United States, overseas doctors form a vital section of the medical staff of many hospitals. Many of them who do not have English as a mother tongue face specific communication problems in their professional life, particularly in the more colloquial and nonmedical language needed in doctor-patient consultations. The course materials described below were designed on the basis of a large number of consultations observed in the casualty (or accident and emergency) departments in twenty hospitals in different parts of the United Kingdom. These observations, supported by audio- and video-recordings and helped by the views of members of the medical profession on the training of overseas doctors and the authenticity of the Doctor-Patient Communication Skills (DOPACS) material, have played a central part in the construction of the course.

The modules use a variety of intensive and self-programming techniques that allow course organizers the greatest possible flexibility in catering to those doctors who wish to improve their skills in doctor-patient communication, particularly in a casualty department setting. The materials concentrate on the complex issues in communication that arise from the contrasting experience and expectations of the local patient and the doctor from overseas. However good the doctor's professional skills, he or she cannot be expected to have full knowledge of the linguistic and cultural conventions that contribute to effective communication in a consultation with a person whose background may differ so radically from the doctor's. To this end there are modules that deal with the central place of language in the consultation; a view of language as communication that brings together language as form and as function; and the status and role of the doctor.

It appears that both instructors and learners (as well as, in a sense, doctors and patients) need to become *sensitized* to these underlying issues, if they are to understand fully the subtle devices of oral (and gestural) communication by which native speakers can give and obtain information, monitor each other's talk, and indicate sympathy, reassurance, and optimism. Attention is focused in the modules upon the communicative effectiveness of different ways of communicating a concept or **FUNCTION** of language, effectiveness seen from the patient's as well as the doctor's point of view. Attention is also drawn to the ways the alternative utterances, which *realize* these functions within the consultation, affect the doctor-patient relationship. For example, should it be:

"Nurse, give this patient anti-tetanus, would you."

or: "I think we'd better give you a little jab, Mr. Smith, just to be on the safe side."

And why?

The materials aim to encourage good doctor-patient relationships by developing the use of appropriate and effective language and will help towards providing the means whereby the doctor from overseas can overcome the linguistic and communicative disadvantage he or she often feels within the profession as a result of problems in communication with patients.

The DOPACS modules are not a beginners course in learning English for a specific purpose; they call upon an already existing medical expertise and a good formal knowledge of English structure and vocabulary. Although there is a Code Characterization section in each module that concentrates on language *form*, this is subordinate to the major concern of the materials, which is for *function* and *communication*, using a variety of interrelated language skills in the work setting.

The background research leading to the present materials is discussed in detail in the four *Working Papers* referred to in the references at the end of this chapter. In summary, Figures 9-1 and 9-2 outline the research and development plan.

The *fieldwork* was broadly in *four* stages. Once it was decided to make casualty departments the setting for the research, an initial period was spent gaining familiarity with the nature and scope of work in such departments. Plans could then be made for a systematic study. Judging that communicative activity in casualty could best be analyzed by reference to the *purposeful work activities* with which it is associated, we wanted first to characterize work routines in treating patients. It would emerge what interlocutions were possible and likely, and subsequent investigation of the doctor's communicative activity in consultations with patients could be approached with an understanding of the institutional and socio-psychological context. Dimensions of variation in the doctor's communicative behavior could then be postulated and tested against data. An adequate set of variables would finally be assigned values based on further data.

Data were collected in twenty casualty departments in hospitals of different regional locations, and took several forms:

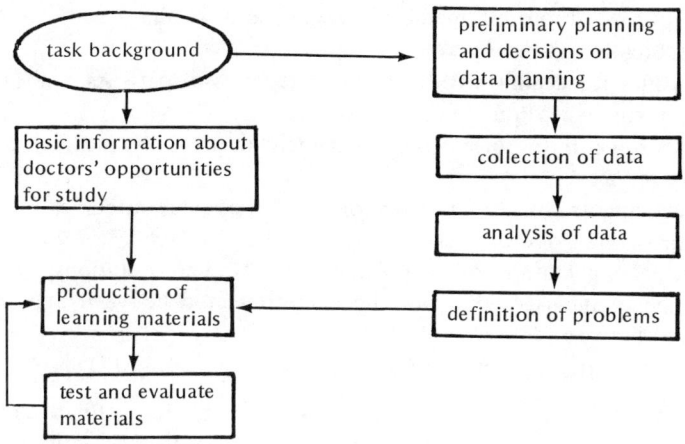

FIGURE 9-1.   SHORT-TERM SCHEME

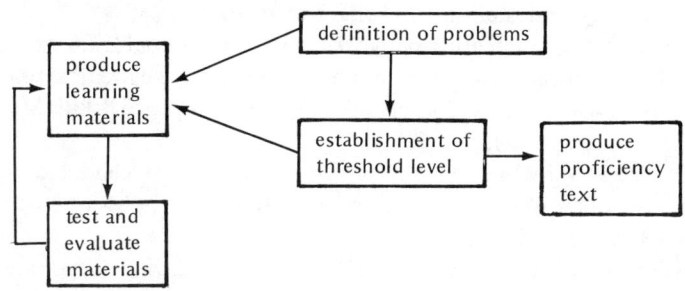

FIGURE 9-2.   LONGER-TERM SCHEME (FOLLOWING FROM 9-1)

Responses by medical nursing staff to systematic inquiries and during informal questioning and unstructured discussion;

Observers' notes, plans, and flowcharts characterizing the spatial and procedural organization of the departments visited;

Observers' real-time analyses of doctor-patient interactions in consultations;

Audio and video recordings of consultations;

Doctors' responses to researchers' questioning on aspects of consultations in which they had been observed.

These subjective and objective data, then, had to do with:

The nature of the work done in each department, and its connections with other medical services in the community;

The physical setting (the layout, equipment, of the department);

The respective duties of medical, nursing, and ancillary staff, and their institutional relationships;

The routines for dealing with different categories of patients, and possible variations on and exceptions to these routines;

Attitudes towards the role of the department in providing medical care and community service;[1]

The participants in, the progression, and possible outcomes of interlocutions involving a doctor;

The mutual expectations of doctors and patients in consultations;

The range of messages that may be communicated between doctors and patients, and between doctors and other staff;

The means of transmission of these messages.

After an initial period of data collection it was possible to postulate a number of variables in terms of which the doctor's communicative activity might be analyzed. A further period of investigation thus involved detailed study of:

The broad range of communication tasks demanded of the doctor at work;

Possible interlocutors of the doctor, the relative frequency of his or her contact with each, and their institutional role-relationships;

The range of communication networks in which the doctor may participate, and the relation, in each, of the communicative role to the medical role;

The relative use made by doctors of each of the language "skills" (speaking, reading, note-taking, etc.);

The channels over which the doctor may transmit and receive messages;

The transactional structure of the consultation, and the socio-psychological framework in which it is enacted;

The repertoire of the doctor's communicative acts during consultations.

Study of doctors' communicative activity in about fifty consultations[2] (an exact figure is not possible, since certain doctor-patient interactions hardly meet a definition of "consultation") showed that a variety of communicative acts (here designated FUNCTIONS) regularly recurred. A set of FUNCTIONS was postulated and set out in checklist form. This FUNCTION set (FS1) was then tested during observation of further consultations. If a doctor utterance was judged to expound one of the FUNCTIONS of FS1, a tick was entered against that FUNCTION. The strengths and shortcomings of FS1 thus became clear, and it could be revised to produce FS2. FS2 was in turn tested and revised to give FS3, and so on. A tolerably workable FUNCTION taxonomy was arrived at in this way during analysis of about four hundred further consultations.

A more powerful notation, which permitted other tests of the FUNCTION taxonomy, was then devised. The *tramline* notation exemplified in Figure 9-3 shows the sequence of FUNCTIONS expounded by the doctor and the addressee (patient or nurse) of each doctor utterance. In the example, which is an analysis of a short consultation, the upper line identifies, by their reference letters, the FUNCTIONS expounded in utterances addressed by the doctor to the patient.

```
D ⟶ P      A B S C E N    N P     V K G P J R
D ⟶ N                      K       K
```

Note: See Appendix II for key.

FIGURE 9-3.   EXAMPLE OF TRAMLINE NOTATION

The lower line does the same for utterances the doctor addresses to the nurse. (A third line recording nurse-to-patient utterances was abandoned after early experimentation.) In this consultation, then, the doctor began by greeting the patient and followed on with an ELICIT. While the patient was responding with general information about the accident the doctor encouraged him with a GO-ON. By means of an INTERROGATE the doctor then initiates another phase in the consultation.

With the use of this notation, a realtime analysis could be compared with subsequent analyses made of audio recordings of the same consultation by several analysts. Where there was inconsistency in the analyses, weaknesses in the taxonomy could be located and further revisions made. Analysts could work also with video recordings of consultations to test the consistency with which nonverbal realizations of FUNCTIONS could be identified and accounted for. The present taxonomy was eventually arrived at, and proved satisfactory in the analysis of a further 400 consultations for a total of 850. The revisions and refinements made during the process described were of four kinds:

1. Finer resolution of one FUNCTION into two or more FUNCTIONS (an INTERROGATE was introduced to account more specifically for questioning, where previously there had been only the QUESTION);
2. Collapse of two over-differentiating FUNCTIONS into one (GREET incorporates, as it were, an earlier PHATIC—which was found, as the data base broadened, not to be practically distinct);
3. Addition of a new FUNCTION to account for utterances not analyzable in terms of any of the FUNCTIONS in the set under test (most of the metacommunicative FUNCTIONS such as REPEAT, FEED-ME-BACK, etc., were additions of this sort);
4. Deletion of a FUNCTION postulated but not validated during tests (a postulated MAINTAIN deleted on the grounds that there was in consultations no "communicative maintaining" that could not be readily analyzed as a REASSURE, a TALK, an ACCEPT, a GO-ON, or a FEED-ME-BACK).

Before outlining the structure of the modular DOPACS materials, it is useful to identify some crucial features of communicative language learning in this context. A communicative approach to the learning of doctor-patient communication skills implies for us a clear awareness of the nature of the consultation as an event, involving an appreciation of its participants and the networks of their communication; and appreciation of the doctor's and the patient's communicative objectives; an ability to handle messages transmitted via a variety of interrelated channels, involving a consequent mastery of interrelated and chained language skills. Above all, to understand these features, the learner has to become sensitive to what Gumperz refers to as *contextualization cues*: to notice the subtle shifts of stress, intonation, and rhythm, as well as the more marked lexical and syntactic choices that all have significance in interpreting and negotiating variable meaning.

Implicit in this approach is the centrality of authenticity: an authenticity, however, both of *data* and of *tasks*. The DOPACS materials seek to *represent* the authenticity of hospital communication and the doctor's tasks. They are however didactic in their aim, and that is why in the discussion on the modules that follows, we make a careful distinction between those exercises that are primarily for formal and functional *practice*, those designed to *sensitize* the learners to the contextualization cues of authentic communication mentioned above, and those that, though *simulative* in their design, are intended to "model" actuality and stimulate authentic discussion and analysis in the classroom and the hospital.

MODULES

A module in the DOPACS materials represents a discrete unit of learning that has been designed in such a way that sections of it can be expanded or shortened or omitted according to the needs of the learner and the situation in which the instruction is taking place. This principle of *flexibility* in the materials extends over both the range of printed activities and exercises within the module as well as the use made of the various accompanying media.

Broadly speaking, there are three types of module design used in the course materials:

The design for SENSITIZATION modules (Modules 1-3), mainly in the form of discussion work with illustrative examples or stimuli.

The design for the FUNCTION modules (Modules 4-23), the main body of the course, which combine illustration, recognition, discussion, teaching exercises, and practice exercises.

The design for the TRANSMEDIATION module (Module 24), again offering illustration, recognition, discussion, and practice exercises but concerned primarily with skill-transfer, or channel-switching from speech to writing and vice versa.

Common to the structure of all the modules are the first *three* elements: ENDS, OUTLINE, and WORKSCHEME.

Ends

This sets out the aims and objectives of the module with a list of modules required to be completed before the module in question; that is, "presupposed."

The aims and objectives are themselves divided into two parts: the *Instructional Goal* and the *Learning Objective*.

Instructional Goal

This is a description in general terms of the new knowledge, skills, abilities, and attitudes that the instructor expects the learner to acquire as a result of his or her instruction. An example of this from the INTERROGATE FUNCTION (Module 7) is:

> To be able to interrogate the patient about the occurrence of his injury or the development of his complaint.

A further example from Module 1, *THE STATUS AND ROLE OF THE CASUALTY OFFICER*, is:

> To make the learner objectify his experience as a doctor from overseas working in an Accident and Emergency Department of a hospital. Emphasis is on the attitudes of doctors from overseas to their status and the roles a doctor has; and on the attitudes of patients and what they expect from a doctor. The learner's attention is drawn to the role of language within a doctor-patient interview.

Learning Objective

This describes in greater detail the behavior expected of the learner after instruction. Typically, each *Learning Objective* refers to Terminal Behavior, Test Conditions, and Standards, features that are picked up and modeled by the module *P-Test* (or Post-Test) (q.v.) to obtain a valid achievement measure.

An example from the GREET FUNCTION (Module 4) is:

> Hearing from each of ten imaginary patients a taped prompt giving details of his/her personal background (age, sex, status) and the time of day, the learner produces each time without hesitation or false starts a GREET which is judged by the instructor to be intelligible and acceptable.

A further example from Module 17, *REASSURE FUNCTION*, is:

> The learner is presented with extracts from ten Doctor-Patient consultations. In each case the patient expresses concern in his response and the learner must reassure the patient verbally and non-verbally in a manner judged by the instructor to be intelligible and acceptable.

In this *Learning Objective* the terminal behavior is that the learner reassures the patient, who is concerned, verbally and nonverbally; the test conditions are that the learner does this for each of ten consultation extracts, and the standards stipulate that his or her utterances are judged to be intelligible and acceptable.

Module "Presuppositions"

These indicate which, if any, of the modules should be worked through and understood by the learner before the module in question is begun. The emphasis here is on precise definition of learning and instructional objectives, presupposing criterion-referenced testing of communicative ability. (Readers are referred, in particular, to Davis, R. H. et al. [1974]).

112 / ENGLISH FOR ACADEMIC AND TECHNICAL PURPOSES

Outline

This is the second element in the module and presents in summary form for the instructor/course planner an overview of all the other elements in the module: the workscheme, the materials, aids, and tests.

An example from Module 7, *INTERROGATE FUNCTION*, is:

OUTLINE

III *Workscheme*		Illustration. Recognition. Discussion. Code Teaching. Production drills. Production Exercises. Simulation Exercise. P-Test.
IV *Instructor Notes*		Tapescripts of tape extracts for illustration and recognition. List of discussion points. List of code points. Substitution table, with description. Substitution drill description and prompts. Description, tapescript, and stimuli for Production Exercises. Description and stimuli for Simulation Exercises.
V *Learner Materials*		Tapescripts of tape extracts for illustration and recognition. Substitution table, with description. Substitution drill with description and examples. (Full write-out of prompts and responses on reverse). Description of taped Production Exercises with examples. (Full write-out of taped stimuli on reverse). Description of Simulation Exercise with example.
VI *Aids*		Audiotapes and visuals. Sample case-cards for Simulation Exercise.
VII *P-Test*		Test with audiotape.

Workscheme

This sets out a *suggested* teaching procedure for the module. The procedure is intended as a guide to one way of working through the module. It does not have to be followed exactly in the way indicated.

In the SENSITIZATION modules, the mode of instruction is largely through discussion, and the *Workscheme* is consequently divided between the stimuli and the discussion points. Here is an example from Module 2, *LANGUAGE IN THE CONSULTATION:*

III WORKSCHEME
1. Begin by raising the points in the first of discussion notes concerning the sequence of operational phases in a consultation.
2. Ask the learners to view the whole *unphased* consultation recorded as Stage 3 after the videotape. Alternatively, listen to any of the *complete* consultations recorded and transcribed in Module 24. Transmediation. (Do *not* use the two consultations from Section 6 of Module 24).

3. Revise conclusions to (1) above on the sequence of operational phases. Aim to isolate (at least) the following:
    1. Greeting
    2. Information-extracting
    3. Examination
    4. Diagnosis
    5. Prognosis/therapy
    6. Leavetaking
4. Ask the learners to view the *phased* consultation recorded as Stage 4 of the videotape.
5. Move on to Recognition exercise I. Ask the learners to listen/view the consultation and isolate the operational phases in the transcript of the consultation. Make any amendments/suggest variants to the conclusions reached in (3) above.
6. Now introduce the points in the second set of discussion notes concerning the relationship between operational phases and language use in the consultation.
7. Ask the learners to view the example of extracts from consultation phases recorded as Stages 5 and 6 of the course videotape. Alternatively, listen to a variety of the consultation extracts recorded and transcribed in Modules 4-23 of the course. Aim to isolate Cognitive, Affective, and Metacommunicative functions of language in the consultation.
8. Now move on to Recognition exercise II. Ask the learners to listen to/view the consultation and suggest functional values for the underlined utterances in the light of their conclusions from (7) above.
9. Using the points in the third set of discussion notes, summarize the language requirements of the operational phases of the consultation, paying particular attention to the three broad functions of language you have isolated.
10. Administer the P-Test.

In the main body of the course, which are the FUNCTION modules, a typical *Workscheme* has the following stages:

(i)	Illustration:	The instructor illustrates the speech function from a number of taped extracts (optionally using slides, illustrations, and videotape).
(ii)	Recognition:	The learners practice recognizing the speech function while listening to other tape extracts.
(iii)	Discussion:	The instructor discusses with the learners the communicative purpose of the speech function and its position in the discourse of the consultation.
(iv)	Code Characterization:	The instructor teaches/revises the code characteristics of the speech function, which may involve work on syntax, lexis, or intonation.
(v)	Production Drills:	The learners use drills to practice what has been learned/revised in *(iv)*.
(vi)	Production Exercises:	The instructor now introduces less controlled exercises leading to Transfer phase work.
(vii)	P-Test:	The P-test is administered to see if the *Learning Objective* has been achieved.

Instructor Notes

This fourth element in the module forms the instructor's teaching materials. It includes a full write-out of all the taped material used; for example, in the Illustration and Recognition phases, in the Production drills and exercises, and in the P-Test. It also provides descriptions of the various drills and exercises/activities, a list of possible discussion points for classroom work, and a set of code points that may need teaching or revising.

Here are some examples from Module 13, DIAG-INFORM FUNCTION:

1. *Illustration*
   Here is a tapescript of the extracts from consultations you can play on the tape, illustrating what the function of the module is. Each DIAG-INFORM is underlined.

2. *Recognition Exercise*
   In the following extracts there are more DIAG-INFORMS. Play the tape and try to recognize and underline them on the tapescript as they occur.

3. *Discussion*
   By using the ELICIT, INTERROGATE, and QUESTION, the doctor will have built up a small case history of the patient's accident or complaint. He is now expected to have some idea of what the complaint is or of what damage has occurred to the patient as a result of the accident. He must now explain clearly to the patient what is wrong with him. The explanation must be given in language the patient understands and in such a manner that the patient isn't disturbed or upset.

   Sensitivity Exercise
   A. Description: In this exercise, you will hear ten DIAG-INFORMS on tape; and from the words and intonation used, you must judge how appropriate each one is, and make your evaluations on the chart below. These are the instructions you will hear on the tape:

Learner Materials

The fifth element in the module forms the learners' materials. It includes tape-scripts for Illustration and Recognition exercises and descriptions and examples of the Production Drills and Exercises. On the reverse of these sheets is a write-out of the Drill Prompts and Responses and of the recorded stimuli.

Aids

This sixth element in the module lists appropriate and available audio and visual aids. This listing is *not* intended to preclude the use of any other aids the instructor may have at his or her disposal.

P-Test

This final element of a module is the P-TEST *(Post-Test)*, which is taken after the module has been worked through. It is designed to discover whether the *Learning Objective* has been attained. Here is an example from Module 13, DIAG-INFORM:

Administration: When two or more learners are tested at one time, the test is most conveniently administered in a language laboratory. It is preferable that learner utterances should be recorded. If it is not possible to use a double-track machine to do this, it is necessary for the Instructor to control the duration of the test for each learner.

Scoring The following criteria may be useful in the assessment of proficiency:
(a) The doctor should not appear unsympathetic.
(b) The doctor presents the DIAG-INFORM in such a way that the patient has confidence in the doctor's diagnosis.
(c) Where it is a provisional DIAG-INFORM, the patient is confident that the doctor is proceeding in the right manner.
(d) The doctor's DIAG-INFORM must be in language that the patient can understand.
(e) The DIAG-INFORM must be syntactically well-formed.
(f) The DIAG-INFORM must be intelligible to a native speaker under conditions of noise.

Transcript of test tape In this test you will hear details of patients' accidents/complaints from five consultations. You must respond with a suitable DIAG-INFORM.
Here is an example:
Prompt: The patient has deep femoral vein thrombosis.
LEARNER: *It looks as if you've a clot in a deep vein in your leg.*
Now here is the test.

Transcript of test tape
1. You think the patient is suffering from intermittent claudication.
2. The patient has a corneal ulcer.
3. The patient has displaced anteriorly the 1st phalanx.
4. The patient has subperiosteal swelling along ulna. The ulna nerve action is intact.
5. The patient has inflamed 1st M.T.P. joint. It is hot, swollen, and purplish. His movement is limited and painful.

Each P-Test is included in *two* forms; one for the Instructor, giving administrative and scoring details, and one for the Learner (the Learner's Copy) simply giving instructions for the Test task(s).

ORGANIZATION

The advantage of a course organized on a modular basis is that it allows a high degree of flexibility in the way in which a course can be organized. It is not our intention that the instructor/course planner should make a class proceed from Module 1 to Module 24 in a strict linear order; nor should he or she have to include *all* the modules; nor should he or she need to complete *all* the sections of *each* module.

Rather the instructor/course planner must organize the modules to fit the needs of the learners, the time available for the course and the situation in which the course is going to take place. At first glance this may suggest that a modular course, like **DOPACS**, has *unlimited* flexibility, so that any learner can move through the course in a way that is exactly suited to his or her needs. This cannot, in practice, be the case, since each of the organizational conditions—the needs of the learner, the time available for the course, and the situation in which the course is to take place— react one upon the other and provide limitations on choice.

Limiting Factors on Flexibility

The time available for the course, for example, is likely to be imposed upon the learner, as indeed will the situation or course location. The course may be extended over a long timespan, say three months; or it may be intensive and limited to three or four weeks. Sessions may range from regular, long sessions of two hours or more, or they may be severely restricted to short sessions whenever learners can be available. Similarly it may be taking place in a school or college where all teaching facilities are available, or, on the other hand, it may be in a hospital in a spare room that happens to be free at the time.

Given these variable conditions and constraints, it is clearly necessary for the course modules to be flexible; equally, and for other course-internal reasons, as we shall see, it is not possible to have *total* flexibility—where any one module can be taught entirely in free arrangement with any other.

Looking at Figure 9-4, we can see three possible variations—among many—that the instructor might have to take into consideration when planning the course. In each case the *Homework* line indicates the time when learners would be free to do any work at home. In the *first* case, the timetable is quite straightforward—there are a regular number of hours, which are the same each week.

In the *second* case the same number of hours are available, but they fall at different times in alternate weeks; and in the second week of each pair, there are more hours available for home study. Such a situation may be made more complex according to the availability of the instructor. If the instructor's own time is less flexible over a two-week period, he or she may have to make use of the home-study periods in Week Two, and plan the use of materials accordingly.

The *third* case is the most complex in that it imagines not all learners being able to come together at the same time. With only one instructor available, for example, it would mean some repetition in the class for those who can come the greater number of times, and more constructive use of the home-study periods for those who can come only the fewer number of class hours.

Inevitably, the number of instructors available is going to affect this kind of organization, together with learner-group size. All these factors affect the freedom of the learner to choose, and the freedom of the instructor to individualize instruction, especially regarding choice of course content.

Diagnostic Test

Whatever the local constraints, however, some student placement in terms of perceived communicative need is going to be necessary. The most suitable way of achieving this is through a *Diagnostic Test* made up of a battery of P-Tests taken from the course modules. We are suggesting here that the function of the module

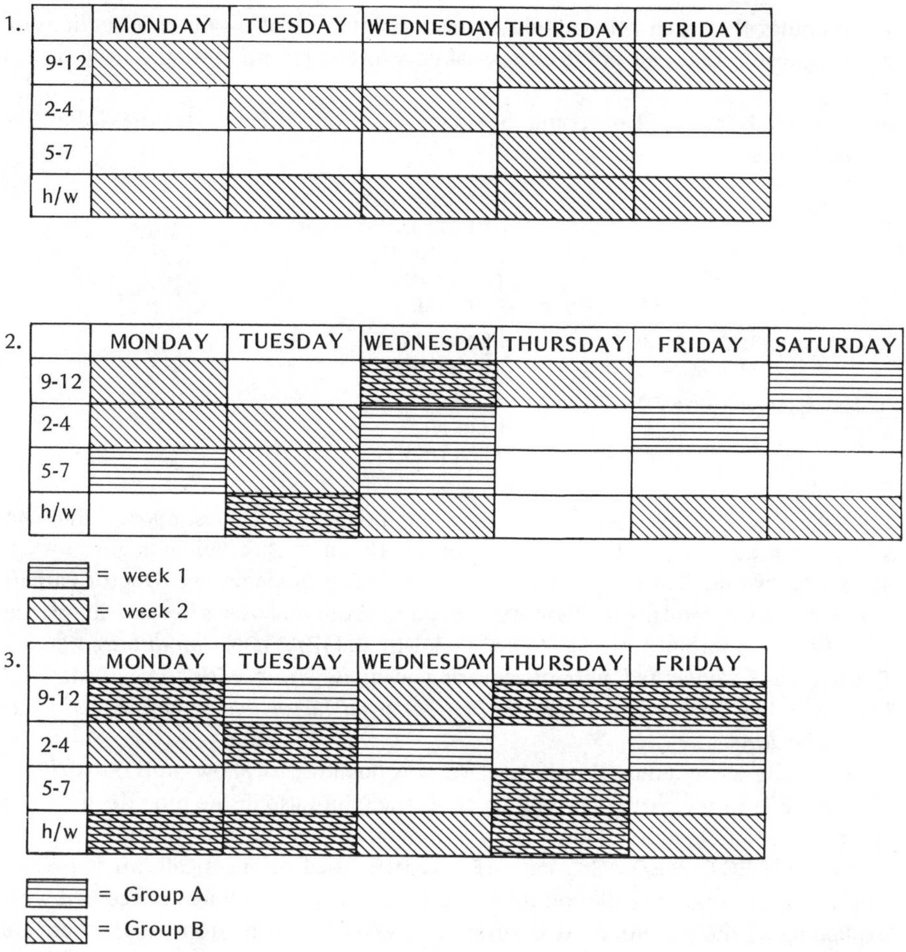

1.

	MONDAY	TUESDAY	WEDNESDAY	THURSDAY	FRIDAY
9-12	▨			▨	▨
2-4		▨			
5-7				▨	
h/w	▨	▨	▨	▨	▨

2.

	MONDAY	TUESDAY	WEDNESDAY	THURSDAY	FRIDAY	SATURDAY
9-12	▨		≡	▨		≡
2-4	▨		≡		≡	≡
5-7			≡			
h/w		≡			▨	▨

▭ = week 1
▨ = week 2

3.

	MONDAY	TUESDAY	WEDNESDAY	THURSDAY	FRIDAY
9-12	≋	≡	▨	≋	≋
2-4	▨	≋		≡	≡
5-7				≋	
h/w	≋	≋	▨	≋	▨

▭ = Group A
▨ = Group B

FIGURE 9-4.   THREE POSSIBLE TIMETABLES

P-Test as an achievement measure for a given module can be matched by its diagnostic function as an entry regulator to a module. Clearly, if a student scores highly on a given module P-Test, taken diagnostically, he or she may not need to be required to study the contents of that module; unless, of course, the student needs to refresh his or her knowledge of another module assumed to have been taught and for which he or she is not prepared.

Such a *Diagnostic Test* should be made up of a selection of P-Tests from the three types of FUNCTION typical to the consultation event: the *cognitive* FUNCTIONS, the *affective* FUNCTIONS, and the *metacommunicative* FUNCTIONS. To a certain extent, the selection is bound to be personal, and learner-directed. However, the instructor/course-planner should take account of any modules that each other module presupposes, so that a failure in sections of the Diagnostic Test can point up a weakness in an area not actually used in the test.

A sample Diagnostic Test could be made up from P-Tests for the following FUNCTIONS:

Cognitive FUNCTIONS:	INTERROGATE
	QUESTION
	DIAG-INFORM
	TREAT-DIRECT
	MED-ASK
Affective FUNCTIONS:	LEAVETAKE
	REASSURE
Metacommunicative FUNCTIONS:	ACCEPT
	REPEAT
	APOLOGY

Looking now at Table 9-1, let us see what modules it is presupposed that the learner has already mastered. To be successful in such a wide-ranging test, a candidate would have to have a very broad proficiency in Doctor-Patient Communication Skills. Furthermore, a good deal of emphasis is necessarily placed on *three* important areas: (1) *the* SENSITIZATION *modules;* (2) *the* FUNCTIONS *concerned with discovering what is wrong with the patient; and* (3) *the* FUNCTIONS *instructing the patient what his or her trouble is and what should be done.*

By noting where failure is taking place, it is possible to show not only that the failure is in the particular module concerned, but also in the modules assumed to have been taught. Thus, if a candidate fails in the P-Tests for the TREAT-DIRECT, MED-ASK, and REASSURE, used diagnostically, it is reasonable to suppose that instruction is needed on *all* the FUNCTIONS concerned with explaining to the patient what is wrong and what has to be done, since there are

TABLE 9-1. MODULES PRESUPPOSED TO EACH OF TEN FUNCTIONS

INTERROGATE	1	2	3		5						
QUESTION	1	2	3			6	7				
DIAG-INFORM	1	2	3			6	7		10	12	
TREAT-DIRECT	1	2	3				7		11 12 13 14		20
MED-ASK	1	2	3						13 14 15 16		
LEAVETAKE	1	2	3	4							
REASSURE	1	2	3	4	5	6	7		13 14 15 16		22 23
ACCEPT	1	2	3			6	7	8			
REPEAT	1	2	3			6	7		10	14 15 16	
APOLOGY	1	2	3		5	6			9	11	14 15

Note: See Appendix I for key.

points from Modules 12 to 16 that he or she does not seem to grasp. On the other hand, a candidate who scored badly in the QUESTION, DIAG-INFORM, REASSURE, and ACCEPT would seem to need instruction in those modules concerned with eliciting information from the patient, since the "failed" modules have those modules in common that are assumed to have been taught previously.

Course Intensity

It is not adequate merely to divide courses simply into Intensive and Extensive courses without considering the frequency of sessions within the course. A short intensive course can mean two weeks of several contact-hours daily (Instructor-learner sessions); or it can mean two weeks of only a few contact-hours, with much of the learning being done by the learners themselves in follow-up self-study sessions.

We can imagine, therefore, two types of courses, as shown in Figure 9-5.

Extensive Courses could be similarly organized. An extensive course over twelve weeks with frequent contact sessions will require instructors to supplement the existing course material with additional material they devise. This might well take the form of transfer work calling on the specific communication demands of their local hospital, with a good deal of local, authentic support material. With less frequent contact sessions it will be necessary for the instructor to divide the existing material into classwork and homework exercises.

(Each timetable is for a period of two weeks.)

:A:

	Monday	Tuesday	Wednesday	Thursday	Friday
9-12	▨	▨	▨	▨	▨
2-4	▨	▨	▨	▨	▨
5-7					
h/w	▨	▨	▨	▨	▨

:B:

	Monday	Tuesday	Wendesday	Thursday	Friday
9-12		▨		▨	
2-4	▨				
5-7			▨		
h/w		▨	▨	▨	▨

FIGURE 9-5.   TWO INTENSIVE COURSE TIMETABLES

Sequence

Although there is a good deal of sequencing variety possible within the modular design, the fact that the modules themselves fall generally into *three* broad types, the SENSITIZATION *modules,* the FUNCTION *modules,* and the TRANSMEDIATION *module,* has implications for Module sequence in a course.

Accepting, for example, that learners will come from varying socio-cultural backgrounds, it is essential *before going on to the main part of the course* that they become aware of the particular U.K. socio-cultural setting in which they will be/are working. The SENSITIZATION modules are therefore an essential element at the outset of any course, although different groups of learners will need different lengths of exposure to the ideas within the modules concerned. The FUNCTION modules, in turn, depend upon this sensitization, which, as we point out, may be known to the learner and merely need refreshing quickly in some cases.

The TRANSMEDIATION Module (Module 24) is chiefly concerned with the transfer of skills, or channel switching. This might seem to presuppose much of the work done in the central FUNCTION modules, and consequently to be done *after* they have been completed. This does not seem to be the best procedure since in practicing a transfer from writing to speech (as in the case of speaking from casenotes, for example), the doctor is concentrating on a limited set of consultation FUNCTIONS. The same is true when he or she is speaking on the telephone. It may be a good deal more suitable for the instructor to bring aspects of the TRANSMEDIATION module into the teaching of various FUNCTION modules. For example, practice in noting down case histories (taken from the TRANSMEDIATION module) can be linked into the module INTERROGATE.

Example (TRANSMEDIATION - Module 24 - Exercise 8)
                 IV INSTRUCTOR NOTES/LEARNER MATERIALS
8. *Transmediation Practice (Written to Spoken)*
   A: Description: In this exercise, for each of the case cards provided, you should simulate a situation with a colleague where a patient is *representing* at Casualty. Your consultation should continue from the point reached in the case card in question, making free use of the spoken consultation FUNCTIONS you have practiced.
   B: Case cards:
      (i)
      (ii)
      (iii)
      (iv)
      (v)
      (vi)

Although, then, outside factors will limit the flexibility of module arrangement for each individual course, each course should nonetheless be considered separately, and the instructor/course planner should design a program most suited to the instructor's own and the students' interests.

The following timetable (Table 9-2) is taken from a short three-day program that was organized to pilot some of the DOPACS materials. *It should be regarded simply as an example of how modules can be assembled into ONE short course, not as a general model to follow.*

TABLE 9-2. SAMPLE TIME-TABLE FOR A THREE-DAY DOPACS COURSE

	THURSDAY	FRIDAY	SATURDAY
9:15-10:45	Modules 1-3[1]	Modules 8 and 9 GO-ON ACCEPT	Module 24 TRANSMEDIATION[3]
	Coffee Break		
11:15-12:45	Modules 1-3[1]	Modules 10 and 11 QUESTION MAKESURE	Modules 13 and 14 DIAG-INFORM ACTION-INFORM
	Lunch Break		
2:00-3:00	Modules 4 and 5 GREET LEAVETEAKE	Module 12 DIRECT	Modules 15 and 16 PROG-INFORM TREAT-DIRECT
	Tea Break		
4:00-5:30	Modules 6 and 7 ELICIT INTERROGATE	Module 17 REASSURE	Simulation Exercise with patients (VTR) Post-course Feedback
Evening		Individually assigned work [2]	

Note: 1. Using VTR facilities, with a simulated patient, in a hospital location. Discussion of sensitization using VTR playback.

> Module 1 = Status and Role of the C.O.
> Module 2 = Language in the Consultation
> Module 3 = Form and Function

2. Individually assigned sections from various modules for self-study with cassette recorder, supplemented with non-DOPACS general pronunciation and spoken English practice.

3. Although on this occasion TRANSMEDIATION had a separate timetable slot, elements could well be introduced as support to the individual FUNCTION modules, as suggested above.

PRESENTATION

Modules

One of the objectives of the DOPACS course is to allow individual students to adopt their own speed of learning and learning strategies while maintaining a general instructional control over the work of the class as a whole.

Clearly, where exercises can take place in a language laboratory, individual interests can be served very directly; equally, group work within the class can stimulate cooperative communication among individual learners—it is not necessary for the class as a whole to work chorally on the production exercises, or, indeed, to have each member answering a question in turn, through the teacher.

> Example 1   PROG-INFORM FUNCTION (Module 15)
> Production Exercise (2) :
> Divide the class into several small groups of three members. Each group is given a number of the items in the exercise (dependent on how many groups there are) and the group has to decide on the appropriate responses, including alternatives in each case. This kind of procedure has the class as a whole examining each item more thoroughly than if each item had been answered by an individual giving only one response, either in the class or in a laboratory.

Often class discussion can be merely instructor-talk. In the DOPACS materials it is important that the learners not only understand the points made in the discussion sections of the modules, but also realize their work-relatedness. The class could again be divided into groups, with each group discussing one of the Discussion points, and then each group would report on their attitudes, to be then taken up and examined by the rest of the class.

> Example 2   REASSURE FUNCTION (Module 17)
> Discussion Points:
> There are five major points for Discussion. Before beginning the module, divide the class into five groups. While the illustration tape is being played, the class not only recognizes where the REASSURE is used but each group considers the REASSURE within the context of its own Discussion point. In this way it is possible to give the discussion a practical basis with the learners able to illustrate their points with examples.
> This method for dealing with discussion points could be adopted for all the modules.

Remember that individual module workschemes only present one way of organizing the classroom learning.

Exercise Types

Following the section marked *Code Characterization*, the FUNCTION modules make use of *six* different exercise types, at various times and places within the module:

(i)   *Drills*
(ii) *Tables*
(iii) *Identification exercises*
(iv) *Sensitivity exercises*
(v)   *Production practice exercises*
(vi) *Simulation exercises.*

The general movement is from the very controlled exercises to the noncontrolled, as in the simulation exercises.

The *identification* and *sensitivity* exercises are different from the others; instead of prompting oral production, these two types are *perceptual* exercises in that they require the learner to become aware of the contextualization cues (both in terms of language and paralanguage) through which it is often possible to arrive at the communicative value of utterances. Such cues are frequently realized by intonational choice, and these exercises frequently follow exercises in intonation practice.

In particular, the *identification* exercises are concerned with enabling learners to distinguish utterances with appropriate intonation patterns from those where the language is grammatically well-formed but with inappropriate intonation.

Example 3
A: Description

GO-ON FUNCTION (Module 8) Identification exercise:
In this exercise, the learner will hear five extracts from Doctor-Patient interviews. The patient is telling the doctor about his accident/complaint, and the doctor responds with a series of GO-ONS. In each extract, there are four DOCTOR responses. Each GO-ON is lexically correct, but sometimes the intonation used is inappropriate. The learner must decide whether the doctor's response is suitable, and indicate this on a chart—an example of which is shown below.

	Appropriate	Inappropriate
FIRST EXTRACT		
1st response		
2nd response		
3rd response		
4th response		
SECOND EXTRACT		
1st response		
2nd response		
3rd response		
4th response		
THIRD EXTRACT		
1st response		
2nd response		
3rd response		
4th response		
FOURTH EXTRACT		
1st response		
2nd response		
3rd response		
4th response		
FIFTH EXTRACT		
1st response		
2nd response		
3rd response		
4th response		

B: Tapescript.
   1. P: . . . we were all climbing together.
          D: Mm-mm. . .

124 / ENGLISH FOR ACADEMIC AND TECHNICAL PURPOSES

    P: ... and I slipped on something.
    D: Yes. ...
    P: I didn't think about it. I sat there and laughed.
    D: And. ...
    P: Well, I went to get up and I could hardly move.
    D: So. ...
2. P: It were just an old biro.
    D: Really ....
    P: ... I was bored in the lesson and was playing with it.
    D: Uh-uh. ...
    P: ... it was only an old biro.
    D: So. ...
    P: ... as I opened it, the spring shot out.
    D: And ....
3. P: I wasn't goin' fast.
    D: No. ...
    P: I think me trouser must've caught.
    D: Yes. ...
    P: It was round the roundabout.
    D: Right. ...
    P: My trousers caught and the bike went over.
    D: I see. ...
4. P: It's happened several nights.
    D: Yes. ...
    P: Well, I just get into bed, then it starts.
    D: Then. ...
    P: I just can't lie there. It's like pains shooting through my foot.
    D: Uh-uh. ...
    P: The wife said I got to come.
    D: So. ...
5. P: I don't actually feel bad.
    D: No. ...
    P: But sometimes in the early evening.
    D: Yes. ...
    P: Well, I feel sort of dizzy. I been to my own doctor.
    D: Uh-uh. ...
    P: He can't work it out. Gave me some pills.
    D: And. ...

The *sensitivity* exercises differ in that the learner has to judge not only which utterances are acceptable, but also what degree of acceptability and appropriateness there is in each utterance, *in the learner's view*.

Example 4   LEAVETAKE FUNCTION (Module 5) Sensitivity exercise
A: Description   The learners will hear ten LEAVETAKEs on tape, and from the words and intonation used, they must judge how appropriate each one is. The Instructor must issue the learners with copies of the chart shown below, on which they make their evaluations. After hearing the tape, the learners will discuss their results with the Instructor, giving reasons for their selections. These are the instructions they will hear on the tape:

"You have been given a chart on which you must show your evaluations on the ten LEAVETAKEs you are about to hear. If you think the example is very good, you should put a tick in column five; if it is very poor, put a tick in column one. If it is neither very good nor very poor you should put a tick in one of the middle columns, depending on how good you think it is. When you have finished, discuss your results with your Instructor, giving reasons for your selection.

Now here are the examples. Listen carefully and don't forget that the intonation is as important as the actual words used."

Acceptability

LEAVETAKE	1	2	3	4	5
(i)					
(ii)					
(iii)					
(iv)					
(v)					
(vi)					
(vii)					
(viii)					
(ix)					
(x)					

B: Tapescript

1. P: Thank you.
   D: Thank you.
   P: Thank you very much. I don't need to come any more.
   D: No need to come again unless you're worried.
   P: All right, all right.
2. P: We're going on holiday on Friday; we're away for one week.
   D: Can you get your dressing done there in somewhere in hospital?
   P: Yeah.
   D: All right then you'll be coming back after one week then?
   P: Yeah.
   D: Er, see you in a week; if that's like not yet healed, it's all right.
3. D: You'll feel a bit sore. I don't think you've broken any bones or anything, but it might be a bit more sore tomorrow than it is today.
   P: Yeah.
   D: Now if anything odd turns up come and see us, but if you're quite happy, then, er, let nature do the job. Bye-bye Mr. Clarke.
   P: Goodbye.
4. P: Well I've been off a couple of days now.
   D: When do you want to start again?
   P: I'm starting in't morning.
   D: Do you need a note?
   P: No, no.
   D: Oh, you're all right, are you; don't do it too often; you don't need to come in again, bye-bye, Mr. Johnson.
5. D: So we'll give you some ointment to apply three times a day.
   P: Yes.
   D: For three days and you can come back here if you still have any difficulty.
   P: Right.
   D: Right, thank you.

6. D: That often takes the weight on; that should be all right they're pretty springy at this age, just as well; but the collar bone takes the weight from the arm onto the body. So there we are, you're going to have your picture taken.
    P's M: That's it, come on.
    D: Do you know where to go?
    P's M: erm...
    D: I'll show you and we'll see you later Helen.

It is possible for both these exercise types to be practiced in a language laboratory or in a classroom. It is important, however, on completion of the exercise, for the learners to discuss their results with the instructor in the case of the *sensitivity* exercise by dividing the learners into groups and discussing each item as it occurs.

The *drills* are traditional substitution and progressive drills, to be located in the classroom or the laboratory. They can be used for general class practice or to provide differentiated exercises for those students who need more exposure to formal language work. The *substitution tables* can be used in a similar way, either orally with the whole class, or on an individual and group basis, using blackboard, the book materials, or the overhead projector.

Although the orientation of the DOPACS materials is towards a functional and communicative view of language and language learning, with a major emphasis placed on the authenticity of the language data and tasks, it would be foolish to ignore the need to provide formal language practice for many learners. Such formal work is located in the Code Characterization Section of each FUNCTION module, and is practiced in the drills and substitution tables. This leaves the less controlled practice exercises to develop a functional and communicative language control, mirroring the authenticity of the Illustration and Recognition Sections, made overt and objectivized in the sections on Discussion Points and Sensitivity.

The *production practice* exercises gradually become less controlled. In many cases we advise that they be done in a language laboratory; strictly speaking, this is not necessary. Some, such as those that make use of short *dialogues,* give an opportunity for Pair-Work; while others, such as those incorporating *picture-stores*, give opportunities for whole groups to work together. In these exercises, when the students have completed their work on the story in a group, one member of the group should be selected to give the group's response to the story to the rest of the class.

Finally, in the *simulation exercises,* learners are given freedom to demonstrate their own knowledge of the language within the given situation and the required functions. These exercises can either be done with the instructor playing the part of the patient, and the learner the doctor's role or with learners playing all the roles. Depending on the ability of the class as a whole, time can be set aside for learners to prepare the simulation before the class. After the simulation exercise, (which can very usefully be video-recorded) the class should discuss the appropriateness of the language used, following the techniques of the Sensitivity exercises. It is important that such discussion concerns itself only with the language involved, and *not* with clinical matters, with which the learners as trained doctors may disagree — not simply because they are right or wrong but because of the different clinical background and training the learners may have had. A program for one module may take (at least) two different forms:

Example 5　　　　　　　DIAG-INFORM FUNCTION (Module 13)
MODE A
(i) Divide class into three groups: each group is given one Discussion Point to consider.
(ii) Play through the Illustration Section to all learners, isolating realizations of the DIAG-INFORM.
(iii) The class divides into groups, each group considering its Discussion Point.
(iv) Play through the Recognition Section to all learners. After each example, the groups collate part of the work in the discussion groups using the examples to illustrate their points.
(v) Go on to the Sensitivity exercise; in discussing learner's evaluations, relate them to the previous discussion.
(vi) Code points can be taught/worked through as necessary, making use of the Substitution Table for homework.
(vii) Quick review using the Substitution drill.
(viii) Reassemble in groups; each group to find appropriate responses for the Production Practice items.
(ix) Collate the groups' responses with discussion.
(x) Administer the P-Test.
MODE B
(i) Teach/review the Code Characterization points, using the taped Illustration Section for examples.
(ii) Go through the Recognition exercise in small groups.
(iii) Work on the Sensitivity exercise in small groups.
(iv) Use the language laboratory for substitution drill leading to production practice.
(v) Reassemble in a class for discussion of the DIAG-INFORM and its function in the consultation.
(vi) Administer the P-Test.

In a sense the DOPACS materials appear to end at a *simulative* stage of language performance; this is deliberate, since actual *transfer* to authentic communication is guaranteed, given the work-experience of the doctors and the work-relatedness of the course materials. We would expect an interaction between work and study, where study cycles and procedures both mirror, simulate, and prepare for the actuality of hospital communication. It is obviously desirable for instructors/course planners to make as close a connection as possible between *learning/teaching* communication and *practicing* communication in real time. The audiovisual media of the DOPACS course are there to provide a convenient pedagogic link to the doctor's world; they are stylized and *represent* the authenticity of his or her own environment, rather than seek to *replace* it.

Finally, in this section, it is worth recalling that the advantage of a modular course, operating in discrete Units, which can be omitted and reordered, is that each module can be expanded or shortened according to learner and teacher need.

A Diagnostic test will throw up areas where work is needed. It may not be the case, however, that in *all* areas *all* learners need to perform a similar amount of work, which would be the case if the instructor worked repeatedly through each module as it came. It may well be that learners are easily able to grasp the problems of the DIAG-INFORM, so that only the Production Practice exercises at the end are necessary, whereas with a metacommunicative FUNCTION such as the GO-ON, the learners may require a good deal of practice, especially in the controlled exercises. The instructor may wish to add his or her own, local hospital-specific material. The modular system allows this to happen; and the exercises should be considered as a guide. An important objective of the DOPACS modules is that they should be *permeable* and admit freely of additional material.

SELF STUDY

Although, as we have seen, many sections of the DOPACS modules can be used for self-study activities, the course as a whole is not designed primarily for independent learner use. It would be difficult, and less than profitable, for the learner to work without instructor guidance. In the "instructional" as opposed to the "practice" section of the modules, for example in the teaching of the code points, the instructor has been left to devise his or her own effective methods of teaching and explanation.

However there are areas where the learner may usefully do part of the module at home, given access to a cassette recorder. For example, Illustration and Recognition exercises may usefully be done away from the class before the Instructor begins the discussion on the module. If the learner has been prepared in advance by being told the main points of the discussion, after going through the Illustration and Recognition in his or her own time, the learner may be more able to enter fully into the discussion.

Once again, where learners require extra work on drills or production practice, these can usefully be done out of class; as can the exercises for which there is only a minority need among the class. In this way, the course materials can be made to provide more hours for the learner than the actual available class time. On long extensive courses, where there is a long time lapse between each contact session, work at home can usefully bridge the gap between classes.

It is important to realize, however, that a communicative understanding of the social and interpersonal significance of doctor-patient language is most likely to derive from small group interactive discussion, where alternative interpretations as to doctor and patient meaning can be cooperatively worked upon and shared. The transfer to effective communicative performance likewise thrives in such an environment, although, clearly, time must be made available for individual study and practice.

APPENDIX I: KEY TO TABLE 9-1

MODULE TITLES

Module 1:	*Status and Role of the Casualty Officer*
Module 2:	*Language in the Consultation*
Module 3:	*Form and Function*
Module 4:	*Greet FUNCTION*
Module 5:	*Leavetake FUNCTION*
Module 6:	*Elicit FUNCTION*
Module 7:	*Interrogate FUNCTION*
Module 8:	*Go-On FUNCTION*
Module 9:	*Accept FUNCTION*
Module 10:	*Question FUNCTION*
Module 11:	*Makesure FUNCTION*
Module 12:	*Direct FUNCTION*
Module 13:	*Diag-Inform FUNCTION*
Module 14:	*Action-Inform FUNCTION*
Module 15:	*Prog-Inform FUNCTION*
Module 16:	*Treat-Direct FUNCTION*
Module 17:	*Reassure FUNCTION*
Module 18:	*Repeat FUNCTION*
Module 19:	*Feed-me-back FUNCTION*
Module 20:	*Restate FUNCTION*
Module 21:	*Med-Ask FUNCTION*
Module 22:	*Admin-Ask FUNCTION*
Module 23:	*Apology FUNCTION*
Module 24:	*TRANSMEDIATION*

APPENDIX II: KEY TO FIGURE 9-3

(List of speech FUNCTIONS used to make live, realtime analyses of a doctor's utterances during casualty consultations)

Doctors' speech FUNCTIONS *in Casualty*

A = GREET: D: "Hullo";
                      D: "Good morning".;
                      D: "Mrs. Jones?" etc.

B = ELICIT: (to get broad description of accident with some circumstantial detail):
                      D: "Can you tell me what happened?" . . . etc.

C = INTERROGATE: (to probe circumstances of trauma relevant to diagnosis . . .):
D: "Do you remember if your whole weight was on the foot?"
D: "Did you bend right back when you fell?". . . . etc.

D = QUESTION: (to get information during examination):
D: "Does this hurt?";
D: "Can you bend it?" etc.

E = MAKESURE: (to make sure that what Dr. understands is what P meant):
D: "Does it hurt here?"
P: "No, not really."
D: "It doesn't hurt?"
P: "No."

F = EXTEND: (to test a deduction made from P's information):
D: "Can you walk all right?"
P: "Yes."
D: "So it doesn't hurt to put your weight on it?"
P: "No."

G = ACTION-INFORM: (to let the patient know what is being done/going to be done):
D: "I'm going to put in a couple of stitches."
D: "I think we'd better have an X-ray, to make sure . . ." etc.

H = DIAG-INFORM: (to let the patient know the diagnosis):
D: "You haven't broken anything" . . . etc.

I = PROG-INFORM: (to let the patient know how the condition is likely to progress):
D: "It should heal up quite quickly." etc.

J = TREAT-DIRECT: (to tell the patient what to do to help the cure):
D: "Take plenty of rest." etc.

K = DIRECT: (to tell the patient what to do so that medical attention can effectively be given):
D: "Can you just lie down a moment."
D: "Take this with you to X-ray."
D: "Come back in five days." etc.

L = APOLOGY: (to apologize for hurting patient or otherwise inconveniencing):
D: "Sorry. Did that hurt?" etc.

M = TALK: (to give information not strictly relevant to the consultation in hand):
D: "I've seen rather a lot of these lately."
D: "Little girls tend to do that sort of thing."

N = MED-ASK: (to get information relevant to clinical aspects of consultation):
D: "Are you allergic to penicillin?"
D: "Have you been vaccinated against tetanus?" etc.

O = ADMIN-ASK: (to get information not relevant to *clinical* aspects of consultation):
D: "Do you use this hand in your work?"
D: "Did you come here on foot?" etc.

P = REASSURE: (to reassure patient)
D: "Nothing serious here."
D: "Don't worry, it's all right." etc.

Q = ACCEPT: (to acknowledge receipt of communication):
D: "... Yes ..."
P: "I sort of twisted it round ... you know ... like ..."
D: "Twisted it. I see."

R = LEAVETAKE: (to end the consultation):
D: "Right, thank you, Mrs. Jones."
D: "OK? Thank you."
D: "Good. See you after the X-ray then ..."

S = GO-ON: (to encourage patient to continue the story):
P: "Well, I was playing football, ..."
D: "Mmm ..."
P: "And ..."

T = ANSWER: (to reply to query raised by patient/nurse):
P: "Does that mean it's broken?"
D: "Yes, I'm afraid it's broken just here."
N: "Shall I do an elastic bandage, Doctor?"
D: "Yes, I think that's all it needs."

U = REPEAT: (to get the patient/nurse/addressee to repeat what he/she said):
D: "What?"
D: "Sorry?" etc.

V = RESTATE: (repeating what was said because the patient didn't catch it):
D: "Can you swallow all right?"
P: "Can I ... ?"
D: "... Swallow, all right."

W = FEED-ME-BACK: (to check that the patient/nurse/addressee has understood/is listening):
D: "Do you follow me?"
D: "OK?"
D: "Is that all right?" etc.

Source: Candlin, Bruton, and Leather (1976a) pp. 269-271.

Notes

1. Patient attitudes were not directly investigated. Since our chief interest was the *actual* communicative behavior of the casualty doctor, there was a limit to our interest in what to the consumer might be an ideal service. A study of patient attitudes, to have validity, would have needed more time in design and execution than we could afford. Also, patients presenting at casualty are in no mood to oblige researchers, whatever their aims, and we thought it claim enough on their goodwill to seek their consent to an observer's presence at their consultation.

2. Observation of consultations could be relatively unobtrusive. The consent of the participants was sought at the start of an observation session. An observer in a white coat made notes during the consultation, without active participation of any kind. There was no perceptible inhibiting effect on the interactions in question. In contrast to the general practitioner's consultation, it is common enough in the hospital setting for unidentified people to come and go while the doctor is seeing a patient. There may be communication between two or more speaker-hearers such that the set of speaker-hearers, their roles in the communication event, and the means of transmission of their messages are constants in the institutional setting. Each such configuration of constants constitutes a different network.

References

Candlin, C. N., C. J. Bruton, and J. H. Leather. 1974-75. *Doctor-Patient Communication Skills: Working Papers I–IV,* University of Lancaster Mimeo.

———. 1976a. "Doctors in Casualty: Applying Communicative Competence to Components of Specialist Course Design." *IRAL* 14.3. pp. 245-272.

———. 1976b. "Doctor Speech Functions in Casualty Consultations: Some Quantified Characteristics of Discourse in a Regulated Setting." *Proceedings of the III AILA World Congress (1975),* ed. G. Nickel. Stuttgart Hochschulverlag.

Candlin, C. N., C. J. Bruton, J. H. Leather, and E. Woods. 1977. *Doctor-Patient Communication Skills Vols. I and II.* Graves Medical Audio-Visual Library, Chelmsford, England.

Davis, R. H., L. T. Alexander, and S. Yellon. 1974. *Learning Systems Design.* McGraw-Hill.

Editorial Comments

This chapter provides a summary of a larger study on oral interactions in a medical context, one of the few studies we know of, in fact, working on *oral* English for Specific Purposes (ESP). (Other work includes Schmidt (this volume) and Levine (University of Minnesota).) The authors present a framework for a thorough needs analysis of doctor-patient interactions, drawing extensively on sociolinguistic assumptions and techniques. A very helpful discussion is included here that describes the procedures and problems involved in the development of a taxonomy of specific purpose functions that seem to occur in this kind of doctor-patient interaction; this taxonomy may prove to be helpful in analysis of oral interactions in other ESP contexts as well.

In our view, this discussion should also help to argue against what we term the *ESP fallacy*: the belief that the notion "learner needs" is unambiguous, a view attacked by Widdowson and Mackay (chaps. 1 and 10, respectively). For one thing, there are the "present needs" of (a variety of) learner-types in the ESL classroom, as distinct from "future needs" on the job or in the academic classroom. For another, as Devon Woods (personal communication) points out, the term *needs analysis* seems to imply to many people that: "there are in fact needs out there which can be *simply* analyzed." Perhaps what we are involved with is a philosophy-of-science problem, the common situation in science in which existence of a name implies a hypothesis. In any case, from the Candlin et al. discussion about the difficulties of creating a series of functional categories, one is reminded of the phenomenon in linguistic and anthropological fieldwork, that in a complex, empirical, real-life domain, it is very difficult to create a descriptive framework that "fits" the data. We raise this issue again in our comments on the next several chapters.

One of the values of this chapter for us is that it demonstrates one way in which to build on a functional needs analysis (once you have one that appears to work) in developing teaching materials for instruction in communicative skills and in using interactional learning objectives. We find particularly valuable the detail provided here in summary form and alluded to in the references.

The discussion of the importance and practical value of a modular approach to curriculum development in ESP contexts such as this seems to us, intuitively, to be highly instructive and potentially very useful. This discussion provides for the practicing teacher, the syllabus designer, and the course director something unfortunately quite unusual for our field — a detailed, tested model.

L.S.
E.T.

10
Developing a Reading Curriculum for ESP

Ronald Mackay

The purpose of this chapter is to trace the case history of a project in English for Specific Purposes (ESP) that began in 1975 and is still in operation. This chapter encompasses the whole of the "ESP operation" (as conceived for the purposes of this project) to show the reader the interrelationship between the rationale behind the activities involved in the conception, planning, development and mounting, and subsequent evaluation of one ESP program. Our[1] principal aim is to stress the cohesive nature of the stages involved in the entire project rather than to provide exhaustive details on any of its individual phases in particular. At the same time, we would acknowledge that the development of any ESP program, the one reported on included, can, and indeed, should never slavishly follow a preordained plan. Planning and implementing curricula in education involves dealing with real teachers, real students, real data, and coping with real circumstances. This inevitably means that the planners must be willing to take the changing aspects of the environment into consideration and modify their original plans to accommodate them. Nevertheless, an informed plan of action permits the planner to identify the points at which compromises can be made with least damage to the program as a whole.

It would seem reasonable to assume that the more closely a second language teaching program is based on the identified uses to which a specific group of students will put the language, the more successful and effective the course will be (Selinker, Trimble, and Vroman 1972). This is one rationale underlying specific purpose language teaching—but see Widdowson and Crofts (chaps. 1 and 11, respectively). The aim of this chapter is to trace the case history of a project in

ESP to show the steps and decisions involved in preparing and teaching one example of an ESP course to near beginners at the university level in Mexico.

The project discussed here was one of several resulting from the establishment of a cooperative link between the Centre for the Teaching of Foreign Languages (CELE) at the National Autonomous University of Mexico (UNAM) and the Department of Linguistics, Edinburgh University. The link was supported jointly by the Mexican and British governments. This cooperation, begun in 1975, had three distinct though related purposes: (1) to develop and test materials intended to provide students with English language skills as a tool in their academic/ professional studies; (2) to document the progress and stages of the project so that the procedures followed could, possibly in a modified form, be used as a model upon which other projects with similar purposes could pattern themselves; and (3) to train local personnel at every stage of the project so that a cadre of well-qualified and experienced applied linguists could be built.

In particular, the project discussed below deals with that part of the work carried out cooperatively between CELE, UNAM, and the Faculty of Veterinary Medicine and Animal Production (FMVZ) at UNAM. Its goal was to provide undergraduate animal scientists and veterinarians with that variety of English and those English language skills that would be of most professional use to them during their studies. Such a goal, it was hypothesized, would be appropriate for any project carried out in any of the other faculties and schools of UNAM (e.g., Law, Economics, Chemistry, Architecture, Dentistry, etc.). However, a starting point had to be made somewhere, and it was decided by CELE to develop a prototype ESP project in conjunction with the Faculty of Veterinary Medicine and Animal Production (FMVZ), because of the enthusiastic support for the project given by the Dean and his staff. Moreover, the role played by the FMVZ (and comparable faculties in other Mexican universities) in increasing food production in Mexico is felt to be of enormous importance to the country and its people. A joint project between Mexico and Britain in the field of animal production was already in progress and developing, and was based in Chetumal, Quintana Roo. Importantly, we had the full cooperation of the scientists involved in that project and the English teacher, Joanne Preston, (now at the University of Yucatan) who already had experience with English for animal production during her teaching career in Cuba.

It was felt that besides functioning within a suitable environment, the project would be meeting real needs in an important area contributing to the internal development of Mexico.

A MODEL FOR ESP CURRICULUM DEVELOPMENT

The first step in the project, after selecting the personnel to be involved both in CELE and the PMVZ, was to establish an operational framework within which the project could be carried out. It was necessary to draw up a procedural model that would allow different individuals to work in different stages of the project at the same time while ensuring that these different components could be finally fitted together to make an integrated whole. Hence a set of procedures was established, which began with the gathering of information about the students and about their needs for a language other than Spanish, and ended with an evaluation and revision of the materials developed to meet these identified needs. Similar practical attempts to model the numerous activities involved in foreign or second language syllabus design are discussed in Wilson (1976). While operational models have their uses, it must be borne in mind that there is no "ideal" procedure for the planning and preparation of a syllabus. The steps will inevitably depend upon specific factors in the situation in question. But a well-planned procedural model does help to ensure that no essential steps are left out of the project, and the model presented in Figure 10-1 developed out of this experience.

The Basic Information Gathering Stage

Initial examination of purported needs amply demonstrated that there is an inadequate distinction made between current real needs, future real needs, and future hypothetical needs in ESP work in syllabus planning. It is not uncommon for future hypothetical needs to influence the nature of the program with the result that current needs are overlooked altogether and only a very small proportion of those taught ever find a use for the costly and lengthy instruction given.

Another category of "need" that tends to add to the confusion, is that "imposed" by a well-meaning teacher reflecting the teacher's desires for certain kinds of instruction, independent of any identifiable need on the part of the students.

Given these complexities, a questionnaire was therefore prepared for both the subject-matter teachers and the students in the FMVZ (Mackay 1978b). Previous experience had shown the inadequacy of information-gathering instruments that were left for the students to complete; they were returned with the answers to some questions left blank, while misunderstanding of questions was obvious from conflicting answers, and anomalous answers were difficult or impossible to follow up for explanation.

It was decided that the questionnaire should be conducted as a structured interview in which a trained interviewer would put the previously determined questions directly to the staff member or student being interviewed and note his or her answers. In this way it was expected that deficiencies in the type of questionnaire mentioned above could be overcome.

After a pilot version of the question battery had been tried out on a sample population, and the questions and scales modified in the light of the outcome, the structured interview was conducted individually with forty-two professors and fifty-two students selected at random, and representing every field of study and every semester in the undergraduate degree in the FMVZ. The results seemed to provide us with a clear picture of the needs of the students as represented by both

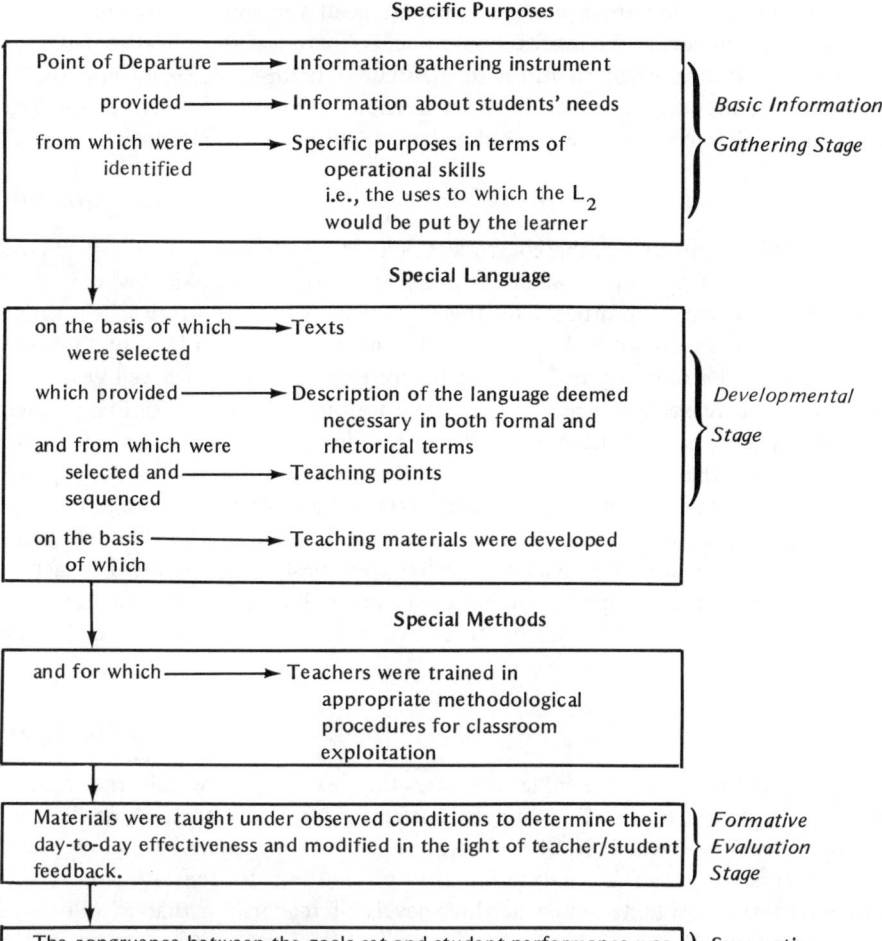

FIGURE 10-1. A PROCEDURAL MODEL FOR ESP SYLLABUS DESIGN

the staff and student body. In essence, the results indicated that a knowledge of *no language other than Spanish* was necessary for a student to complete professional undergraduate studies satisfactorily. However, it was felt by 78% of the staff and 58% of the students interviewed that a reading knowledge of English would permit students to increase the quality of their academic and professional knowledge significantly. No skill other than a reading skill emerged as a real need for undergraduates during the entire course of their academic study in the FMVZ.

Despite the fact that there was no apparent need for any foreign language to satisfy the examiners in the professional subjects, there was an obligatory language requirement students had to fulfill to graduate. The disservice arbitrary foreign language requirements do for both professional schools and service-language departments has been pointed out elsewhere (Sculthorpe 1974; Mackay 1976a).

The Students

The students for whom the course was being prepared were all undergraduates in the Faculty of Veterinary Medicine and Animal Production. Most were in their late teens or early twenties and their previous exposure to English varied enormously. Virtually all had studied English as a subject for at least two years in high school but a minority had had English for five, six, and even seven years. For administrative reasons, it was not possible to group students according to their proficiency on a standardized test. The only criterion for selecting students for the course was that they have completed at least three semesters of undergraduate studies. This meant that we could at least count on a certain minimum knowledge of the principles underlying animal science and make use of the student's knowledge of the subject to lead him or her to a mastery of English. The lack of homogeneity in the groups is not ideal but so far has not presented itself as a major problem. The groups met for three two-hour sessions per week for thirteen weeks.

The Texts

In an attempt to determine whether the texts upon which the reading instruction should be based should be authentic target discourse or an "easier" discourse variety, we experimented with texts differing along two dimensions, viz., readership aimed at and familiarity of content to the student. It was discovered that of texts aimed at three levels of readership; that is, (1) those written for a high-school level of readership, (2) those written for an undergraduate level of readership, and (3) those written for practicing veterinarians, the last two categories motivated the student more strongly. Related to this outcome was, no doubt, the relative familiarity of the students with the content of the texts. High-school biology was already familar to them, and so the task of struggling with the language only to retrieve information already possessed was felt not to be worth the effort. On the other hand, the reward of gaining new, but related, information from a text was regarded as being well worth the struggle involved with the language.

The use of authentic reading materials also allowed us to identify the characteristic organizational principles of texts dealing with animal science as well as the formal characteristics in terms of sentence structure and specialized vocabulary. The topics dealt with included Behavior and Clinical Disorders in Farm Animals, Preconditioning Cattle for the Feedlot, Gastrointestinal Parasitism in Ruminants, and so forth (FMVZ/CELE 1975).

Two techniques were used to identify some of the "reading difficulties" of Spanish-speaking students reading English so that special attention could be given to these areas of difficulty. One technique used cloze and modified cloze tests, and the other used translation. These pieces of research are still continuing. Until the results of these and other techniques could provide us with teaching points more objectively arrived at, our selection of difficulties was inevitably based on informed intuition and on observations made by the teachers experimenting with the pilot materials as well as the results of student introspection.

The Exercises

The exercise types used to practice the teaching points were also arrived at as a result of prior experience and familiarity with successful practices. Exercise types included *anticipation exercises* intended to encourage an attitude of expectancy in the reader. We saw this as developing habits of "prediction" in reading that, according to current psycholinguistic theory, are characteristic of successful readers. These appear to "prime" the student for the kind of information to expect and the way in which it is organized. An example of one such anticipation exercise is:

> The diagram below represents the way in which the information in the text you are about to read, is organized. Translate the headings into Spanish. Discuss, in Spanish, the kinds of information you would expect to find under each heading:
>
>   Foreign Bodies in the Esophagus
>   (Small Animals)
>
> Examples of foreign bodies   (i)
>   (ii)
>   (iii)
> Obstruction characteristics   (i)   complete
>   (ii)   partial
> Clinical signs depend on   (i)
>   (ii)
>   (iii)
>   (iv)
> Means of detection   (i)
>   (ii)
>   (iii)
> Now, go on to read the text and see how many of your expectations are fulfilled.

Lexical exercises included rephrasing, word-building, the use of contextual clues, and the use of lexical relationships to relate one part of the discourse to another (Berman 1975). In *rephrasing exercises,* the student is provided with simple paraphrases of difficult vocabulary items or phrases and is asked to underline the corresponding word or phrase in the text, for example:

> The link between altered behavior and the diseased stage in farm animals is very close. Thus there is a tendency for obviously abnormal behavior which presumably occurs in response to an abnormal physical state, to be used as the identification index for particular disorders. For this reason, a number of diseases are known by behavioral descriptions. Examples of these include staggers, gid, and lockjaw.

Rephrasing: underline the words in the text which correspond in meaning to the underlined words in the following sentences:
1. There is a close <u>relationship</u> between the <u>pathological condition</u> and <u>modification of conduct</u> in farm animals.
2. There is a <u>general inclination</u> to use abnormal behavior as <u>the means of naming</u> particular diseases.

In such exercises the student is not being asked to supply synonyms of difficult words but is being provided with glosses of difficult terms contextualized within a sentence, and his or her attention hopefully is being focused upon the items *in use* rather than in isolation.

Word-building exercises help the student to become familiar with affixes and how they alter the meanings of words, for example:

Complete the sentences below so that they agree with the information given in the text you have just read.
  (i) Supportive treatment is _____ to cure acute cases of equine encephalitis.
                             sufficient/insufficient
  (ii) A biological vector is _____ by an agent of a disease.
                             infect/uninfected
  (iii) A medical cure for equine encephalitis is at present _____
                             unavailable/available

Syntactic exercises focus on sentence-level grammar, as well as on relationships between sentences as opposed to within sentences. Exercises on the use of logical connectors provide the student with practice in identifying words that link information in a logical way and permit the reader to "follow the argument" of the text, for example:

Read each word or phrase below:
because   porque
however   sin embargo
therefore   por consiguiente
that is (to say)   es decir/o sea
such as   tal (es) como

Now write the most appropriate word or phrase from the English list into each of the spaces in the text so that the information conforms to that in the passage you have just read.
(a) At birth, the pig's gut is sterile, _____ , it is free from all micro-organisms.
(b) _____ it is flooded with lactobacilli within a few hours.
(c) After a few days, a large number of micro-organisms _____ bacteria, protozoa and viruses are present in the alimentary system.

Information-extraction exercises encourage students to take structured notes, often in diagramatic form, and look similar in format to the anticipation exercises.

Translation-type exercises encourage the students to reproduce the basic information in the text in their mother tongue, Spanish, for example:

Translate the headings and complete the diagram in Spanish by re-reading the text.

Feedlot Facilities include

Feeds	Equipment for	Holding Facilities and	Facilities for Moving Cattle
(i) _____	_____	_____	(a) _____
(ii) _____	_____	_____	(b) _____
_____			

Despite the climate of disapproval surrounding the use of translation as a learning strategy, we felt that this kind of exercise was justified. After all, although the students had to read in English, the information gained had to be employed *in Spanish* and integrated into their existing knowledge *in Spanish*.

Our observations and the feedback from our teachers who were using the materials did permit us to sequence the exercise types within any instructional unit to lead to what we considered to be optimum learning on the part of the student. It was generally agreed by the team that the most functional sequence for the exercises was:

Anticipation Exercise
Text — Rephrasing incorporated into text
Contextual Reference
Word-building/re-ordering of words/sentence completion
Intrasentential connectors
Intersentential connectors
Note-taking
True/False
Translation — Reproduction type exercise

It was felt that this sequence helped to order the exercises in such a way as to provide the learner with the maximum use of the one preceding it and the maximum opportunity to make a contribution to the one following it.

Methodological Procedures in the Classroom

It will be evident to the reader by now, that a great deal of Spanish must have been used in our classrooms. Because the students' need for English did not extend beyond the ability to read, we felt that it would have been unduly costly in terms of time, and uneconomical in terms of effort, to insist that the language of the classroom should be English only. Our teachers were bilingual and were encouraged to ask a question in English followed immediately by the same question in Spanish. If a student felt he or she could respond in English, the student did. If not, he or she answered in Spanish and no class time was taken up with the teacher eliciting oral English responses from students. Since the goal of the course was to train students to demonstrate their understanding of English texts related to their studies in their mother tongue, the lack of spoken English was not seen as a drawback in any way to achieving this goal. To ensure that the students had an internal "model" of how the text would be read in English, the teachers read the passages aloud several times as students followed with their eyes.

Formative Evaluation Stage

Feedback at this stage of formative evaluation was provided in two ways. Detailed *evaluation sheets* were completed by the teachers of the experimental program, which took into consideration their reactions to the texts, the teaching points, and the exercise types. However, the project director sat in on some of the classes, observing the interaction among teacher, student, and materials. It was possible to alter materials and procedures in conscious ways in a fairly controlled manner as opposed to making arbitrary changes in the hope that improved teaching or learning might follow.

The Summative Evaluation

Finally the materials and course of instruction, which lasted one semester (seventy hours approximately), were evaluated in terms of the students' ability to read and understand academic and professional discourse in their field of study. Criterion-referenced tests were prepared employing texts representing target discourse. These were tests designed not to compare the achievement of one student with that of another, but to demonstrate their effectiveness at extracting information from texts dealing with animal science and written in English. Tests were conducted before, during, and at the end of the course of instruction.[2]

Briefly, it was found that 94% of the students who received instruction showed improvement in English reading comprehension over the period of the course. Since due to administrative constraints, we were unable to make provision for a control group against which to compare the final reading proficiency of our initial group of students, it is of course not possible to say that the improvement was due entirely to the course of instruction. However, students reported informally that by the end of the course they were less fearful of consulting textbooks written in English. It is fairly certain that the course had at least served to overcome the initial unwillingness experienced by many students to attempt to read books written in a language with which their school encounters may have been far from confidence-building.

An additional advantage occurring from this ESP course was the reduction in the dropout rate. Whereas "general English" courses at that time had a 50% dropout rate, this tailor-made course had a dropout rate of only 4% (i.e., 6 students out of 153 dropped the semester long course). Subsequent courses using these materials have likewise had lower than average dropout rates.

CONCLUSION

There are many problems to be ironed out in the preparation of specialized courses for scientists, technologists, or others who require some proficiency in the English language as an auxiliary to those professional or vocational skills they already possess or are in the process of acquiring. The matter of nonhomogeneous groups; the extent to which it is feasible, practicable, even desirable to teach skills in isolation; the provision of appropriate instruments to determine the effectiveness of the materials, the teaching, and the learning; classroom procedures appropriate to the goals, materials, and maturity of the students; the identification of what it is that constitutes a difficulty for non-native speakers learning specialized English; the provision of pertinent training for teachers; all these are matters that must be carefully examined if ESP courses are to be consistently improved with experience.

There is recent evidence that some of these matters are already beginning to attract the attention of researchers, and new techniques are being employed to provide data to answer the questions. Selinker's suggestions (1979) for the use of informants have provided the approach for a number of studies investigating the kinds of difficulties encountered by students (e.g., Cohen et al. 1978). The effectiveness of certain types of exercises on reading comprehension has been examined by Alderson and Richards (1977); the effects of different kinds of teaching materials on the discourse produced in class was reported upon by Phillips and Shettlesworth (1975); and Long, Adams, McLean, and Castaños (1976) described the differences in quantity and quality of discourse produced by students organized in a lockstep manner as compared to working in small groups.

All of these studies, as well as those edited by Pike (1977), are of primary importance because of the research methodology they propose or employ and there is evidence that they are encouraging objectivity and rigor in the way in which questions of importance to ESP are being formulated and answers sought.

However, even the limited success of our pilot ESP project in the FMVZ and our gropings towards ways for the organization and close documentation of our professional activities reflected in our occasional R & D Unit Reports have sufficiently encouraged the authorities to authorize the continuation of research and the preparation of additional specialized courses for other faculties and schools of UNAM.

Notes

1. I would like to acknowledge the contribution of my colleagues, G. Alvarez, L. Cas-Romero, S. Bastien, M. Chasan, R. Kemp, B. Klassen, T. Garst, D. Litvak, S. Richards, and M. Williamson for contributing at every stage of the project and for making it a success.

2. R & D Unit Report No. 6, *Student Performance as a Means of Evaluating the Reading Comprehension Programme for Undergraduate Students in the Facultad de Medicina Veterinaira y Zooternia, at U.N.A.M.* prepared by Mackay, R., Cas-Romero, L., Kemp, R., and Williamson, M. August 1976.

References

Alderson, J.C., and S. Richards. 1977. *Difficulties which Students Encounter When Reading Texts in English, R & D Unit Report No. 8,* CELE, UNAM, Mexico.

Berman, R. 1975. "Analytic Syntax: A Technique for Advanced Reading." *TESOL Quarterly* 8.

Cohen, A. D., H. Glassman, P. R., Rosenbaum, J. Ferrara, and J. Fine. 1978. "Reading English for Specialized Purposes: Discourse Analysis and the Use of Student Informants." Paper presented at Twelfth Annual TESOL Convention, Mexico City.

FMVZ/CELE. 1975. "Inglés para Objectivos Especificos, Lectura de Comprehension." Published jointly by the Centre for the Teaching of Foreign Languages (CELE) and the Faculty of Animal Sciences (FMVZ), National Autonomous University of Mexico, Mexico City.

Long, M. H., L. Adams, L. McLean, and F. Castaños. 1976. "Doing Things with Words: Interaction in Lockstep and Small Group Classroom Situations." *On TESOL 1976*, eds. J. Fanselow and R. Crymes.

Mackay, R. 1976a. "A Project in English for Specific Purposes." *Research and Development Unit Report No. 2*. CELE, National Autonomous University of Mexico, Mexico City.

———. 1976b. "English for Science and Technology in Mexico: Problems and Principles." *MEXTESOL Journal* 1.1, pp. 54-65.

———. 1978a. "Practical Curriculum Development and Evaluation in ESP/EST." *EST Newsletter*.

———. 1978b. "Identifying the Nature of the Learner's Needs." *English for Specific Purposes: A Case Study Approach*, eds. R. Mackay and A. Mountford. Longmans.

Phillips, M. and M. Shettlesworth. 1975. "Questions in the Design and Use of Courses in English for Specialized Purposes." *Proceedings of Fourth International Congress of AILA*. Stuttgart.

Pike, K. L. 1977. "Pilot Projects on the Reading of English of Science and Technology." *University of Michigan Papers in Linguistics: Special Publications in Applied Linguistics No. 1*.

Sculthorpe, M. A. L. 1974. "Intensive Courses: Towards a Strategy for Teaching." *Teaching Languages to Adults for Special Purposes: CILT Reports and Papers No. 11*, ed. G. E. Perren.

Selinker, L. 1979. "On the Use of Informants in Discourse Analysis and 'Language for Specialized Purposes.'" *IRAL* 17.3, pp. 189-215.

Selinker, L., L. Trimble, and R. Vroman. 1972. *Working Papers in English for Science and Technology*. Office of Engineering Research, University of Washington.

Wilson, G. H. (Ed.) 1976. *Curriculum Development and Syllabus Design for English Teaching*. SEAMEO/RELC and Singapore University Press, Singapore.

Editorial Comments

Mackay reports here on the design and implementation of an ESP program that is part of an extended project in Mexico City. A very useful flow chart is presented (Figure 10-1), which suggests procedures one could follow in setting up a program in ESP. The author shows how these procedures were followed in the very specific circumstances described in the chapter, at a time when (a) the literature in "needs analysis" is very scant indeed, and (b) the need for principles upon which to base practical syllabus design and practical teaching decisions is very great.

Some of the decisions Mackay and colleagues made in the course of designing this program were the focus of fruitful discussions in a graduate seminar one of the editors conducted at the University of Minnesota: (1) the choice of a questionnaire for needs analysis as opposed to linguistic analysis by trained observers *in situ*; (2) the decision to avoid text material that was too familiar to the student (see Crofts, chap. 11); (3) the decision to focus only on reading skills and not on oral skills; (4) the use of exercise materials that seemed to the members of our seminar to exemplify the sort of "process-oriented" approach called for by Widdowson (chap. 1).

Also useful is Mackay's catalogue of unresolved problems still remaining at the end of this part of the project; this listing provides an apparently realistic picture of the sorts of practical dilemmas to be encountered in this field. Mackay's distinctions between "current real needs," "future real needs," and "future hypothetical needs" could be compared to Widdowson's "two interpretations" of "learner needs" discussed in chapter 1 of this volume. These classifications may provide the beginning of a taxonomy of topics to study in the area of "needs analysis."

We believe that careful study of this chapter will prove to be very helpful to the many individuals faced with the prospect of designing, implementing, and evaluating a new ESP program. Mackay's approach allows the reader to set in relief several difficulties with this important field: (1) what we called the "ESP fallacy" (see editorial comments on Candlin et al., chap. 9); (2) what "method" one should use to do needs assessment (see Schmidt, chap. 15, for a quite different approach to ESP needs analysis); (3) the "goal-oriented"/"process-oriented" debate (see Widdowson, chap. 1); this debate will continue.

Finally, we agree wholeheartedly with Mackay's caveat that: "... the development of any ESP program. ... can, and indeed, *should never slavishly follow a preordained plan*" (italics added).

L.S.
E.T.

11 Subjects and Objects in ESP Teaching Materials

J. N. Crofts

The writers of ESP teaching materials seem generally to have taken it for granted that the English of any occupation or academic discipline is best presented and learned in the context of subject matter with which the target students are familiar in connection with the occupation or discipline concerned or which they will learn as they pursue it. This was a natural starting point in the years when English for Specific Purposes (ESP) was beginning to be recognized as a specialist branch of English Language Teaching (ELT) and the small body of ESP pioneers were looking for ways of making their courses more appropriate and attractive to their students than they thought was possible using only general English teaching materials. It must have seemed self-evident that the best vehicles for presenting the English most needed by, say, waiters or students of chemistry were dialogues or written texts closely similar to those these learners were expected to meet in their studies or work. It also must have seemed likely that learners would be more motivated towards their English courses if there was a very obvious similarity between the language-using situations simulated in the English course and those they were meeting or would meet in their occupations or studies. From this sort of thinking sprang the two oldest and biggest series of ESP textbooks, Oxford's *English Studies Series* and Collier-Macmillan's *Special English* series. At that time (the mid-sixties) the important differences between the kinds of language used in different fields were seen mainly in terms of the lexical items that were peculiar to particular fields or especially common in them and grammatical items that were used in a special way or with special frequency. In the last five years or so interest has been focused on the rhetorical structure and the organization of information in texts, and it has been hypothesized that there were significant differences in these respects between different fields (e.g., Selinker et al. 1974 and Widdowson 1979).

It is now about twenty years since ESP textbooks began to appear in some numbers and about ten years since ESP began to gain general recognition. It is time to scrutinize the assumptions I have outlined above in the light of the results of applying them in ESP teaching materials and to compare with them approaches based on practical or other theoretical considerations. I have neither the data nor the time here to offer the full and documented assessment that is needed, but I think that some purpose will be served by pointing out some of the practical weaknesses I have found in using materials based on the assumptions outlined above and by describing some encouraging experiments based on other considerations. I am not suggesting that these assumptions have no validity in any ESP situation, nor do I believe that my own suggestions are universally valid. I believe that ESP situations are infinitely varied and that no principle or practice of any significance can be valid for all of them. What I am going to say is less likely to be valid for situations in which English is being taught for occupational purposes than for those in which it is taught for academic purposes, in which my own experience has been.

The two types of ESP teaching materials that have been most fully advocated in the literature are: (1) so-called *authentic materials* (i.e., texts and *realia* students are expected to meet in the course of their work or studies), and (2) materials simplified in language to the expected level of the students and expected to be very familiar in subject matter, but supposed to present rhetorical items in rhetorical structures typical of those used in the students' specialism[1]; for want of a better name I shall call the latter *elementary materials*. Both types involve assumptions about the students' existing knowledge of their specialism, and the degree of accuracy of these assumptions crucially affects the practical usefulness of the materials to particular students. If the materials writer does not succeed in avoiding both the Scylla of excessive familiarity and the Charybdis of unforeseen ignorance, the student may not be able to use the subject matter in the intended way to learn the intended linguistic and rhetorical points; in extreme cases failure to avoid these dangers may make the materials quite useless and even turn the students against the whole course. When students are very familiar with a topic, they will be bored with any treatment of it as something not familiar, and they will tend to draw on their existing knowledge rather than on the information or point of view presented in the ESP materials. When they do not have already the knowledge that is assumed to be known in the particular treatment of a topic given in the ESP materials, they will be unable to cope with the topic in the intended way without the help of the ESP teacher or some other source of information. The ESP teacher, if he or she is not knowledgeable enough in the specialism, will be unable to give the necessary help, and even if the teacher can give it this may take a disproportionate amount of time from what the course is intended to teach. Authentic materials are especially subject to the second danger and elementary ones to the first. In using published and home-produced materials of both kinds I have found problems arising from failure to avoid both dangers to be extraordinarily common, from which I conclude that both dangers are extremely difficult to avoid when constructing both types of materials. I further conclude that any assumption of specialist knowledge or lack of it is likely to make it difficult to avoid these dangers, and that therefore materials writers, unless they are in a position to find out what the target students do and do not know about their specialism, should look for subject matter that is not expected to be learned as part of the specialism.

A question that has been little discussed in the literature, if at all, and little considered by ESP materials writers, is how far the ESP course is supposed to teach the students' specialism as well as the English they need in that specialism. Some ESP teachers can successfully deal with the subject matter of some specialisms up to their students' level, but this is exceptional. Most of us would be forced frequently to show our ignorance in handling subject matter at this level. Students may accepts such lapses good naturedly, but they must wonder why such an obvious incompetent pretends to present them with anything they know much more about than he or she does. It has been suggested (e.g., Phillips and Shettlesworth 1975) that such cases are an ideal opportunity for the students to produce some genuinely communicative language in explaining points to the teacher. Certainly, when they can; but again sad experience is that usually either none of them can, or they disagree with each other, or they give an explanation that seems wrong and later is found to be wrong. Surely it is better that the teacher should always be in the unambiguous position of fully understanding all the subject matter and being able to expound it and correct mistakes over it. My students actually do ask me to explain points of subject matter, and not only those occurring in the ESP course; and it has always happened when we have asked students at the University of Khartoum for comments on our courses that one of the main points of approval is that our presentation of subject matter helps them to understand the presentation in the specialist courses. We have usually not set out to achieve this at all, but the students seem to think it natural that we should do so, and perhaps they even expect us to. It seems sensible to make our position quite clear, to ourselves and to our students, and if we can usefully teach anything nonlinguistic that the students find helpful in their specialism, we should do so deliberately; if we cannot teach such things, then we must make it clear that we are not trying to teach them, and almost certainly we can persuade the students that we are not doing so only if we avoid completely the subject matter of their specialism. Both authentic and elementary materials tend to have an ambiguous attitude on this point: they consist largely of presentations of subject matter that are didactic in form yet quite inadequate to teach the subject matter because of their incompleteness, disjointedness, and lack of examples and practical exercises.

The final point I want to make about nearly all the elementary and authentic materials published up to now is that, compared with many other recent language-teaching materials, they seem to me unnecessarily dull. This should not be unavoidable, but it seems to be linked to the artificiality of appearing to teach something the students either already know well or expect to learn properly later. Also, presumably, it is often due to the materials writer's inadequate knowledge of the discipline or occupation concerned, so that he or she consciously or unconsciously plays safe, dealing in a way the writer is competent to handle with topics he or she can understand. Even when the materials writer is competent to handle the subject matter at a suitably high level, he or she may be inhibited by the assumption that most ESP teachers who use the materials would be out of their depth in subject matter that is not simple and elementary. Dullness is never easy to avoid, and it can probably never be completely avoided in teaching materials that aim at comprehensiveness; and dull comprehensiveness is surely better than using only material it is easy to make interesting. However, dullness is a major obstacle to motivation and learning, and materials that are uniformly dull are less effective than those that are comparable in other respects but are reasonably interesting.

How then can the difficulties I have mentioned in connection with authentic and elementary materials be avoided, and at the same time the students be adequately prepared to cope with the English of their specialisms? I have already suggested that the ESP teacher's most acceptable and effective role, in addition to that of pure language teacher, is not as a pseudoteacher of subject matter students have previously learned or expect to learn in their specialist studies or occupations, but as a teacher of things *not* learned as part of courses in these specialisms. Such things may either be of intrinsic interest to the students or be seen by them to support the learning they do in their specialisms. I shall describe four applications of this general principle, which have been used in materials produced in the University of Khartoum with somewhat greater teacher satisfaction and apparent student acceptance than published and home-produced materials of the two kinds criticized above. Perhaps this acceptance is partly due to the fact that the importance of correctly understanding and using the English that is the medium for presenting the subject matter is more obvious than when there is ambiguity about whether the subject matter is to be learned or not. Of course many other factors may be involved in these apparent improvements.

The first approach is to supply some of the background to the students' specialisms of which they are largely or wholly ignorant or about which they are misinformed or confused. When such points exist, the teachers of the specialism often take it for granted that the students have the necessary knowledge, and because the students do not have it, they underperform in various ways. If the ESP course successfully teaches such points, the value of the ESP work to their specialist work or studies is obvious, and the value of the English used to teach the points should also be obvious. Once any such points have been identified, the dangers of overfamiliarity and ignorance can more easily be avoided than with topics taken straight from the syllabus of the specialism. There is of course no universal heuristic procedure for identifying usable background points, and still less would we expect to find any universally usable points. This problem rules out approach number one for materials writers who do not have a specific, known group of students in mind. But teachers who produce any of their own materials will find suitable points cropping up in the course of lessons, or they can set out to find them by examining the students' previous education, by conversations with teachers of the specialisms and with the students, or by trial and error.

An actual example will illustrate this approach. In the preliminary planning of a new English course for history students at Khartoum it was hypothesized from what was known of the history they had previously studied they would know little about the geography or previous history of the areas they would be studying in history courses running concurrently with the English course and they would know nothing about the comtemporary history of the surrounding areas. It was also hypothesized from a list of the topics to be covered in the history courses and recommended reading that the emphasis of these courses would be almost entirely on political history, with little on economic or social history. Therefore each English teaching unit would have a theme from one of these background areas and would constitute a fairly complete and coherent chunk of information. When the theme for a unit had been chosen, it was found quite easy to fit the required linguistic points and activities into the theme and to write the materials accordingly.

The second approach is to take subject matter that has probably been learned in the course of studying a specialism and to present it in a different context or in a way that requires the student to adapt or refashion it in some way. For example, facts students have learned about the chemical properties of elements can be related to the physical structure of their atoms, or facts that have been learned in isolation can be related and then generalized. One of the potentially most fruitful applications of this approach is to take knowledge that has been learned verbally and theoretically and to deal with practical applications of it. We have used this approach in a course for physical science students—often with shattering revelations about their real understanding and usable knowledge of basic scientific points. For example, we have presented a text giving first the two physical laws that are applied in refrigerators and then a description of the parts of a refrigerator and the functions of each part. This is followed by comprehension questions, mainly dealing with the relationships between the principles and the parts, and a writing task that involves the application of the principles to a different kind of refrigerator. The two physical principles were familiar, but the practical applications were not. In view of what I have said above about the dangers of taking for granted students' knowledge of subject matter, it is wise when using this approach to give information that has to be worked on by the students.

The third approach is to present points connected with the specialism, but from points of view other than those the students have met before. If, for example, students in their chemistry course are simply presented with facts and expected to learn them unquestioningly, the ESP course can deal with how such facts come to be known, their significance in a wider context, their theoretical explanations, and speculation about them. In short, it can deal with the history, philosophy, and methodology of the specialism; these aspects of it are often of considerable interest and can be a valuable aid to understanding the more factual aspects.

Such approaches have been used in a number of published ESP courses (see, for example, Thornley 1964 and 1965; Close 1965; and Ewer and Latorre, 1969) and can be criticized on the grounds that they do not represent valid samples of the discourse used in teaching and studying the discipline, or examining students in it, and therefore do not sufficiently help the students to cope with such discourse. This criticism can be equally validly leveled at the other approaches I suggest, and it would be a serious one if there had ever been any demonstration that in actual fact students taught with such material were any less able to deal with the discourse of their specialism than students taught with supposedly more genuine material. This is therefore a purely theoretical argument, especially since nobody has yet managed to describe in any thorough yet usable way what really essential differences there are between different types of discourse. It is a fact that very large numbers of people who have learned foreign languages using very general teaching materials have been able to cope adequately, and in many cases extremely well, with specialized discourse of all kinds.

The first two approaches appear most suitable for students who have learned their subjects of specialization in a narrow, largely verbalized way. Students who have been encouraged to learn by activity methods, problem solving, or following their own lines of inquiry may have little to learn about the essential background or about practical applications but might be correspondingly more interested in the history, philosophy, and methodology of these subjects.

The essence of the fourth approach is that every bit of the course materials should be designed to provide teaching and practice in language or related skills. What has sometimes been called the metalanguage of teaching — the teacher's or textbook's explanations and instructions — is a neglected aspect of language teaching, and materials writers tend either to be overwhelmed with guilt at having to use any metalanguage at all or to ignore the problems it usually presents. The former cannot bring themselves to explain anything to the student and give only the shortest possible instructions, while the latter give explanations and instructions that are often more difficult to understand than the points they refer to. I have never seen any published teaching materials in which metalanguage is deliberately exploited in teaching, and I have encountered much opposition from colleagues when I have suggested exploiting it in this way. ESP teachers are apparently quite ready to accept a complex and abstract exposition taken from a physics textbook as a legitimate basis for work in reading comprehension but think that a simpler and more concrete description of the principles of paragraph construction or a set of precise and detailed instructions for a writing task is too difficult. This is doublethink, and if we insist that any skill can be taught and practiced only in a section of the materials headed with the name of that skill, we are wasting a fruitful means of using English in a really meaningful way.

Apart from their intrinsic usefulness as well-contextualized and thoroughly communicative utterances, bits of metalanguage can reveal the extent of students' understanding at least as reliably as any other type of material. It is a sobering experience after some apparently successful oral work to give a simple instruction like, "Now write the other sentences in the exercise," and see blank faces and idle pens; writing the instruction on the blackboard does not necessarily bring any better results. It is perhaps not the English itself that is difficult so much as the fact that the teacher is trying to use it as a means of communication.

Some of the ways in which we have tried to use metalanguage (and other bits of the teaching materials that are not solely and overtly intended for language practice) to promote linguistic and rhetorical learning are: (1) using grammar and vocabulary that is also taught in more specialist contexts elsewhere in the materials; (2) presenting the material in formats visually similar to those used in specialist texts and with the use of conventions and devices typical of such texts, such as tables, graphs, footnotes, cross-references and indexes; (3) presenting expositions of points of language, rhetoric and organization of information in the same sorts of rhetorical structure and wording as are usual in the exposition of points in the specialism; and (4) giving instructions for tasks in which the instructional language of the specialism is used to some extent and close reading is required. If the materials writer is reasonably familiar with texts used in the specialism, he or she should not find it difficult to cast some of the metalinguistic material in a similar form and style. For students whose first language has closely comparable conventions of form, rhetorical structure, and organization to those of English, there is perhaps little actual need for such an approach, but when this is not the case students may be as much disadvantaged by unfamiliarity with such aspects of texts as by actual linguistic difficulties.[2]

Finally, we must not ignore the fact that although probably all published ESP materials use subject matter mainly or entirely taken from the specialism of the target students or from related specialisms, there are a good many institutions in which ESP is taught (sometimes under another name) largely or entirely with general ELT materials. In some cases this is due to ignorance of the existence of special ESP materials, or nonavailability of these, or prejudice, or other reasons other than deliberate and informed choice. In other cases the students have too many and too different specialisms for any specialized approach to be viable. In some cases the choice is made because the students' level of English or of knowledge of their specialism is too low for any of the available materials to be usable and in other cases their level may be too high. In some cases the teachers may have tried using published ESP materials and decided that they were less effective than certain general ones, or the students may have revolted against the ESP materials. Some teachers may believe that it is more practical and useful to teach their students sound study habits and means of extending their English by themselves than to train them for a particular set of uses for an immediate situation. In some cases the English course is regarded as contributing to the students' general education rather than directly (or even indirectly) to their specialist studies and in such cases the subject matter is usually literary or "life and institutions" or background information.

It is easy for those who follow the specialism-oriented mainstream of current ESP theory and practice to regard all supposedly ESP courses in which general ELT materials form the main basis for teaching as more or less inadequate responses to the students' most urgent and important needs. However, on any objective assessment we are still extraordinarily ignorant of what those needs really are, let alone of how best to meet them. I therefore prefer to follow the pragmatic view that the proof of the pudding is in the eating; let us judge all attempts to improve the English of students who need it for a specific purpose by their actual efficiency and effectiveness with the particular students for whom they are made, not by the closeness of their adherence to any set of theoretical principles. Thus we may learn not only how to improve courses in practice but also how to refine our theories so that they become more helpful in designing future courses.

Notes

1. This term is used to designate the academic subject(s) or job area(s) in which the target students are expected to use English.
2. See, for example, articles in ESPMENA Bulletin Nos. 1, 3, and 4 on difficulties of students in various Middle Eastern countries in interpreting scientific diagrams.

References

Close, R. A. 1965. *The English We Use for Science.* Longmans.
Ewer, J. R., and G. Latorre. 1969. *A Course in Basic Scientific English.* Longmans.
Selinker, L., L. Trimble, and R. Vroman. 1974. *Working Papers in English for Science and Technology.* University of Washington.
Thornley, G. C. 1964. *Scientific English Practice.* Longmans.
––– 1965. *Further Scientific English Practice.* Longmans.
Widdowson, H. G. 1979. *Explorations in Applied Linguistics.* Oxford Univ. Press.

Editorial Comments

Based on practical pedagogical concerns, Crofts outlines some inherent weaknesses in the content of current ESP materials. He sees the basic problem as uncertainty as to "how far the ESP course is supposed to teach the students' specialism as well as the English they need in that specialism." This distinction between the content of an ESP course per se and the content of student's specialism is one Crofts focuses on with acumen and one we in ESP ignore at our peril.

It seems to us that both Crofts and Widdowson (chap. 1) have identified a central problem in this field, though from opposite ends of the theoretical/applied continuum – the problem of what the pedagogical goal of an ESP course should be, as distinct from the goal of the specialist course (i.e., the student's specialism). Crofts is not far from Widdowson in suggesting that ESP courses should *not* focus on the *same* content as the specialist course but rather should attempt to teach requisite language skills needed in that specialism. The content of the ESP course should, it is claimed, be related to specialist course content, but be different in kind. Crofts provides helpful suggestions as to how this projected relationship (between the ESP course and the specialist course) might be achieved in a practical context.

As we understand it, the problems alluded to in these comments on Crofts's paper have been debated at length (and often in heated tone) at ESP/EST conferences in various parts of the world. We hope the comments presented here will remove some of the heat and shed some light on what is clearly a difficult set of problems.

L.S.
E.T.

12 ESP Materials in Use: Some Thoughts from the Classroom

M. L. Tickoo

English for Specific Purposes (ESP) materials are being used in tertiary-level institutions in India under two different arrangements: They either serve as alternatives to traditional courses or, in a majority of cases, they influence the design and detail of ordinary courses mainly through additional work on reading passages from these courses. In both cases they are beginning to make an impact on systems of teaching and learning English at this stage.

One way of assessing this impact would be to view ESP as a contribution to curriculum construction. Our curricula have passed through two phases, from one that is primarily literary to another that is grammatically and pedagogically structured and organized. Curriculum developers have now begun to accept the need for semantic, notional, or communicative base to produce a competence that appears to be directly relatable to authentic tasks/roles in specified contexts. Viewed thus, today's ESP is the harbinger of a major shift of focus: from literary-philosophical through grammar-based to communicative.[1] It also appears to be a pointer to a much better organized approach to tertiary-level English Language Teaching (ELT). Such an approach, by accepting the possibilities of basing teaching on "tangibles," brings system and structure into a sphere that has hitherto generally been treated as an unchartable territory, where learning solely depended on an individual teacher's grasp of the subject.

Impact on curriculum construction is however only a small part of ESP at work, although in the long run this may prove to be a most powerful means of reform and reconstruction. The more immediate and noteworthy gains and losses are discernible in course materials in their use in ordinary classrooms, despite the problems that are posed by the fact that published course materials are bound to be products of their authors' understanding, ingenuity, and background as much as of any approach and its emphases.

In this chapter, my purpose is to critically evaluate some published ESP materials based on "inside-the-classroom" experiences in India. I have deliberately stayed away from innovative materials that have been designed and trial-tested in the English-speaking world, most particularly in the United Kingdom for overseas students.[2]

The ESP courses I have focused on here are the ones that have grown either in translating the recently introduced needs- and skills-based curricula at what we call the +2 *stage* (the two years that follow secondary schooling) and the +3 *stage* (the three years of the first degree) or, the courses in communication and remediation envisaged for use at special institutions at the graduate level. Specific illustrative references to a few of these new type courses will be made at appropriate places in this chapter.

The ESP courses in use today are, in the vast majority of cases, either untried trial editions or tentative answers by individuals who own up not only to imperfections but omissions in design and in detail. Their tentativeness makes any definitive conclusions premature; nevertheless there is a sizeable spin-off of (1) perceptible gains and (2) a growing awareness of what might go wrong. I shall refer to these two spin-offs in that order.

One perceptible gain is that in planning syllabus designs for the core courses for school beginners or, in a few cases, for after-school users, there is a growing and openly expressed preference for innovative designs that stay away from an overly exclusive dependence on a "synthetic" (in Wilkins's [1975] sense of the term) structural syllabus with its covert and overt grammar-patterns orientation and the inhibiting practice that accompanies its exploitation by makers of materials or by consumers in classrooms. There is still a lot of resistance to radical change and apprehension about the possible consequences of throwing away the pedagogic baby with the behavioristic bathwater. There is too, as Wilkins (1975) and Widdowson (1975) have admitted elsewhere, no fully viable alternative in sight. Nevertheless even the usual "no-changer," having seen some of the new materials in operation, is now willing to concede the need to experiment in the direction of syllabuses that do not suffer under the tyranny of triviality (e.g., a linear one-item-at-a-time, fixed sequence) that has become part of our practiced orthodoxy. Small steps have already been taken to introduce some elements of a spiraling sequence of notions into an essentially structural framework.

A second gain is more noticeable in those postsecondary or adult-level courses that aim primarily at remediation. There is here great disillusionment with existing materials and teaching that mainly utilize speeded-up structural syllabuses. For this there are two main reasons. One is based on recent insights into the learners' errors that are consequently seen as evidence of what the learner does in using a particular set of rules and categories at a certain stage rather than of how and in what ways he or she falls short in relation to a fixed system of standard usage (see Selinker 1972 and Corder 1975). Errors therefore seem to serve as aids to enrichment and not just roadblocks to perfection; remediation, too, naturally takes on a new character, with a different set of strategies and tasks oriented towards discovery procedures. While such powerful theoretical insights would by themselves have justified a search for alternatives, they have recently gained substantial support in the failures of grammar-usage based courses. In the Indian situation, it is too early to claim that a system that exploits the learners' errors in a planned and organized manner will work better, but it appears to have enough support to make controlled experimentation worthwhile. A welcome feature of our system is that small beginnings have already been made towards the design of such curricular and instructional-materials packages.[3]

A third gain is as follows: Ever since the 1950s when ELT experts exaggeratedly claimed that "learning English is fixing a structural framework" or that "words learned as members of structures can be confidently handled" (Pattison 1951:10), the language-literature divide has been widening, with the two sides taking uncompromising postures—the literature scholar seeing no more than pattern drills and substitution frames in language work and the language-teaching specialists accusing the literature teachers of trading in rehearsed views and borrowed metaphors. Today with the language teacher's espousal of communication and meaning, there is not only much that has brought the two sides nearer—with applied linguists like Widdowson rightly arguing that "literary critics have come closer than linguists to an understanding of the communicative function of language and the ways in which discourse is made" (Widdowson 1975:11)—there is also a tacit admission that what is presently going into the newly emerging curricula for higher order language skills or for tasks-specific objectives may be challenging as the best in literary scholarship of the corresponding levels. If this becomes symptomatic of a new relationship between two estranged but mutually supporting disciplines, ESP may yet have produced a spin-off of unimaginably rich dividends. This kind of counting the blessings is however a little too premature; we have made just a beginning.

These then are a few of the gains that have begun to accrue as a result of the introduction of ESP ideas and materials into the Indian system. Each of them must lead to further efforts towards a sharpening of the tools and a much greater exploitation of the strategies and devices that promise results in the classroom. In the meantime there is another type of feedback, one that calls for either a rethinking on some of what has become associated with ESP or a reversal of the priorities that may not serve the hoped-for objectives.

ESP's "Reading Only" Courses

An example of this problem are courses like the "Stairway Reading Course" prepared at the Central Institute of English and Foreign Languages (CIEFL 1977). Such a course works towards the learners' reading abilities—"to build up their reading vocabulary and to improve their reading comprehension and speed rapidly so that they can use English more efficiently for the study of academic books as well as for pleasure" (CIEFL 1977:ix). For this purpose, it uses passages written in a limited vocabulary, provides detailed comprehension questions (mainly multiple-choice), word tests, speed-reading exercises and, in this case, a companion with glosses on difficult words, and notes in the learner's native language or, in a few cases, in "simple English." In all this, as in the work that it visualizes as taking place in the classroom, the course, thus, appears to provide adequate specific practice in "stimulated situations."

All these strengths notwithstanding, such exclusive concentration on reading does appear to limit the possibilities in the use of such courses in ordinary classrooms and by ordinary teachers. This is largely so because there is a failure to allow for some of the activities, both teacher and learner initiated, that contribute to successful teaching-learning operations. "Reading-only courses" (1) do *not* appear to involve the teacher where he or she can operate best (assuming this is known), (2) *cannot* provide for sufficient interaction among learners (assuming this is known as well) and (3) do *not* allow for that teacher-learner living dialogue that largely sustains good teaching. A part of this problem appears to have been experienced and answered by Swales in preparing his course in scientific writing at the University of Libya: "It seems to me, however, that it does not necessarily follow from the fact that reading has been identified as being the greatest need that it should be assigned the largest proportion of language time. It does not follow because it is equally important to consider what the language teacher can most usefully do in the limited time available to him. In other words, decisions about course priorities should be partly based on an assessment of circumstances under which teacher intervention in the learning process is essential, where it is useful, and where it is of marginal advantage" (Swales 1978:45)[4].

This leads me to my first generalization on types of ESP courses and their use in classrooms. Many of these appear to show some disregard of ordinary teachers' backgrounds, their need to intervene in certain specific ways, and their "sets" or attitudes. By concentrating on reading only, some of these courses force teachers into a sort of verbal inaction where formerly they may have indulged in hour-long lectures. Some others that ask teachers to contribute to and actively participate in the higher order skills of reading *and* writing or to teach important aspects of speech, expect them to rise up to the tasks they may never have performed before. Still others demand of them the ability to teach across a very wide range of specialist subject areas. All of them appear to suggest a failure in defining teachers' roles in a situation where their intervention may measurably count for success.

ESP MATERIALS: TECHNIQUE AND CONTENT:

My second point is perhaps a little more central to ESP materials and I shall draw upon a contrast to make it. Tertiary-level language teaching has for long relied on a strategy whose main instrument is exposure; some call this the "sun burn" approach. Learning here is said to rub off onto learners through their eyes and ears as they take in parts of what they see and hear. ESP's arrival on the scene can be said to have replaced this strategy by one that I have elsewhere called "a linguistic swimming pool" (Tickoo 1976). In it, among other things, dependence on technique takes the place of a total reliance on exposure to subject matter, and a lot of analytical guidance is provided in those areas of language and its learning-teaching that hitherto evaded scholarly scrutiny.

The infusion of "technique" into tertiary-level courses has resulted in a new type of textbook in which the relationship between subject matter and its linguistic exploitation has become almost totally reversed. Where before the text was important, what appears to matter now is what the materials producer *does* with the text. We see this not only in the changed character of the selected texts that once used to be entirely literary, but also, and more importantly for our purpose here, in the ratio between the reading matter and the language exercises that follow it. Let us briefly look at the implications of this change.

A usual anthology, which has hardly changed its content or character over decades, is a book in which the ratio between the reading passage and the notes/ exercises on it is anything between four-to-one and ten-to-one, the exploitation of the passage thus forming only a small, often insignificant, part of the total content of the book. In the type of ESP book that has begun to take its place (e.g., Bhaskar and Prabhu 1975), the ratio has almost totally reversed itself, with exercises that take three-to-six times the space occupied by the text, assuming both greater bulk and enhanced importance. Now let us look at what may happen in the use of such materials in the classroom.

If we must keep the hours of teaching given to this part of the course as constant (which is what the system allows) and allow for the fact that contact with English is confined to the English classroom, we are driven to the following inference: The Indian class that used to spend its time, (say one hundred class hours in the year) on reading about twenty passages (each about 5 pages) and on attempting some rather superficial work on their linguistic exploitation, now spends the same amount of time on ten passages (each about 1.5 pages) and on varied exercises that, at their best, provide opportunities for intensive study and understanding. What are the pros and cons of these two ways of investing the learner's time?

Given a resourceful and suitably trained and equipped teacher, the in-depth study provided through the new ESP book should prove rewarding and equip the reader with much that contributes towards meaningful and mature reading. And if we could also assume that the reader would find a number of opportunities to exercise and transfer the skills thus acquired, the gains would certainly more than compensate for the reduced exposure. But if, on the other hand, and this is true of the vast majority of Indian students, reading in English is largely confined to the work in class, we ought to pause to think about the consequences.

The most noteworthy aspect of the changed situation is that the ordinary teacher now spends a hundred hours with less than twenty pages of reading matter where before he or she used to "teach" one hundred or more pages in the same period. The student, too, unless specially motivated or socially privileged, confines his or her reading to these twenty pages of textual matter. In the hands of the ordinary teacher the language work that follows the book will unfortunately be treated in much the same way as the one-page exercise materials of the usual anthology used to be treated. In spite of its bulk this work, therefore, may not necessarily contribute sufficiently to the development of those skills for which it was specially designed. What is the possible outcome?

One apparent result is that average students read much less, although they could attempt to analyze and understand what they read in somewhat greater depth. In some ways this makes them like cricketers who get to know all about how to handle the bat or to play the ball but have not had enough opportunities to stretch their muscles in doing so. They are thus theoreticians of cricket rather than dependable users of the bat and ball.

Our ESP materials then raise a major question in the teaching of English within defined time schedules — the question of how to use our limited resources to make sure that too great an infusion of technique does not edge out content to the detriment of learning. This may be primarily a question of finding a golden mean between content and technique — the desirable ratio and relationship between them, one that can optimize the output and help the system produce the best possible results in terms of readers who not merely learn how to read but also become its true addicts. A possible answer may come from controlled experiments in ordinary classrooms using materials with different ratios and relationships between these two important aspects of a page of reading. Until that is done the apprehension is that after a point our techniques used on relatively short pieces of writing may be proving counterproductive; the law of diminishing returns must operate here as it does in some other forms of human investment.

ESP AND COURSES IN WRITTEN COMMUNICATION

In some ways our next point is even more central to ESP in operation since what I have to say focuses on ESP materials that are being designed to produce those abilities and that competence that, in most cases, evaded the producers of traditional or structuralist materials. But before I make this point a few clarifications seem to be necessary.

The abilities aimed at in these materials are those of communication in writing. Much like the higher order skills of reading, the different aspects of purposive writing have received a lot of attention and have, as a result, become amenable to specific teaching. But much more than in the case of reading skills there appear to be substantial differences between the analysis of the elements of writing provided by different writers. These differences inevitably lead to different emphases in the materials that may otherwise work towards identical aims. To these differing views of what constitutes communicative competence in writing, we must once again add the variations caused by the differing understandings of the middlemen who translate these ideas into materials for use. The result is a variety of materials that differ as much in the approach to their objectives as in their attention to various aspects that require specific attention. Let us briefly illustrate this point by referring to three of these courses designed for use at the +2 stage (i.e., Classes XI and XII).

A Course in Written English (Ghosh et al. 1978) is designed to help Class XII students in "developing competence in certain communicative needs" by providing training and practice in writing for specific tasks including descriptions of objects, instruments and processes, reports of events and experiments, letter writing, summarizing, essay writing, and so forth. Divided into twelve units, the course exploits a brief (one-to-two pages) reading passage to lead to specific writing tasks that are, in some ways, graded in terms of difficulty and guidance provided. The innovative features of the course are mainly those of passage analysis, which is full and detailed and pays special attention to the organization of paragraphs (especially their rhetorical features) and various linking devices; it also includes notes on usage that explain, in fairly traditional terms, grammatical features that predominate in the type of writing that each unit represents. But, there appears to be a tendency in this course to mistake analysis for teaching, the learner of English language being treated to "lectures" on language analysis and grammar that should serve an initiate into descriptive linguistics. Nevertheless, a lot of work has gone into explaining the salient features of every selected (sometimes written-for-the-purpose) passage.

Freeman's (1977) *Written Communication in English* is based on similar syllabus specifications and is intended to meet the +2 student's academic and vocational needs in writing, essay writing, note-making, and such, but the approach is different in design and in detail. The book provides models of the type of writing that is being taught, helps the learner answer the right sort of questions to gain insights into the significant features of the model, and sets tasks that allow for progression from relative control to relative freedom. Unlike *A Course in Written English* it does not attempt detailed analysis of the texts nor of the features of grammar and usage, although in some of its forty-three units it does provide some useful guidance on the organization and arrangement of the models.

Narayanaswamy (1979) works towards similar objectives in a series of three books that lay emphasis on exemplifying the processes of communication rather than on analysing them. Models are provided and briefly analysed for their prominent discourse features, and tasks are set with guidance that appears to use what programmers call *fading* — a process wherein the learner is allowed to do more and more and is given progressively diminishing assistance.

These three courses are thus different manifestations of an ESP approach whose twin essentials — a specificity of purpose and a quest for changing the learner's dominant linguistic ability into communicative competence — are basic to all three. Further, in spite of several differences between them that owe their distinctiveness to their authors, the books are designed for similar classrooms, the same quality of teaching, and towards a similar range of abilities. A critique of the three courses singly and in comparison is a separate task not attempted here. My object here has been to spell out some of the things that may warrant a rethinking of the way in which some such materials seek their avowed aims.

The approach to communication through writing implicit in these materials appears, in some important respects, to be similar to the one that has been used with some success in more easily analyzable tasks of language acquisition. Let us take a couple of examples to explicate it. To teach a reference skill (e.g., the use of a dictionary) one analyzes the tasks that are involved in each such skill by studying the source materials (in this case a good dictionary) and noting down all that a proficient user succeeds in getting out of it.[5] Having thus arrived at an understanding of the complete task (viz., the best possible use of a good dictionary), one attempts to set out the steps that lead the learner step by step to this degree of proficiency. The learner's task should be made easier by a process of simulation that combines analysis by the materials producer with guided application by the learner. The result at the end of the total exercise is, or should be, the learner's active ability to use a good dictionary for everything it has to offer for his or her specific but growing needs.

A different set of skills is involved in one's ability to take notes. But once again it may be possible to atomize the tasks that constitute efficient note-taking and, as in the case of reference skills, the approach to teaching these tasks takes the learner through an ordered set of steps that combines an analysis of what appears to be involved in the 'goal-oriented' task (See Widdowson, chap. 1), with guided exercises in performing each individual subtask. All this should lead the learner on to independent note-taking from different types of prose (cf. Freeman 1977, Units 19-24, and Tickoo and Sasikumar 1979). The main strength of such sets of materials apparently lies in the analysis of the tasks that are to be performed and in the success of the simulated exercises that are provided to help the learner reach a degree of perfection in attempting each and all of them. This is also true of the sets of materials that have been designed for competence in writing for specific purposes. And as in the case of good reference or note-taking materials, there is always both explanation and exercise to enable the learner to reach self-sufficiency in specific tasks of writing.

WHAT THEN ARE THE PROBLEMS?

Apart from the ones that are related to the author's failure to visualize the book's use in the classroom already referred to above, these can be seen as shortfalls rather than failures. I raise them here to suggest that the price that the system now pays in this much needed movement away from lack of guidance to precise analytical guidance towards writing tasks may be reduced if pioneers see the need for adjustments and adaptation to real classroom situations. In the history of educational innovation it has often been seen that pioneers can be so satisfied with their pioneering efforts that they lose sight of the other possibilities or even of the possible omissions and commissions in their wares. But let us now move on to some possible limitations of the entire genre.

New type ESP courses in reading and communicative writing are based on a strategy, briefly illustrated above, whose common core is a combination of analysis with exercise (in differing proportions) towards simulated tasks. This type of exercise appears to guarantee a minimum level of performance, but it also appears to breed uniformity. For the vast majority of learners it is, for example, extremely helpful to learn about the rhetorical structure of a paragraph and to understand the need for making the appropriate choice of intrasentential and intersentential linkers. These essentials appear to provide the ground on which learners can shape and organize their ideas in writing reports, descriptions, expository essays, and other forms of composition. But there is a doubt: in building towards precision and correctness, do these courses stand in the way of originality and individual style? That is, there is something to what Polanyi (1969:146) points to in a similar though not directly related context: "By concentrating attention on his fingers, a pianist can paralyze himself; the motions of his fingers no longer bear then on the music performed, they have lost their meaning." The point is that attention to the subskills that are said to constitute purposive writing may have a similarly paralyzing effect on the student of communication through writing.

Another point is particularly true of only some of these courses. *A Course in Writing* (Ghosh et al. 1978), for example, provides a great deal of explanation, both linguistic and rhetorical and also a lot of "do's and don't's." This will naturally occupy the bulk of the limited time that is allowed in the classroom for writing, leaving very little time for either guided or free composition. The result may be that the teacher and the learner have very few opportunities for genuinely challenging compositional tasks.

The cumulative effect of these problems is that there is at times an openly expressed dissatisfaction from the brighter student with what amounts to routinized and repetitive chores. There can be no two views on the fact that structured "communicative" tasks, being more meaningful and more akin to real-life English, are better than the structured drills in usage and grammar that they have replaced. But even these more interesting tasks must lack some of the excitement of the unexpected as they lack the romance of free writing. Moreover, such rigorously organized courses also add to the teacher's teaching time (as opposed to learner's learning time), which in a system like ours, where the teacher does all the talking and the learner gets fed on rehearsed views and pronouncements, is something that cannot do much good. The major difference in this case is that the explanations sooner or later give place to meaningful practice.

In looking forward to ESP materials on aspects of purposive writing, it may therefore pay to keep the following points in mind. One, communicative writing may not be entirely amenable to the same sort of analysis or the same degree of atomization as the different subskills of some "lesser" language-learning tasks.

Secondly, the processes of synthesizing (which must be largely those of the learner) will in this case always be much more challenging since what comes out of the analysis does not *by itself* add up to a wholesome, integrated composition. Lastly, there seems to be a need for some rethinking on the time and attention that is given in some of these courses to "teaching time" as opposed to "learning time."

CONCLUSION

In all that has been said above, there is an inevitable tentativeness caused by the fact that I lack the objectivity and hindsight that distance and time lend to academic pursuits. All of us are a party to what looks like being a worthwhile advance in ELT planning and practice, and all of us are also partisans to one or another way of approaching the ESP tasks. What I have tried to do here, despite such obvious limitations, is to view the movement through some of the representative products that have become available in the last few years from something like a front-of-the-classroom viewpoint. The focus here has been more on inadequacies and excesses than on the gains (which certainly outnumber the inadequacies since a main aim is to restore the balance in a situation where pioneers may tilt it too much or too soon.

Notes

1. A brief evolutionary analysis is provided in MacMillan (1976). For a slightly different view see Tickoo (1976).
2. Accounts of several such courses are being made available in recent British publications. For several case studies of such courses see Mackay and Mountford (1978).
3. Although we have no books that are based on a fully defined notional/semantic framework, a few authors of textbooks have incorporated some elements of the approach. For one such book, see Coffey (1978).
4. Michael Sharwood-Smith makes this point differently: "The four skills are to some extent facets of the same diamond. We must not separate them too rigidly for the purposes of constructing specific teaching materials" *(English Teaching Forum* 1974, vol. 12, p. 8).
5. Such a set of graded exercises on the use of the dictionary is available in NCERT (1977).

References

Allen, J. P. B., and S. P. Corder. 1974. *Techniques in Applied Linguistics. Edinburgh Course in Applied Linguistics 3.* Oxford Univ. Press.
Bhaskar, W. W., S., and N. S. Prabhu. 1975. *English Through Reading*, vol. 1. Macmillan.
CIEFL, 1977.*Stairway Reading Course: Reader 1.* Orient Longman.
Coffey, B. 1978. *English Reader: Class 10.* Govt. of Andhra Pradesh.
Corder, S. P. 1974. "Error Analysis." In Allen and Corder 1974. Pp. 122-54.
Freeman, S. 1977. *Written Communication in English.* Orient Longman.
Ghosh, R. N., K. Moody, and S. R. Inthira. 1978. *A Course in Written English.* The National Council of Educational Research and Training.
Mackay, R., and A. Mountford. 1978. *English for Specific Purposes, Part 3.* Longmans.

Macmillan, M. 1976. "Teaching English to Scientists of Other Languages." *CILT Reports and Papers 7.* 19-30. Centre for Information on Language Teaching and Research.
Narayanaswamy, V. R. 1979. *Organized Writing-2.* Orient Longman.
NCERT 1977. *English Reader: A Textbook for the Core Course, Class 11, Semester 1.* Frank Brothers.
Pattison, B. 1951. *English Teaching in the World Today.* Evans Brothers.
Polanyi, M. 1969. *Knowing and Being.* Ed. M. Greene, Routledge, and K. Paul.
Selinker, L. 1972. "Interlanguage." *IRAL* 10.3 pp. 204-31.
Swales, John. 1978. "Writing Scientific English." In Mackay and Mountford 1978, chapt. 3.
Tickoo, M. L. 1976. "Theories and materials in EST: a View from Hyderabad." In *Teaching English for Science and Technology,* ed. J. C. Richards. Singapore Univ. Press.
Tickoo, C., and J. Sasikumar. 1979. *Writing with a Purpose,* Oxford Univ. Press.
Special Reference to Science and Technology: Problems and Perspectives, pp. 3-10. The British Council, ETIC.
Wilkins, D. A. 1975. *Notional Syllabuses.* Oxford Univ. Press.

Editorial Comments

This chapter provides the reader with a much-needed critical evaluation of some ESP curriculum materials in reading and writing that have recently been produced. What seems to the editors to be of particular interest is Tickoo's concern that current ESP materials seem to focus too much on *conscious analysis* of the skills involved in reading and writing and too little on the *actual use* of those skills as they occur together in realistic situations. The student becomes like "a theoretician of cricket rather than a dependable user of the bat and ball." The author calls for a more holistic approach, in which form and content are taught together, and students are given more practice using the requisite "ESP skills" (assuming these are known; see our comments on the previous three chapters). Tickoo's conclusion here appears to contradict Crofts's suggestion that ESP courses should not focus on the same content as the specialist course. We leave it to the reader to work out how this apparent contradiction relates to process approaches and the convergent/divergent distinction of Widdowson.

We agree with Tickoo that some of the insights provided by Trimble's rhetoric, as well as the work of Widdowson and Ewer, with their emphasis on the interrelationship of content and grammatical form, may be of value in moving curriculum materials toward a more integrated and holistic approach. Tickoo joins Crofts (chap. 11) in presenting a useful taking-off-point from which scholars interested in these practical concerns could explore the relationship between the ESP course and the specialism course. Much work needs to be done in this area.

L.S.
E.T.

13

Teaching the Use of the Article in EST

Thomas Huckin, Leslie Olsen

In 1977-78, there were 235,509 foreign students in the United States. Many of these students, especially the approximately 203,300 students from Asia and the Middle East,[1] have moderate to severe problems with the use of articles in English. Unfortunately, many of these students are placed in traditional composition and technical writing courses taught by teachers with no materials or training for teaching the use of articles.

To help alleviate this problem, we have prepared the following pedagogical discussion.[2] The discussion treats both the indefinite article, *a/an* (section 1) and the definite article, *the*, (section 2) and includes graded exercises appropriately spaced. It can be used either by teachers or by advanced students (for self-instruction).

Our approach reflects the fact that most foreign students in the United States are studying scientific or technical subjects:[3] Most of the examples and exercises are taken from basic or popular works in science and technology;[4] the discussion is more detailed and explicit than in standard ESL treatments; and a flow chart is used to summarize the rule-governed procedure aspects of article choice.[5]

One other feature of our approach deserves mention, namely its rhetorical rather than sentence-level orientation. This stems from our conviction that most article choices reflect larger contextual (or even extratextual) considerations. Accordingly, we have deliberately chosen many paragraph-length examples and exercises to illustrate various points.

166 / ENGLISH FOR ACADEMIC AND TECHNICAL PURPOSES

We should note that many of the exercises are "graded" so that an A-level example conforms to an American fourth-grade science text, a B-level exercise to an American eighth-grade science text, and a C-level exercise to printed material for general adult readers.

THE INDEFINITE ARTICLE (a/an): NONUNIQUE REFERENCE

To understand the use of articles, one must first understand a basic property of common nouns, namely, the property of "reference." We all know that nouns refer to objects or concepts *at different levels of generality*: the same noun that refers to an entire category of objects in one sentence may refer only to a particular, unique object in another. For example, consider the word *window* in a sentence like *"Every room in this building has a window."* The writer of this sentence probably is not thinking of any particular window but of windows in **general**: each room has an object belonging to that general category. On the other hand, in a sentence like *"The window in room 303 is broken,"* the writer is singling out a **particular** window, one that has a unique identity.

Here, we will use the term "nonunique reference" to describe examples of **general** reference like the first one above, and the term "unique reference" to describe examples of **particular** reference like the second. This section (1) deals exclusively with cases of nonunique reference; it points out that no article is used unless the noun is a singular "countable" noun (in which case *a* or *an* is used).[6] Section 2 then describes many cases of unique reference, showing that the definite article *(the)* is used in each case.

Uncountable Nouns

Many English nouns represent objects or concepts that do not have a defining shape or form: *water, rice, gravity, magnetism, information, engineering*. Such nouns are called "uncountable" nouns because they are customarily not counted; for example, one does not normally say *"five waters"* or *"eight rices"* or *"fifteen magnetisms."*[7] In fact, one does not normally use the plural form at all for such nouns.

Some common types of uncountable nouns are:

1. Those representing an amorphous physical mass (a mass without definite shape): *sugar, sand, salt, rice, flour,* any liquid or gas, and so forth.
2. Those representing an abstract concept: *gravity, information,*[8] *curiosity, happiness, magnetism,* and so forth.
3. Those representing a continuous process: *photosynthesis, pollution, osmosis, conbustion,* and so forth.
4. Those representing a field of study: *mathematics, chemistry, physics, engineering,* and so forth.

Rule: Whenever an uncountable noun is used with a nonunique (general) referent in mind, no article is used.

Examples:
"*Magnetism* is the force that causes iron filings to be attracted to a magnet."
"My nephew says he wants to study *engineering*."

We can represent the above rule with the flow chart in Figure 13.1.[9]

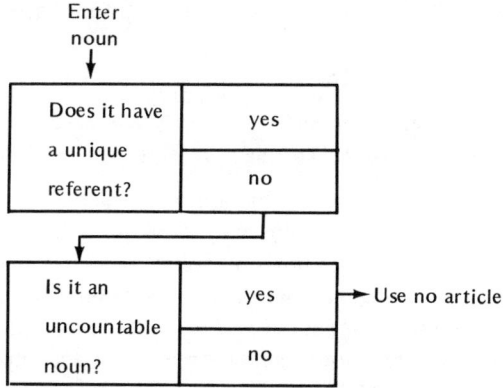

FIGURE 13-1.   PARTIAL FLOW CHART FOR CHOOSING THE CORRECT ARTICLE (STEP 1)

Countable Nouns

In contrast to uncountable nouns, there are many nouns in English that represent concepts or objects that have a defining shape or form. These are the so-called countable nouns. Some examples of countable nouns are *book, automobile, molecule, computer,* and *microscope*. Unlike uncountable nouns, words like these readily occur:

1. In the plural form *(books, automobiles, molecules)*.
2. With numbers *(four computers, nine microscopes)*.
3. With adjectives like *several, many,* and *few (several books, many microscopes, few molecules)*.

In addition to these nouns, English has some abstract nouns that are countable. Examples of such nouns include *idea, concept, theory,* and *hypothesis*. These nouns obviously do not have a physical shape or form though you may wish to argue that they do have some shape or form.). However, as do the nouns above, these abstract nouns often occur:

1. In the plural form *(ideas, concepts, theories)*.
2. With numbers *(three hypotheses, two concepts, four theories)*.
3. With adjectives like *several, few,* and *many (several ideas, few theories, many hypotheses)*.

Of course, countable nouns often occur in the singular. In such cases, if the writer is not thinking of a unique or particular referent, it is appropriate to use the indefinite article: *a book, an automobile, a molecule,* and such. (Incidentally, the indefinite article derives historically from the Old English word for *one*; that is why one never finds both the indefinite article and the word *one* used together (e.g., *a one computer*).

Rule: Whenever a countable noun is used with a nonunique referent in mind: (a) the indefinite article is used if the noun is singular; (b) no article is used if the noun is plural.[10]

Examples:
> The Apollo-16 X-ray and gamma-ray spectrometer observed *a gamma-ray event* on April 27, 1972, at approximately 10:50 GMT. (Trombka 1975:119)

By using the indefinite article, the author implies that although the spectrometer only observed one actual gamma-ray event, there may well have been **other** gamma-ray events that the spectrometer did **not** observe. Remember that the indefinite article *a/an* is used only with **singular** countable nouns; **plural** countable nouns stand alone without any accompanying indefinite articles. For instance, in the sentence above, the singular countable noun *gamma-ray event* is accompanied by the indefinite article: *a gamma-ray event.* If the author had observed more than one gamma-ray event, he might have written:

> The Apollo-16 X-ray and gamma-ray spectrometer observed *gamma-ray events* on April 27, 1972, at approximately 10:50 GMT.

If the author had wanted to be more specific, he might have specified the number of observed gamma-ray events. However, to do this he would have used a specific number such as *three* or an adjective such as *several*, **not** an indefinite article.

> The Apollo-16 X-ray and gamma-ray spectrometer observed *three* (or *several*) *gamma-ray events* on April 27, 1972, at approximately 10:50 GMT.

In summary, then, one uses the indefinite article *a/an* with singular, countable nouns to indicate that the object or concept in question is **not unique**.[11]

In certain contexts this nonuniqueness can readily be generalized so that the noun or noun phrase refers to **any** (i.e., **all**) members of the class. Consider the following:

> *A well-constructed building* that is properly maintained does not wear out quickly.

The phrase *a well-constructed building* refers to **any** *well-constructed building* (hence **all** *well-constructed buildings*) and is accordingly not unique.

Other Examples:
> *An ideal machine* is one that has no friction.
> Bill hopes to buy *a computer* someday.
> An effective way of learning mathematics is by working on *problems.*
> *Valence electrons* are those located in the outermost shell of an atom.

Adding this rule to our previous flow chart, we have the situation as represented in Figure 13-2.

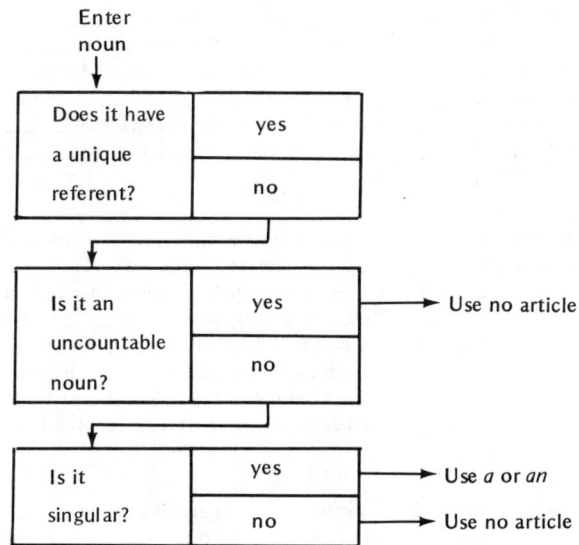

FIGURE 13-2. PARTIAL FLOW CHART FOR CHOOSING THE CORRECT ARTICLE (STEP 2)

Exercise 1: Mark each of these nouns as being countable or uncountable:

rocket	program
engine	pollution
inflation	satellite
lever	molecule of CO_2
CO_2	ecology
wheel	engineer
friction	radar
gravity	combustion
atom	motor
computer	engineering
aluminum	book
weather	meter
machine	sodium nitrite
information	photosynthesis

Mark each of the italicized nouns as being countable or uncountable:
1. The acceleration of *gravity, g,* is the *acceleration* imparted to a *body* by its own *weight.*
2. If *friction* could be eliminated, no force at all would be necessary to keep an *object* in motion, once it had been started.
3. The *coefficient* of friction just before *motion* begins is larger than the coefficient of friction when there is actual sliding of one *surface* over the other.

170 / ENGLISH FOR ACADEMIC AND TECHNICAL PURPOSES

Exercise 2: In the following passages, insert indefinite articles *(a* or *an)* where necessary. (Use figure 13-2 as an aid.)

A: Storing Electric Power

In _____ space the sun is always shining, so there is no problem with storing _____ electricity. On Earth, however, the sun shines only half the time in _____ good weather and not at all in bad. Thus, _____ electricity must be stored for _____ sunless periods. Currently this is done with _____ lead-acid storage batteries, similar to those used in _____ automobiles. _____ day's electricity for _____ average single-family house can be stored in _____ batteries occupying the space of _____ closet; _____ row of such "closets" in the basement stores _____ power for _____ sunless periods. (Adapted from Morris 1977:40).

B: Power Requirements in an Average Home

_____ average single-family residence (_____ four-person, 1,500-square-foot, non-air-conditioned house) uses about _____ 700 kilowatt hours per month, the equivalent of _____ one-kilowatt generator running continuously. Because this average house needs _____ one kilowatt of _____ average power, it requires _____ five kilowatts of _____ peak power. This, in turn, would require about _____ 500 square feet of _____ solar cells at _____ present efficiency levels under _____ optimum conditions. The Energy Research and Development Administration (ERDA) says 1,500 square feet would now be required in _____ northern city like Boston. (Adapted from Morris 1977:41).

C: Vectors and Scalars

Vectors are _____ quantities that have both _____ magnitude and _____ direction. Examples of _____ physical quantities that are vectors are _____ force, _____ velocity, and _____ acceleration. Thus, when one states that _____ car is moving north at 100 kilometers per hour, with respect to _____ coordinate system attached to the Earth, one is specifying the vector quantity velocity with _____ magnitude (100 kilometers per hour) and _____ direction (north).

Scalars are _____ quantities that have _____ magnitude only. Examples of _____ physical quantities that are scalars are _____ mass, _____ distance, _____ speed, and _____ density. Thus, when one states only the fact that _____ car is moving at 100 kilometers per hour one has specified _____ scalar, _____ speed, since only _____ magnitude (100 kilometers per hour) is given (that is, no direction is specified). (Adapted from Sears 1950:4).

Counters

Although uncountable nouns themselves cannot be counted, they can usually be modified by certain types of phrases—called *counters*—that **can** be counted. One example of such a counter is *cup of* _____. It can be used to modify an uncountable noun like *water,* thereby creating a countable noun phrase, *cup of water.* Thus, although one cannot say "a water" or "two waters" or "three waters," one **can** say "a cup of water" or "two cups of water" or "three cups of water."

Counters are typically composed of a countable noun and the preposition *of,* so that the complete noun phrase has this structure:

The countable noun should represent a unit of measure that is **appropriate** for the object or concept represented by the uncountable noun. For example, liquids are customarily measured by putting them into containers having a certain capacity. The countable unit of measure might be *cups* or *liters* or *quarts* as in five cups of milk.

Even uncountable nouns referring to more abstract concepts can usually be modified by appropriate counters. For instance, electric current is measured in terms of *amperes* (*25 amperes of electric current*); information can be measured in terms of *pieces* (*a piece of information*); processes can be measured in units of time (*three months of experimentation*).[12]

Exercise 3: A list of uncountable nouns follows. Insert appropriate counters or measure phrases so that you change these uncountable nouns to countable units. The first two examples are done for you. (You can easily complete some examples in this exercise by using the appropriate unit for measuring the noun. For instance, electric power is measured in watts.)

Uncountable	Countable
oxygen	3 liters of oxygen
	3 moles of oxygen
	3 molecules of oxygen
electric power	3 watts of _____ electric power
current	_____ current
force	_____ force
work	_____ work
pressure	_____ pressure
temperature	_____ temperature
liquid	_____ liquid
pollution	_____ pollution
chemistry	_____ chemistry
electrolysis	_____ electrolysis
radar	_____ radar
combustion	_____ combustion
friction	_____ friction
oxygen	_____ oxygen
electric potential	_____ electric potential

Two-Way Nouns

Many nouns in technical English can refer to either countable or uncountable concepts. Such *two-way* nouns all have one thing in common: when they are used in the uncountable sense they refer to a **general** concept, but when they are used as countable nouns they refer to a **specification** of that general concept. Consider the word *metal* for example: it is commonly used in an uncountable sense to mean the general class of matter that is opaque, ductile, and fusible, and that typically consists of only one or two chemical elements (e.g., "Chisels are usually made of *metal*"). But it is also sometimes used as a countable noun to mean a *type of metal*. For example, the sentence "Brass is an alloy composed of two *metals*, zinc and copper" means the same thing as "Brass is an alloy composed of two *types of metal*, zinc and copper." Some other two-way nouns that usually have the meaning *type of* __X__ in the countable sense (where X is the name of a class) are *fuel, acid, soil, material,* and *gasoline*. Note, for instance, the following:

1. The vast majority of American automobiles run on *gasoline*. (Here *gasoline* is general, uncountable.)

    Our local service station usually carries several *gasolines:* leaded regular, leaded premium, unleaded regular, and unleaded premium. (Here *gasolines* is specific, countable.) Note that you could have said: Our local service station usually carries several *types of gasoline* or *(grades of gasoline)*: leaded regular, and so forth.

2. Railcars transporting *acid* must be specifically designed. (Here *acid* is general, uncountable.)

    Electrolytic action in an automobile battery produces an *acid* that can lead to corrosion of the terminals. (Here *acid* is specific, countable. You could have said: Electrolytic action in an automobile battery produces a *type of acid* that can lead to corrosion of the terminals.)

In many other cases, however, the specification of a two-way noun does not mean *type of* __X__ but may instead mean *amount of* __X__ . Note this example:

 The two circuits have different *resistances.*

Here *resistances,* a word that is commonly used as an uncountable noun referring to **general** opposition against electric current, refers specifically to the **amount** of opposition: So the above sentence means, in effect, "The two circuits have different *amounts of resistance.*" Some other two-way nouns that usually mean *amount of* __X__ in the countable sense are *mass, velocity, force, pressure, power,* and *acceleration.*

Sometimes the specification of a two-way noun means, roughly, a *complete process of* _____ . For example, the word *distillation* normally is used to refer to the general process of distillation and is thus used as an uncountable noun. But sometimes the writer wants to focus on one or more specific applications of the process, as in the sentence: "At the refinery, the crude oil undergoes *two complete processes of distillation.*" He or she can shorten the sentence: "At the refinery, the crude oil undergoes *two distillations.*"

There are still other possible interpretations that can be attached to the specification of a two-way noun; it is advisable to exercise caution in your own writing and not to perform a specification that you are not sure of.

 Exercise 4: Mark each of the italicized nouns as countable or uncountable. Examples 1-2 in C have already been done.
  A: 1. *Water* expands when it is heated in a *container.*
    2. Chemistry *students* study the *concept* that *matter* is made up of *particles.*
    3. *Molecules* occupy *space.*

	4.	*Velocity* and speed are both the *ratio* of a length to a time.
	5.	The unit of *velocity* (or speed) in the English system is one *foot* per second.
B:	1.	Approximately 99 percent of the *matter* making up the *sun* and other *stars* is a *mixture* of the *elements* hydrogen and *helium*.
	2.	The earth is about 150,000,000 *kilometers* (93 million *miles*) from the *sun*—one astronomical unit in the *language* of *astronomers*.
	3.	If the *earth* were at some other *distance* from the sun, we would receive more or less of the sun's *energy* than we do.
	4.	A positive *velocity* indicates *motion* toward the right, and a negative velocity indicates motion towards the left.
	5.	In the *year* 1624, Sir Isaac Newton (the famous *physicist*) was born and Galileo died.
C:	1.	Mechanics is the branch of physics and engineering that deals with the interrelations of *force*, matter, and motion. (uncountable)
	2.	We can exert a *force* on a body by muscular effort; compressed air exerts a *force* on the walls of its container; a locomotive exerts a *force* on the train that it is drawing. (countable in all instances italicized)
	3.	The newton is equal to a *force* of 0.224 pounds, a *force* that imparts to a mass of one kilogram an acceleration of one meter per second, per second.
	4.	*Mass* is a quantitative measure of inertia.
	5.	*Mass*, as used in mechanics, refers to that property of matter that in everyday language is described by the word inertia.
	6.	The newton is a force that imparts to a *mass* of one kilogram an acceleration of one meter per second, per second.
	7.	We may derive the relation between *pressure* and *elevation* in a fluid.
	8.	*Pressure* is expressed in lbs/ft^2, $newtons/m^2$, or $dynes/cm^2$.
	9.	A *pressure* of 1.013×10^6 $dynes/cm^2$, or 14.7 lbs/in^2, is called one atmosphere.

Informal Usages

There are certain informal usages that you are apt to hear spoken in conversations or lectures but you rarely see in writing. It is important to avoid such usages in your writing, since they are stylistically inappropriate for anything but the most informal level.

For example, in the informal situation of the chemistry lab or small discussion group, student chemists sometimes talk about normally **uncountable** nouns, such as the names of elements and molecules, as if they were **countable** nouns. A student might read aloud this equation, for instance:

$$Ag_2O + H_2O_2 = 2Ag + O_2 + H_2O$$

as "*one silver oxide* plus *one hydrogen peroxide* yields *two silver(s)* plus *an oxygen* plus *a water*." Similarly:

$$Cu + 2H_2SO_4 = CuSO_2 + SO_2 + 2H_2O$$

could be read aloud as "*one copper* plus *two sulfuric acid(s)* yields *one copper sulfate* plus *one sulfur dioxide* plus *two water(s)*." Although this type of rendition is frequently heard in informal settings, it would be highly unsuitable for formal purposes. A more formal reading of the same formula would be "*one* **atom** *of* *copper* plus *two* **molecules** *of sulfuric acid,*" and so on.

A second example of informal usage, frequently heard, is the use of the indefinite article instead of *per* in measured-rate expressions like the following:

A small car should get at least 35 miles *a* gallon.
Northern Michigan averages 5.2 hours of sunlight *a* day.

More formal versions of these two sentences would be "A small car should get at least 35 miles *per* gallon" and "Northern Michigan averages 5.2 hours of sunlight *per* day."

THE DEFINITE ARTICLE (the): UNIQUE REFERENCE

In English, the definite article *the* is used to show that a noun or noun phrase refers to a **unique (particular)** object or concept. The definite article may occur with any type of noun—singular or plural, countable or uncountable. (Note that this contrasts with the use of the indefinite article described in section 1; the indefinite article is used to show that a noun or noun phrase is nonunique, and it occurs only with singular countable nouns.)

A noun or noun phrase modified by *the* may be unique in one of several ways. In some cases, the referent of the noun or noun phrase is unique by its very nature. We have called this **inherent uniqueness** because the uniqueness exists in the very nature of the referent itself (see below for discussion). In other cases, the referent of the noun or noun phrase is defined to be unique by a given context. We have called this **contextual uniqueness** (discussion follows). In still other cases, the referent is unique only because this uniqueness is implied. We have called this **implied uniqueness** (discussion follows).

Inherent Uniqueness: Special Adjectives

When certain adjectives are attached to nouns, they modify the noun so that, for any given context, the noun must have a unique referent. In other words, such a noun refers to **only one unique** person, place, or thing.

Superlative adjectives, for example, modify nouns in such a way. Superlative adjectives are words like *tallest, fastest, heaviest, most valuable, least important.* In any given context, there is normally **only one** *tallest building;* **only one** *fastest car;* **only one** *most valuable person;* **only one** *least important point.* Thus, each of these nouns has only one unique referent and must take the definite article: **the** *tallest building,* **the** *fastest car,* **the** *most valuable person,* **the** *least important point.*

Similarly, ordinal adjectives like *first, last, second, fifth, nth,* and so forth, each represent a unique position in an ordering: given any ordered set, there can be only one first position, only one last position, only one second position, and so on. Consequently, whenever a noun or noun phrase is modified by such an adjective, it usually requires the definite article: *the first attempt, the last investigation, the second stage,* and such.[13]

Some other adjectives by their very nature also restrict nouns to a unique referent and therefore normally occur with the definite article. Examples of such adjectives are *only, sole, exact, current,* and *present.* Three of these adjectives can be found in the following report on the surface sampler for the Viking mission to Mars.

> The Viking lander's surface sampler is **the** *only means* for acquiring small "bites" of Martian soil and then delivering them to the three analytical instruments located deep inside the lander: the biology instrument, the gas chromatograph—mass spectrometer, and the X-ray fluorescence spectrometer (see "The Vikings are coming," June 1976, p. 48). Without directly acquired samples of the Mars surface, the *sole use* for these instruments would be to analyze windblown dust that might accumulate in them over a long time—a very unattractive alternative. Thus, on sol 2 (a sol is a Mars day of 24 hours, 40 minutes), when the surface sampler jammed during its initial operation, a team of experts at the Viking mission control center immediately sprang into action to remedy the situation.
>
> **The** *exact nature* of the problem became evident during tests on a full-scale lander mock-up, known as the Science Test Lander (STL), at the Jet Propulsion Laboratory in Pasadena, California. (Spitzer 1976:92)

In this passage, *only* and *sole* restrict their nouns so that each can refer to only one unique (particular) referent. *The only means* (for acquiring small bites of Martian soil) can refer to only one particular *means* and that is *the Viking lander's surface sampler.* Similarly, *the sole use* (for these instruments) can refer to only one particular *use* and that is *to analyze windblown dust that might accumulate over a long time.* As a result the definite article is used in each case: **the** *only means,* **the** *sole use.*

Similarly, *the exact nature* (of the problem) has a unique referent. *The exact nature* refers to only the one "true" nature and not to the many apparent natures of the problem. *Exact* is used with many conceptual nouns like *nature, effect, purpose,* or *reason* in this way and requires the definite article.

Inherent Uniqueness: Special Nouns

There are certain nouns that we usually think of as referring to unique events, nouns like *advent, commencement, beginning, future,* and so on. Because of this such nouns almost always occur with the definite article.

For example, we generally assume that there is only one beginning, one middle, and one end for any given process. Consequently, when talking about a given process, we refer to *the* beginning, *the* middle, *the* end. Note this example:

> Technical writing classes ... teach students to make the results of their investigations and in particular their generalizations, their conclusions, readily available to busy and inattentive readers. This means that these generalizations cannot be buried somewhere in **the** middle or **the** end of a report; they must come at **the** beginning of the report where they are most easily found. (Olsen 1977:176)

Similarly, we think of certain aspects of our common existence as being unique: *the past, the present, the future, the 1940s, the early 1970s, the sky, the earth, the ground.* Thus, as illustrated below, such a noun used in its unique sense requires the definite article.

> During *the early 1970s,* the U.S. Postal Service tested several computer-controlled reading and sorting systems to speed up mail delivery. These systems were later installed in post offices in New York City, Boston, and Cincinnati. (Mennie 1976:41)

Exceptions to such use of the definite article occur only when the noun is modified to refer to a nonunique existence:

> Our company hopes that next year will be *a good year.*
> Sailors like to see *a sky full of stars* rather than *a sky full of clouds.*

Notice, for instance, that in the first sample sentence, *a good year* does not refer to a unique year but to **any** year that happens to be good. It could refer to a year in which the company made a 6 percent profit, an 8 percent profit, or a 12 percent profit.

> Exercise 5: In the following passages, find all the examples of the special adjectives and nouns just discussed. Be prepared to classify the various **definite article plus noun** and **indefinite article plus noun** units and to explain your classification.
>
> A: Aluminum and Charles Martin Hall
>
> In the 1880s, if anyone had invented a way of making aluminum cheaply, that man could have benefited the world—and made a fortune. At that time, aluminum was very expensive to make. Although aluminum is the most abundant metal in the earth's crust, it was then very difficult to separate from the earth's crust. The first man to discover a way of separating aluminum from the earth's crust was a man named Charles Martin Hall. The way he did this used electricity to separate out the aluminum (adapted from Brandwein 1972:48).
>
> B: The Planets: Origin and Orbit
>
> The earth is a planet moving in orbit around the sun. It is not the sun's only planet. There are other planets, in other orbits, moving around the sun. The earth is merely the third planet from the sun. All the planets, including the earth, move in the same direction around the sun. All the orbits lie in nearly the same plane—except the outermost orbit (Pluto's), which is tilted.
>
> How did this remarkable collection of moving objects get this way? How did the objects come to have orbits in nearly the same plane? How do the objects maintain the present order? Why does the furthest planet, Pluto, have a tilted orbit? Is there something special about an outermost orbit that makes it different from other orbits? Did the solar system come together bit by bit from different directions in space, at different times? Or did it have a single origin? These are some of the questions which astronomers try to answer (adapted from Brandwein 1975:198).
>
> C: An Introduction to 3-D Radar
>
> Air-traffic radars of the 1950s could readily determine the direction of incoming and outgoing aircraft, but not their height above the ground. The planes might be a mile apart in altitude or on the verge of colliding—but air-traffic controllers on the ground had no way of obtaining this information from current radar data alone, or without some previous radar history on both planes before they entered the same range-azimuth "capsule." Recognizing this obvious deficiency, the Airways Modernization Board (the forerunner of the FAA) decided to investigate the radar "height finder" as a likely solution to the problem.

The new air-traffic radar would have to resolve targets to within 1000 feet at fifty miles and be able to determine whether two aircraft, approaching each other from opposite ends of the sky, might pose a threat to each other. This meant that the radar had to measure the altitude of each aircraft before it entered the range of another and to allow for any distortions in the target's return signals due to blending in the atmosphere.

Looked at another way, the problem was to hold steady a lever fifty miles long—the length over which the radar beam had to be effective to do its job. Designers had to contend with wind, temperature, and humidity variations, and even the light, imperceptible seismic motions of the ground itself.

In addition to these structural problems, the major problems facing the designers were "ground clutter"—the bane of all radars—and, unexpectedly, system noise. However, an unexpected benefit of the system was the height finder's unique ability to track targets in the rain (Terrese 1976:49).

Exercise 6: Insert *the*, *a*, or *an* where appropriate in the following passages and be prepared to justify your choice.

A. Aluminum and Bauxite

Aluminum is _____ element, _____ substance made up of one kind of _____ atom. _____ aluminum happens to be _____ element that joins with other elements easily and firmly. In other words, _____ aluminum easily and firmly combines with _____ other elements to form _____ compounds. _____ compounds are substances, as you might know, in which different kinds of _____ atoms are combined. And once it gets into a compound, _____ aluminum atom is different to get out.

This can easily be seen in bauxite. Bauxite is _____ claylike material containing aluminum. In _____ bauxite, aluminum is very tightly bound to _____ oxygen (adapted from Brandwein 1972:49).

B. The Formation of Our Solar System

The nebular hypothesis and _____ collision hypothesis each describe one way _____ solar system might have been formed. However, these hypotheses proved to be unsatisfactory for _____ number of _____ reasons. In _____ first place, they did not account for _____ fact that the orbits _____ planets are nearly circular and in nearly _____ same plane. If the masses that became _____ planets were violently pulled out of _____ sun, their orbits would have been _____ long narrow ellipses, and each orbit would probably be in _____ different plane.

Another objection is that _____ astronomers have not found _____ star that could have met with _____ sun at about the time that _____ earth was formed. Here is _____ instance of how observations can upset _____ hypothesis. Scientists demand that hypotheses fit the facts, even _____ most attractive hypothesis (adapted from Brandwein 1975:200).

C. The Big Dish Radio Telescope

"One of _____ most challenging engineering problems of _____ century" . . . "Dwarfing anything constructed in _____ past for the study of the universe" . . . "_____ largest movable land-based structure ever constructed in _____ world."

These were only three of the descriptors enthusiastically applied to the U.S. Navy's attempt in _____ late 1950s to build _____ mammoth radio telescope with _____ 600-foot diameter antenna that would be fully steerable. The structure, which would have been twice as large as any fully steerable telescope built since, would have towered sixty-six stories above _____ ground on _____ 7-acre foundation near Sugar Grove, West Virginia. Unfortunately for eager astronomers, however, in 1961-62 original cost estimates of $52 million were reevaluated and reestimated to be between $200 and $300 million for _____ future. As a result, the so-called Big Dish was abandoned in 1962, _____ victim, proclaimed one engineering magazine, of galloping obsolescence. Now all that remains of that dream to see more of _____ sky and further into space than ever before is the concrete foundation for the telescope tracks and the pintle bearing (Wolff 1976:89).

Inherent Uniqueness: Generics

The definite article is sometimes used generically, that is, to indicate that a countable noun or noun phrase refers to an entire class-type. In such usage, the noun or noun phrase is always in the singular, and it is usually found in a context that defines or characterizes the class. Consider the following example:

> For simplicity and efficiency, **the** *Hawker Siddeley Harrier* is one of the best present-day VTOL [Vertical Take Off & Landing] aircraft. This plane uses the concept of "vectored thrust" where four rotating exhaust nozzles are used to deflect the exhaust from vertically down to directly behind (Talay 1975:149).

The author is not referring here to a single plane but to an entire class of planes, namely, those known as Hawker Siddley Harriers. (Notice how the **defining characteristics** of Hawker Siddeley Harriers are being discussed here.) Since there is only one such type of plane, the reference to this type is by its very nature unique. This is why the definite article is used.[14]

Contextual Uniqueness: Previous Mention

In contrast to cases like those just discussed, where a reference is unique by its very nature, there are other cases where a reference is unique because of shared knowledge between the writer and the intended reader. In such cases, the writer establishes a context and then uses a noun or noun phrase that refers to (some referent in) this context.

One type of such "shared knowledge" occurs in the form of a **repeated** noun or noun phrase. The first mention of a noun or noun phrase establishes it in a given context. Further mention of it refers to this first mention. Consider the following example:

> Soil physicists have characterized the drying of a *soil* in three stages. They are:
> * The wet stage, where the evaporation is solely determined by the meteorological conditions;
> * An intermediate or drying stage where the *soil* occurs in the wet stage early in the day, but then dries off because there is not a sufficient amount of water in the *soil* to meet the evaporation rate; and
> * The dry stage, where evaporation is solely determined by the molecular transfer properties of water within the *soil*.
> There is a striking change in the evaporation rate as the *soil* dries during the transition from the wet stages to the drying stage (Schmigge 1975:2-3).

In this example, the first mention of the noun *soil* does not have a unique referent. The author is randomly referring to **any** soil, and so marks the noun with the indefinite article: *a soil* (ln. 1).

The author then uses the randomly selected soil as a model for the soil-drying process. In doing so, he refers back to the model soil several times. Each of these later mentions of the word *soil* thus has a specific, unique referent—namely, the soil sample randomly selected at the beginning. To make this reference clear to the reader, the author uses the definite article with each of these later mentions: . . . **the** *soil* . . . **the** *soil* . . . **the** *soil*.

Not all cases of "previous mention" *the* involve repetitions of the exact same noun, however. In many cases, the repetition involves a synonymous noun or variant form and the definite article is still used. In the following paragraph, for example, the three noun phrases in italics vary slightly in form but all refer to the same *expanse of glass*.

> The simplest approach to passive space heating is through direct gain of solar radiation by means of *a south-facing expanse of glass*. This approach works best when *the south window area* is double-glazed and when the building has considerable thermal mass in the form of concrete floors and masonry walls insulated on the outside. What results is, in effect, a live-in solar collector thermal storage unit. If *the south-facing window area* is vertical, seasonal temperature control is basically automatic . . . . (Pacific Regional Solar Heating Handbook 1976:82).

Here, as in the previous example, the first mention of the noun phrase *south-facing expanse of glass* does not have a specific, unique referent. Hence, the indefinite article is used: *a south-facing expanse of glass*. Then, the author uses this *expanse of glass* as a model and refers to it twice. The first time he calls it *the south window area*; the second time he calls it *the south-facing window area*. In form, these are both slight variants of the original *south-facing expanse of glass*, but they both refer uniquely to that particular *expanse of glass*. Thus, the definite article must be used: . . . **the** *south window area* . . . **the** *south-facing window area*.

Contextual Uniqueness: A Following Modifier

The most frequent and therefore most important use of the definite article occurs when the writer gives a noun a unique referent by modifying it. In such cases, the modifier usually follows the noun, forming a **noun phrase**. Consider, for example, the noun *father*. This word, by itself, is not unique, since there are many fathers in the world. But if we find it in a context like *father of Michelangelo,* we then have a unique referent, since Michelangelo had only one father. Because of this uniqueness, the definite article is used: **the** *father of Michelangelo*. As long as the noun phrase (noun plus modifier) describes a unique reference, the definite article is used, as can be seen in the following examples:

> The father of Michelangelo was a minor government official.
> The Italian government decided to honor *the father of Michelangelo*.
> Many people are not aware that *the father of Michelangelo* lived in Florence.

However, sometimes the noun phrase unit is broken up, so that the noun no longer has its uniqueness-defining modifier in its own noun phrase. Then the definite article usually should not be used. For example, consider the sentence: "Michelangelo had *a father* who was a minor government official." Here *father* and *Michelangelo* are no longer linked together in the same noun phrase; instead, *father* is modified by the clause *who was a minor government official*. This latter clause does not refer to a unique referent: There was probably more than one father in Michelangelo's day who was also a minor government official. Thus, since *father* does not have a unique referent, the indefinite article is used instead of the definite article: Michelangelo had *a father* who was a minor government official.

It should be clear from the above example that a modifier following a noun and joining with it to form a noun phrase serves as part of the context of a noun and can thus limit the noun to a unique referent. For other examples of this phenomenon, consider the following passage:

> At *the time the Mariner-9 spacecraft began its Martian orbit, in November 1971,* an intense, planet-wide dust storm was in progress. *The infrared spectroscopy experiment which was carried on the spacecraft* obtained information on the thermal structure of the atmosphere, both during a portion of the dust storm and during its subsequent dissipation (Conrath 1975:135).

In the first sentence, the noun *time* does not refer to just any time but rather to a single, specific time, namely, the time when Mariner-9 began its Martian orbit (November 1971). Because of this unique reference, the definite article is used: *the time*....

Similarly, in sentence 2, the noun *experiment* is modified so that it refers not just to any experiment but to a specific one, namely, the one that was carried on the spacecraft and used infrared spectroscopy.

> Exercise 7: Find all the examples of *the* used for generics, previous mention, or a following modifier (*the* discussed above). Be prepared to classify the various **definite article plus noun** and **indefinite article plus noun** units and to explain your classification.
> A: Steel in the Tin Can
> The tin can is really made of steel, not tin. The can is made of steel because steel is strong. However, steel corrodes so the steel in the can must be protected from corrosion. The metal tin does not corrode. Thus, a thin coating of tin is put on the steel to make the "tin" can. The tin saves the steel from corroding (adapted from Brandwein 1972:82).
> B: The Composition of the Heavenly Bodies
> The composition of the heavenly bodies is not uniform. About 99 percent of the matter making up the sun and other stars is a mixture of the light gaseous elements hydrogen and helium. The other 1 percent of the matter consists of the heavier elements—oxygen, iron, aluminum, nitrogen, and others.
> The distribution of elements in our solar system is quite different. The distribution falls into two distinct groupings: the distribution in the inner planets (Mercury, Venus, Earth, and Mars) and that in the outer planets (Jupiter, Saturn, Uranus, and Neptune). For the inner planets, only about 1 percent of the matter consists of the lighter elements; the other 99 percent is made up of the heavier elements. In contrast, the outer planets contain a great deal of the lighter element hydrogen and relatively small amounts of the heavier elements. (The chemical make-up of the planet Pluto is not yet known.) (adapted from Brandwein 1975:200).

C: An Introduction to the Physics and Physiology of Acceleration
   In the days of the frail canvas-covered aircraft that flew at slow speeds and could not take stresses easily tolerated by the human body, acceleration was not much of a problem. Today, aircrafts of much stronger construction travel at sonic and supersonic speeds and thus can impose tremendous forces for appreciable periods of time on the now relatively frail human occupant. Since aviation medicine has as yet little understanding of these important forces, a study of the fundamental principles involved in the physiology of acceleration is needed. Such a study should proceed through the following stages:
(1) The history of acceleration and its relation to aviation medicine should be described.
(2) The physiological effects and the clinical response to such forces should be understood by the flight surgeon.
(3) The conventional terminology for discussing these forces and their effects must be established (NATO 1967b:1).

Exercise 8: Insert *the*, *a*, or *an* where appropriate in the following passage, and be prepared to justify your choice.
A: Awareness of Technological Revolutions
   It is easy to be aware of _____ revolution brought by _____ internal combustion engine. _____ effects of _____ revolution are part of our world. Most of us own _____ car and know something of _____ piston, _____ cylinder, and _____ horsepower. It is also easy to be aware of _____ revolution brought about by _____ electronic tube. Most of us own _____ radios and _____ television sets and know something about _____ waves and _____ electrical interference. Unfortunately, it is harder to be aware of _____ chemical revolution because its products are hidden. Yet this revolution is important because it is _____ basis for the other revolutions. _____ automobile could not run without fuel, which is a chemical. _____ car or _____ electronic tube could not be built without _____ metal, fabric, adhesive, glass, paint, and plastics, which are _____ chemicals or _____ results of chemical processes. If we are to understand our world, we must be aware of _____ chemical revolution.

B: Newton and the Universal Law of Gravitation
   Isaac Newton was born the same year that Galileo died, 1642. Newton was only 24 years old when he solved _____ problem of what holds the solar system together. The story, as you probably know, is that _____ falling apple set Newton thinking in _____ right direction. It was not _____ question of why _____ apple fell that interested him. Everyone knew that gravity pulled things toward the earth. Gravity made _____ apple fall, of course.
   It was at this point that _____ observant questioning man produced _____ great scientist. Newton went on from _____ observation that gravity pulled things to the earth to ask other questions. Was the moon falling, too? Did _____ force of gravitation reach from the earth to the moon? Did it reach from the sun to the planets?
   After much work, Newton concluded that _____ force of gravitation did reach from the earth to the moon and hold them together. In fact, gravitation held together the whole solar system and universe. _____ now famous conclusion is known as Newton's Universal Law of Gravitation (adapted from Brandwein 1975:208).

C: The Dynamics of Rotation Applied to the Centrifuge
   _____ classic treatment of rotational physics usually found in _____ engineering textbook and in _____ advanced text on gyrodynamics are ordinarily quite rigorous in their mathematical treatment of _____ subject. This paper is intended to present _____ subject in such manner, first, as to relieve _____ physicians and medical officers of _____ labor required to gain _____ rigorous

insight into _____ subject and, second, to strip away _____ non-essentials associated with _____ classic developments which are not pertinent to _____ work at hand.

To this end, _____ treatment used in this paper will be _____ largely intuitive, extensively graphical one, and _____ use of mathematics beyond algebra will be studiously avoided (NATO 1967a:1).

Contextual Uniqueness: Shared Knowledge

Often the writer and intended readers share certain knowledge of the world because they belong to the same culture. (*Culture,* in this case, can be defined broadly or narrowly, depending on whether the writer is addressing a broad, general audience or a narrow, specialized one.) Sometimes the writer uses a noun or noun phrase that has only one referent in the real world and believes that the reader knows about this uniqueness of reference. In such a situation, the writer can use the definite article to mark the noun or noun phrase accordingly. Consider the following passage, for example, which begins a report presented to a group of aerospace scientists and engineers at a NASA symposium:

> This paper presents the preliminary results from *the Goddard-University of New Hampshire cosmic-ray experiment* during *a recent Pioneer-11 encounter with Jupiter.* Before continuing, however, I would like to say a few words about *the other Goddard experiment* on Pioneer-10, *the flux-gate magnetometer.*
>
> This experiment performed flawlessly throughout the encounter, and it observed a maximum magnetic field strength of 1.2 gauss just prior to occultation. A preliminary spherical harmonic analysis has been performed, and it indicates that *the simple offset dipole model* is only a fair representation of the field . . . (Teegarden 1975:157).

Now it happens to be a fact that each of the italicized noun phrases in this passage has a unique real-world referent: there was only one Goddard-University of New Hampshire cosmic-ray experiment on Pioneer-11, there was only one Pioneer-11 encounter with Jupiter, and so on. Of course, not everybody knows these facts. But in the author's immediate culture—that is, in his circle of fellow scientists and engineers, the ones he's addressing in this case—these facts seem to be *common knowledge*: Everyone in the group knows that there was only one such experiment, only one such encounter, and such. Consequently, even at first mention, the author marks these noun phrases with the definite article.

If this writer had been addressing a broader, more general audience of readers, he might have chosen to use the indefinite article instead:

> This paper presents the preliminary results from *a Goddard-University of New Hampshire cosmic-ray experiment* during *a recent Pioneer-11 encounter with Jupiter.* Before continuing, however, I would like to say a few words about *another Goddard experiment* on Pioneer-10, *a flux-gate magnetometer.*
>
> This experiment performed flawlessly throughout the encounter, and it observed a maximum magnetic field strength of 1.2 gauss just prior to occultation. A preliminary spherical harmonic analysis has been performed, and it indicates that *a simple offset dipole model* is only a fair representation of the field . . . .

In deciding whether to use the definite or indefinite article, therefore, you sometimes have to consider *two* things: (1) whether or not the noun or noun phrase has a unique referent and, (2) whether or not your reader *shares* this knowledge with you. If you do not know who your readers are likely to be, or if there is a great variety of backgrounds among your readers—as is often the case with technical reports, for example—you cannot depend on the sharing of specialized knowledge.

Implied Uniqueness

A less frequent use of the definite article occurs when the writer wants to imply that a noun or noun phrase has a unique referent even though the reader may not know of this uniqueness. This implied uniqueness is not often used intentionally by most writers of scientific and technical works. However, it seems to appear frequently when a reader deals with a text whose content is too difficult for the reader's level of technical expertise. As an example, consider the following passage from a repair manual for the Hewlett Packard Preset Counter, Model 5330 A/B.

> The counter measures frequencies to 10Mhz. Direct readouts of rates such as gallons/minute, revolutions/second, miles, hour, etc., can be obtained by normalizing with *the time base. The rate mode* is similar to *the frequency measurement mode* of a conventional counter except for *the preset time base. The gate length selection* is (10^{-6} sec. x M)N. N is the setting of *the N switch* and can be set from 1 to 100,000. When *the N switch* is set to 00000, N = 1,000,000. M is *the MULTIPLIER switch*, and can be set to x1, x10, x100, or x1000 (Hewlett Packard 1969:3-1).

If the reader does not know anything about the operation of a preset counter (such as this Hewlett Packard machine) several definite-article-plus-noun units are at first confusing: *the time base, the rate mode, the frequency measurement mode, the preset time base, the gate length selection, the N switch,* and *the MULTIPLIER switch.* It is probably not at all clear to the unknowing reader that any of these nouns should necessarily be unique; the reader must simply accept the writer's implication of uniqueness. From the writer's point of view, it is important to establish that there is only one of each of these items, and he or she efficiently does this by using the definite article.

As illustrated in the above example, this use of the definite article is aimed at a reader lacking specific knowledge of the subject being discussed. It tells him or her that a particular item (e.g., *the rate mode*) exists and that there is only one of it. For the more knowledgeable reader, this information is not necessary because of his or her prior cultural knowledge. For instance, an electronics specialist familiar with the Hewlett Packard Preset Counter already knows that each item in the above example is unique. For this specialist, the definite articles are examples of contextual uniqueness through shared knowledge. The articles are not the instances of implied uniqueness seen by the unknowing reader.

184 / ENGLISH FOR ACADEMIC AND TECHNICAL PURPOSES

This last discussion illustrates a situation sometimes seen with the definite article — that any given use of the definite article may have more than one valid explanation depending on the previous knowledge the reader brings to a particular text.

A FLOW CHART FOR ARTICLES

Reviewing the main points of this chapter, we find:

1. The indefinite article *(a/an)* is used with singular countable nouns having a nonunique referent (see Figure 13-2);
2. The definite article *(the)* is used with **any** noun (excluding proper names) that has a unique referent;
3. Nouns or noun phrases can be judged to have a unique referent for any one or more of several different reasons: (a) The uniqueness is **inherent**; (b) The uniqueness is dictated by the **context**; (c) The uniqueness is **implied.**

If you are undecided as to which article to use, try using the diagram in Figure 13-3 ("Flow Chart for Choosing the Right Article"). It tells you not only when to use *the* or *a/an* (or no article at all) but also when to use the demonstrative *this* (pl. *these*). For an illustration of how to use Figure 13-3, see Figure 13-4 and the explanation immediately following it. To see how this flow chart works, let us consider some of the noun phrases in the following introductory paragraph from a report by the United States Energy Research and Development Administration:

> *The continuing depletion of domestic fossil fuels* may be a signal of one of the most significant long-term issues facing the United States as it enters its third century. The impacts of decisions made today concerning our remaining natural resources will persist for generations, beyond the lifetime of today's children. *Solar energy* will be an important part of *these decisions* (ERDA 1977:V).

In the first sentence, the main noun of the italicized noun phrase is *depletion*; the other words of the phrase are its modifiers. If we were the authors of this paragraph and were not sure about which article to use, we could begin by asking ourselves the first question on the flow diagram (in the upper left-hand cell) "Does it have a unique referent?" Here the answer is "yes," (1) because the following modifier *of domestic fuels* identifies a particular kind of depletion, and (2) because, in our culture, when we talk about this kind of depletion we are all talking about the same thing. (Incidentally, if the writer wants to talk not about the **present** continuing depletion of fossil fuels but about some **hypothetical** depletion in the **future,** he or she might then want to use the indefinite article (and a future form of the verb): *A continuing depletion of domestic fossil fuels would be a signal of*.... The indefinite article would be appropriate in such a case because the noun phrase would have only a hypothetical, and therefore

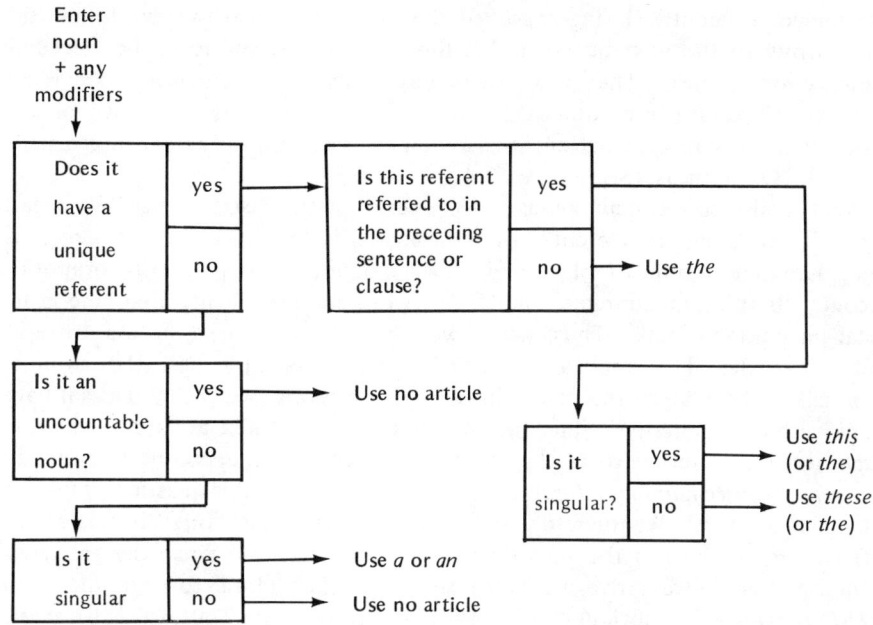

FIGURE 13-3. FLOW CHART FOR CHOOSING THE RIGHT ARTICLE

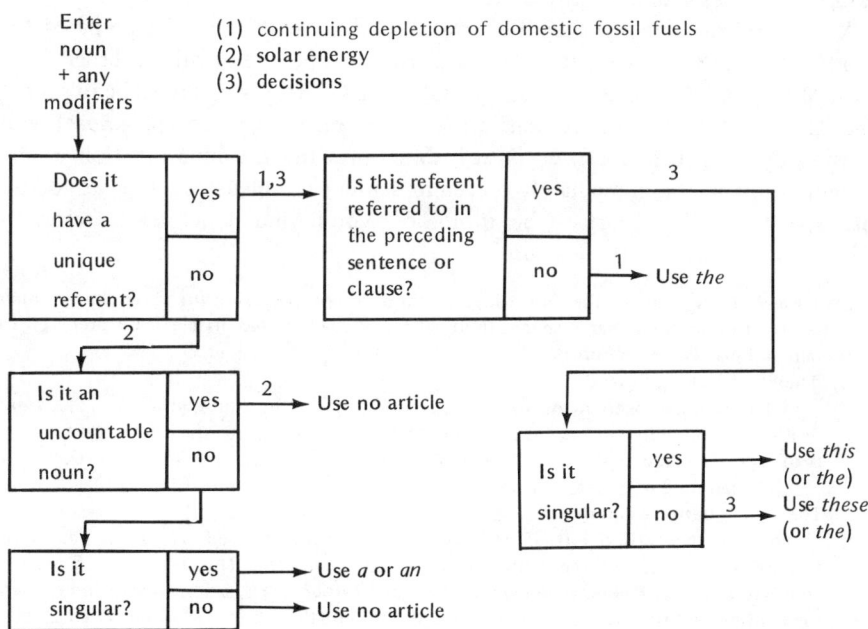

FIGURE 13-4. USE OF FLOW CHART WITH SAMPLE NOUN PHRASES

nonunique, referent.) Having answered the uniqueness question, we follow the "no" arrow to the next question: "Is this referent referred to in the preceding sentence or clause?" The answer here, obviously, is "no," since there is no sentence or clause preceding this noun phrase. We therefore arrive at the instruction, "Use *the*," which accords, as you can see, with the actual choice made by the ERDA authors. (See Figure 13-4.)

Next, consider the noun phrase *solar energy* in the last sentence. We begin, "Does it have a unique referent?" Here the answer is "no," because *solar energy* is being used here to refer to solar energy in general, not to any particular form of it. Second, "Is it an uncountable noun?" The word *energy* is being used here in its usual uncountable sense. Thus, we answer "yes" to this question and arrive at "Use no article." This result agrees with the choice made by the ERDA authors.

Finally, let's analyze the noun phrase *these decisions*. We begin, "Does it have a unique set of referents?" Since the decisions referred to here are presumably the same decisions referred to in the preceding sentence (i.e., *decisions made today concerning our remaining natural resources*), the answer to this question of unique reference is "yes." We therefore go on to the next question: "Is this set of referents referred to in the preceding sentence or clause?" Since the answer is obviously "yes," we arrive at, "Is it singular?" The plural form of the noun *decisions* gives us an obvious "no" answer to this question. Thus, we arrive at the instruction, "Use *these* (or *the*)." (*These* is usually preferred, probably for phonological or other stylistic reasons: Notice that the ERDA authors chose *these*, which does sound slightly better than *the*.)

A word of caution in using this flow chart: Be flexible, and be prepared for occasional exceptions. No natural language can be as precise or rule-governed as an artificial language like mathematics or FORTRAN. Exceptions are to be expected especially in the use of demonstratives, for example, *that* (pl. *those*) will occasionally substitute for *this (these)*; sometimes the previous mention of the referent is not in the immediately preceding sentence or clause. As long as you do not expect the flow chart to be foolproof, you'll find it helpful in resolving dilemmas about which article to use.

Exercise 9: Now look at the following text and determine, using the flow chart, which article to use for each blank space. (**Not all** blank spaces **need** articles.) Be prepared to explain and justify your choices.

A: The Steel-Making Process

After iron has been made in _____ blast furnace, the iron contains _____ good deal of carbon. This makes _____ iron break easily. So _____ steel, which is stronger than iron, is made from _____ iron. This occurs in _____ steel-making process. At _____ beginning of _____ process, most of _____ carbon is burnt out of _____ iron. Then _____ definite amount of _____ carbon is added.

To burn the carbon out of iron, different furnaces are used. The most important furnace is _____ furnace which converts iron to steel. This is _____ Bessemer converter. _____ Bessemer converter is shaped rather like _____ egg; it can be tilted for loading and unloading. It is loaded with molten (that is, melted) iron. Then _____ air is blown through _____ molten iron. The oxygen in _____ air combines with _____ carbon and some other materials in the iron. This makes the iron even hotter. It also makes _____ fiery blast of hot gases that spout from the converter.

When _____ carbon has been burnt out of _____ iron, a measured amount of carbon is added. This is _____ final step of _____ steel-making process. The iron has become steel (adapted from Brandwein 1972:77-8).

B: The Effect of Velocity on the Path of a Moving Body

Imagine a cannon on top of _____ highest mountain on the earth. It is firing _____ cannonballs horizontally. _____ first cannonball fired follows its path. As _____ cannonball moves, _____ gravity pulls it down, and it soon hits _____ ground. Now _____ velocity with which each succeeding cannonball is fired is increased. Thus, the cannonball goes farther each time. Cannonball 2 goes farther than cannonball 1 although each is being pulled by _____ gravity toward the earth all the time. _____ last cannonball is fired with such tremendous velocity that it goes completely around the earth. It returns to _____ mountaintop and continues around the earth again and again. _____ cannonball's inertia causes it to continue in motion indefinitely in orbit around _____ earth. In such a situation, we could consider _____ cannonball to be an artificial satellite, just like _____ weather satellites launched by _____ U.S. Weather Service (adapted from Brandwein 1975:209).

C: Standard ESSA Wind Observations

By far _____ most complete wind data available in _____ United States reside in _____ records of _____ U.S. Weather Bureau (ESSA) stations, which number more than 1,000. Many of _____ stations have been in operation for one or more decades, and ESSA has provided _____ excellent repository and processing center at Asheville, North Carolina, so that data can be retrieved and reprocessed readily.

_____ typical "surface" wind observation is usually obtained from _____ sluggish cup anemometer and vane assembly, mounted in _____ well-exposed location about 30 feet above _____ ground or _____ building structure. _____ vast majority of _____ sites are at airports, and urban observations are comparatively rare. _____ standard observation procedure is to note _____ indicated wind speed and direction for _____ brief period once each hour, and record them to $10°$ (formerly 16 compass points) and _____ nearest knot or mile per hour. Normally _____ contacting device is associated with _____ anemometer, from which one can obtain _____ time required for one mile of wind flow to pass _____ instrument. Observations called PIBALS or RABALS are taken at many of _____ stations, using either visual or electronic tracking of _____ rising balloon several times per day to determine _____ variation of wind with height. _____ data are processed to reflect _____ wind at 1,000-foot intervals above sea level (Singer and Smith 1970:23).

FINAL TESTS ON ARTICLES

Test A: Find and classify all the noun phrases. Be prepared to explain why each one does or does not have an article.

Manned Flight: A Success Story

On December 17, 1903, Orville and Wilbur Wright successfully achieved sustained flight in a power-driven aircraft. The first flight that day lasted only 12 seconds over a distance of 37 meters (120 feet). This is about the length of the Space Shuttle Orbiter. The fourth flight of the day (and the longest flight) traveled 260 meters (852 feet) in 59 seconds. The initial notification of this event to the world was a telegram to the Wrights' father.

Sixty-six years later, a man first stepped on the lunar surface. An estimated 500 million people throughout the world saw the event on television or listened to it on radio as it happened. This was surely an historic event.

Historic events are spectacular. The space program, however, has always been much more than a television spectacular. Today, space transportation is working in many ways for us all, and we have come to expect this.

A whole new era of transportation will come into being in the 1980s with the advent of the Space Shuttle. As a transportation system to Earth orbit, it will offer the workhorse capabilities of such earthbound carriers as trucks, ships, and airlines. It will be as vital to the nation's future in space as the more conventional carrier of today is to the country's economic life and well-being (adapted from Lyndon B. Johnson Space Center 1976:v-vi).

Test B: Insert articles (and *this* and *these*, if you wish) where appropriate. Be prepared to explain and justify your choices.

The Edsel: A Modern Anti-Success Story

Not since Ford's introduction of _____ Model A, 30 years earlier, had so much fanfare accompanied _____ arrival of _____ new car. When _____ same company formally unveiled _____ Edsel in September 1957, it had already invested _____ quarter of _____ billion dollars in development, production, _____ distribution, and promotion of the new venture. The amount, according to _____ account of the day, made _____ Edsel _____ costliest consumer product in _____ history. Ford counted on selling at least 2,000,000 Edsels _____ first year.

However, a little over two years and two months later, Ford had sold only about 100,000 Edsels, and _____ auto maker permanently discontinued production. _____ total loss to _____ company reached $350 million, according to some estimates. _____ loss was equivalent to that which would be incurred were Ford simply to give away 110,000 models of its comparably priced car, _____ Mercury.

_____ conventional wisdom has held that _____ rapid decline of the Edsel was due to the company's over-reliance on _____ results of public-opinion polls and motivational research. According to _____ view, _____ results were slavishly adhered to in _____ way the Edsel was promoted, in _____ way it was named, and also in the way _____ car was designed. It is further argued that such efforts are doomed to failure, for when _____ car-buying public perceives itself pursued in _____ overly calculated manner, it will invariably turn away in favor of _____ more spontaneously attentive competitor.

When conceived in _____ late 40s, _____ the idea that eventually led to the Edsel was one of putting on _____ market _____ new and completely different medium-priced car. It would be designed to keep _____ upwardly mobile owners of _____ Fords, intent on trading in their symbols of low-income earnings, in _____ Ford family.

_____ Edsel design was certainly different. A novel radiator grill, in _____ shape of _____ horse collar, was set vertically in _____ center of _____ conventionally low, wide front end. _____ unique rear end was marked by widespread horizontal wings. Another striking aspect, within _____ driving compartment, was a cluster of _____ automatic-transmission push buttons on the hub of _____ steering wheel. _____ push buttons controlled what was then _____ most powerful engine (345 horsepower) for _____ automobile at _____ time of its introduction.

The Edsel's failure has been attributed to _____ rather long time lag between conception and market introduction. Forced by _____ Korean War in 1950 to postpone the car's development, Ford came out with the Edsel precisely at _____ time hindsight reveals the car-buying public was moving decisively toward _____ smaller, less powerful compacts. Moreover, within two years, _____ stock market would nose-dive, marking _____ beginning of _____ 1958 recession, and _____ automobile industry would end its season with _____ second largest number of unsold cars in history (Christiansen 1977:94).

Test C: Insert the articles (and *this* and *these*, if you wish) where appropriate. Be prepared to explain and justify your choices.

The Role of Standard Reference Materials
in Environmental Engineering

_____ provisions of _____ Clean Air Act Amendments of 1970 and _____ Federal Water Pollution Control Act of 1972 include _____ requirements to limit _____ emissions of _____ pollutants from various points of _____ discharge such as _____ automobile tailpipe and _____wastewater effluent. It is fairly obvious that such measures are required if we are to maintain our air and water in _____sufficiently clean state for protection of _____public health and welfare. What is not obvious is _____exact extent to which it is necessary to limit _____ discharges in order to reach _____ sufficient purity. As long as _____ costs rise exponentially with degree of _____ purification, we may expect only enough public pressure to control discharges for adequate protection and no more. _____economic fact underlines the critical necessity for _____development of _____valid environmental measurement system.

There are two fundamental elements to such _____system. First, we must establish as accurately as possible _____ dose-response relationships so that _____ most proper ambient air and water quality standards can be set. Secondly, we must establish _____ relationship between _____ pollutant concentrations at _____ point of discharge and at _____ point of human contact. Basic to _____ measurement system are requirements that:

(1) _____health effect can be measured with requisite accuracy.
(2) _____accurate model is available.
(3) _____ pollutant measurements at ambient and source concentrations are internally consistent.

_____ part of _____ measurement system with which we at _____ National Bureau of Standards have been primarily concerned is _____ third of these. In the discussion that follows, it is presumed that _____other two requirements are met (EPA 1976:58).

Notes

1. "The 235,509 foreign students in the United States were from more than 175 countries. More than half of the students, 55.6%, came from Asia, and nearly one-third, 31.2%, were from the member nations of the Organization of Petroleum Exporting Countries (OPEC)." Open Doors 1977/78: "Report on Internation Education Exchange." *Newsletter of the Institute of International Education,* Nov. 1978, p. 2.

2. Although this treatment will not account for every single instance of article use, it approaches what we feel to be the limits of thoroughness in a pedagogical setting.

3. *Open Doors 1977/78,* p. 3.

DISTRIBUTION OF FOREIGN STUDENTS IN THE UNITED STATES
BY FIELDS OF STUDY

	1977/78	Percentage	1976/77	Percentage
Engineering	67,870	28.8	48,990	24.1
Business and Management	39,540	16.8	34,810	17.2
Natural and Life Sciences	23,360	9.9	22,980	11.3
Social Sciences	23,310	9.9	20,890	10.3
Education	12,470	5.3	12,030	5.9
Mathematics and Computer Science	12,300	5.2	9,610	4.7
Fine and Applied Arts	12,240	5.2	8,930	4.4
Humanities	11,810	5.0	14,370	7.1
Health Professions	10,820	4.6	11,840	5.8
Agriculture	8,660	3.7	6,490	3.2
Other	13,130	5.6	12,130	6.0
TOTAL	235,510	100.0%	203,070	100.0%

4. Any passage that is not noted was written by the authors to illustrate the particular point(s) under discussion. Note also that we have simplified several passages for pedagogical suitability without, hopefully, *over*simplifying. (But cf. H.G. Widdowson, *Explorations in Applied Linguistics,* London: Oxford Univ. Press (1979) chs. 14-15 for discussion of the dangers of simplification.)

5. The flow-chart approach was chosen because it illustrates, in visual form, the step-by-step procedure of article choice and because students in science and technology are generally accustomed to having such visual aids in their instructional materials.

6. *A* is used before words beginning with a consonant sound: *a meter, a unit, a handle,* etc.; *an* is used before words beginning with a vowel sound: *an atom, an experiment, an hour,* etc.

7. See discussion of Two-Way Nouns and Informal Usages for some exceptions.

8. *Information* deserves special attention from students speaking French, Italian, German, and Spanish, since the corresponding noun in these languages is countable.

9. The flow chart should be used as follows: Taking the example, "Magnetism is the force that causes iron filings to be attracted to a magnet," let us consider the noun (properly speaking, noun **phrase**) *magnetism.* We first ask of it, "Does it have a unique referent?" The answer to this question is "no" (since magnetism in a general, not particular, sense is meant here), so we follow the arrow from the "no" cell to the next question, "Is it an uncountable noun?" The answer here is "yes," and so we follow the "yes" cell to the final instruction, "Use no article." The other flow charts in this chapter are used in similar fashion.

10. Certain verbs, especially verbs of volition, can allow a "specific" interpretation for a following noun with an indefinite article. For example, the sentence, "John wants to marry a Norwegian," can be interpreted as meaning that John has a specific person in mind that he wants to marry, who is of Norwegian nationality (as opposed to an alternative reading according to which one of John's requirements for **any** future spouse is that she be of Norwegian nationality). This "specific" reading, focusing only on the nationality of John's intended spouse, should not be confused with cases of unique reference (as embodied, for example, in "John wants to marry **the** Norwegian"), where complete identity (of John's intended) is implied.

For further discussion of this distinction between specificity and **uniqueness,** cf. Lyons 1977:187-192.

11. A critical problem for both the student and the teacher is how to determine when there is or is not unique reference. In the subsequent discussion of The Definite Article, seven different ways are described in which a noun phrase may be said to have a unique referent, and many examples are offered; hopefully, the student will gain an intuitive understanding of the concept by working through these examples.

Ideally, of course, we would want to offer some heuristic to deal more directly with this problem. But the concept of unique reference is so much intertwined with culturally conditioned perceptions that no such single heuristic, in our view, is possible. This is especially true of cases of "implied uniqueness," where the writer's implication that there is only one referent in the universe-of-discourse will be accepted by the reader only to the extent that it conforms to that reader's experience in that particular culture. For example: "I took a stroll in the park yesterday and sat down for a while next to the person" sounds distinctly odd unless you have already identified which person you mean. On the other hand, "I took a stroll in the park yesterday and sat down for a while next to the bandstand (drinking fountain, softball field, etc.)" sounds all right because in our culture many parks contain only one bandstand (drinking fountain, softball field, etc.). Although this entire matter is a very important one and deserves detailed study and exposition, it is unfortunately beyond the scope of the present study.

12. Obviously, a writer must know what units of measure are customarily used if he or she wants to modify an uncountable noun by a counter. Providing such units of measure should pose no problem, however, since such units are part of the basic vocabulary in any field. A writer who knows enough about a subject to write about it certainly knows the field's basic units of measure.

13. It should be pointed out that ordinal adjectives do occasionally occur with the indefinite article: "There are several problems that need to be resolved before we can make progress on this project. One problem is that. . . . **A second problem** has to do with the

auxiliary generator. . . ." In such cases, we would argue, the adjective is not being used in a truly "ordinal" sense but rather in an "enumerative" one. In the example cited above, for instance, the author does not seem to be presenting the problem as a rank-ordering but rather as simply an unordered set.

These comments are entirely speculative, however, and further study of the matter is called for, particularly with regard to the rhetorical factors involved.

14. Of course, generic reference can also be achieved through the use of the indefinite article or the article-less plural:

"For simplicity and efficiency, a Hawker Siddeley Harrier is one of the best present-day VTOL aircraft."

"For simplicity and efficiency, Hawker Siddeley Harriers are one of the best present-day VTOL aircraft."

In such cases, the writer is not focusing attention directly on the class of Hawker Siddeley Harriers but rather on representative individuals; the genericity is achieved only indirectly, by implication.

In many cases these three kinds of generics are mutually substitutable. In many other cases, however, they are not. Distinguishing the proper conditions of usage for these three generics is an extremely complicated matter, not only for the ESL instructor but even for the theoretical linguist; to our knowledge, no adequate pedagogical treatment of this subject exists. (For some theoretical discussion, see Burton-Roberts 1976 and Herschensohn 1979.)

References

Brandwein, P. F. 1972. *Concepts in Science*. 3rd ed. Harcourt Brace Jovanovich.
———. 1975. *Matter: An Earth Science*. Harcourt Brace Jovanovich.
Burton-Roberts, N. 1976. "On the Generic Article." *Language,* 52:2. June 1976.
Christiansen, D. 1977. "The Edsel: A Modern Antisuccess Story." *IEEE Spectrum*, 14:11. Nov. 1977.
Conrath, B. J. 1975. "Dissipation of the Martian Dust Storm of 1971." *Significant Accomplishments in Science and Technology: Goddard Space Center, 1974*. NASA: Scientific and Technical Information Office.
EPA. 1976. *Health, Environmental Effects, and Control Technology of Energy Use*. U.S. Environmental Protection Agency. Report No. 600/7-76-002.
ERDA. 1977. *Solar Energy in America's Future: A Preliminary Assessment*. 2nd ed. Energy Research and Development Administration (Division of Solar Energy). Washington, D.C. March 1977.
Herschensohn, J. 1979. "On Generics." Cornell University Linguistics Department. Unpublished Manuscript.
Hewlett Packard. 1969. Hewlett Packard Present Counter, Model 5330 A/B, Repair Manual, No. 313-476-6400. Santa Clara: California.
Los Alamos (N.M.) Scientific Laboratory. Solar Energy Group. 1976. *Pacific Regional Solar Heating Handbook*. Univ. of Cal.
Lyndon B. Johnson Space Center. 1976. "A New Era in Space." *Space Shuttle*. Washington, D.C.: NASA: Scientific and Technical Information Office.
Lyons, J. 1977. *Semantics*. Cambridge Univ. Press.
Mennie, D. 1976. "A Try at Automated 'Zip.'" *IEEE Spectrum,* 13:10. Oct. 1976.
Morris, D. 1977. "Solar Cells Find their Niche in Everyday Life on Earth." *Smithsonian,* Oct. 1977.
NATO: Advisory Group for Aerospace Research and Development, Biodynamics Committee. 1967a. "The Dynamics of Rotation Applied to Centrifuges." *Principles of Biodynamics:*

As Applied to Manned Aerospace Flight, Section A, Prolonged Acceleration: Linear and Radial. Paris.

———. 1967b. "An Introduction to the Physics and Physiology of Acceleration." *Principles of Biodynamics: As Applied to Manned Aerospace Flight, Section A, Prolonged Acceleration: Linear and Radial.* Paris.

Olsen, L. A. 1977. "Computer-Assisted Writing Analysis: An Introduction." *Technical and Professional Communication: Teaching in the Two-Year College, Four-Year College, and the Professional School.* Professional Communication Press.

Open Doors 1977/78: "Report on Internation Education Exchange." *Newsletter of the Institute of International Education.* Nov. 1978.

Schmigge, T. J. 1975. "Measurement of Soil Moisture Utilizing the Diurnal Range of Surface Temperature." *Significant Accomplishments in Science and Technology: Goddard Space Center, 1974.* NASA: Scientific and Technical Information Office.

Sears, F. W. 1950. *Mechanics, Heat, and Sound.* Addison-Wesley.

Singer, I. A., and M. E. Smith. 1970. "The Adequacy of Existing Meteorological Data for Evaluating Structural Problems." *Wind Loads on Buildings and Structures.* U.S. Dept. of Commerce, National Bureau of Standards.

Spitzer, C. R. 1976. "Unlimbering Viking's Soops." *IEEE Spectrum,* 13:10. Oct. 1976.

Talay, T. A. 1975. *Introduction to the Aerodynamics of Flight.* NASA-SP-367.

Teegarden, B. J. 1975. "Late Results from the Pioneer-11 Flyby." *Significant Accomplishments in Science and Technology: Goddard Space Center, 1974.* NASA: Scientific and Technical Information Office.

Torrero, E. A. 1976. "The Big Pan of 3-D Radar." *IEEE Spectrum* 13:10. Oct. 1976.

Trombka, J. I. 1975. "A Gamma-Ray Burst from Apollo-16." *Significant Accomplishments in Science and Technology: Goddard Space Center, 1974.* NASA: Scientific and Technical Information Office.

Widdowson, H. G. 1979. *Explorations in Applied Linguistics.* Oxford Univ. Press.

Wolff, M. F. 1976. "The Navy's Big Dish." *IEEE Spectrum,* 13:10. Oct. 1976.

Editorial Comments

Fitting in with Trimble's practical interest in the teaching of EST grammar/rhetoric, Huckin and Olsen here present some new suggestions for the teaching of the English article. This chapter is an excellent example of "goal-oriented" (see Widdowson, chap. 1) textual/grammatical analysis. Interestingly, their analysis attempts to present grammar in a textualization sense; that is, their generalizations are supported by reference to samples of actual EST texts (in this case introductory science and technology textbooks, as well as some popular-science genre material) in a functional framework.

A key contribution of this chapter is the clear, well-documented discussion of the factors that condition article choice in EST discourse—a discussion that should be of particular interest to any teacher who has tried to untangle this knot (and who hasn't?) for a class of foreign learners, especially advanced learners. The flow diagram (Figure 13-3) presented here should prove helpful in classroom use.

We believe that Huckin and Olsen present here some uses of English articles that may not have been recorded before: some informal uses of the article with noncount nouns, the uses of the definite and indefinite article when a postmodifier occurs either within or outside the same noun phrase, and implied uniqueness rules.

Finally Huckin and Olsen present in this chapter a rather extended series of sample exercises, which have been classroom-tested, in the rhetorical patterning of the English article. (One may write to the authors for a description of their EST program that is ongoing in an American engineering college, a situation very similar to Trimble's in Seattle. See Affiliations page for address.)

L.S.
E.T.

Interpretation of "Information Transfer"

14

from a Diagram

Ljerka Bartolić

Technical information may be conveyed in two ways, either by a text (the verbal form of information) or by different kinds of graphic presentation (the nonverbal form of information) [see e.g., Widdowson 1978]. Both of these forms are usually accompanied by mathematical symbols used in the calculation of the technical problems to be solved. Obviously, which of these two forms will be used depends largely on the kind of information to be conveyed.

This chapter will deal only with diagrammatic information as used in mechanical engineering English. The interpretation of diagrams (see Bartolić 1975) presents difficulties to students of English when explaining diagrams in a foreign language. Diagrams are used either at the level of obtaining information, in other words in "reading" diagrams, or they may serve as a basis for some discussion of an engineering problem. In the former case the student interprets the diagram for himself or herself and does that in his or her mother tongue, while in the latter case the student must be provided with the knowledge of technical terminology and language mechanisms that will enable him or her to explain the technical data given by a diagram. We are interested in the second case and also in the problem of the process of interpreting the diagram from the language point of view. So our starting point may be formulated in terms of two questions: What volume of information does the reader and interpreter of the diagram obtain, and at what level, and which language items and structures are of interest in the process of information transfer from the diagram (the nonverbal form) to a verbal form, which in turn may be either in the form of oral or written reproduction?

For the purpose of exemplifying our proposed teaching procedure we shall take a simplified schematic heat flow diagram of a steam power plant, a diagram that is commonly found in engineering practice.

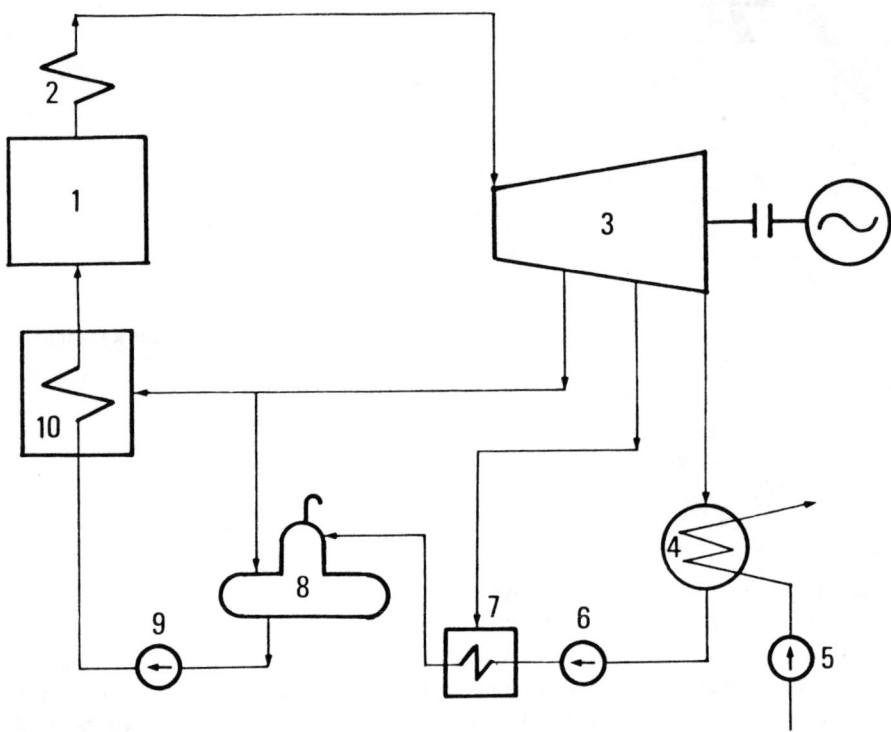

1 steam generator
2 superheater
3 steam turbine (turbogenerator)
4 condenser
5 circulating pump

6 condensate pump
7 low-pressure heater
8 deaerator
9 feed water pump
10 high-pressure heater

Editor's note: This diagram was designed by the author and drawn by a student in her department. This is "such a basic diagram that it can be found in any standard book dealing with heat power plants" (Bartolić, personal communication).

FIGURE 14-1. HEAT FLOW DIAGRAM

When he or she first glances at it, we hypothesize that the reader of the diagram makes mental statements that may be formulated approximately as:

The identification of symbols in the diagram;
Symbol—technical term correspondence;

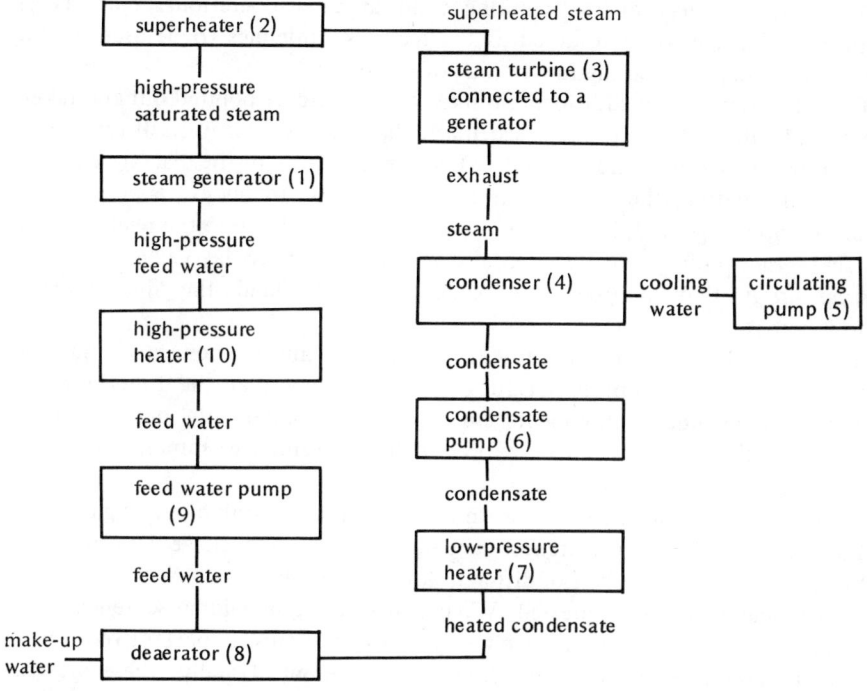

Editor's Note: This diagram was created by the author.

FIGURE 14-2.   LANGUAGE BLOCK DIAGRAM

The identification of components in the system and their individual functions;
The identification of the working fluid and the characteristic features of its state;
The identification of the flow of the working fluid and its direction;
The visualization of the functioning of the system (a synthesis).

These statements should not be taken as individual or separate statements but in their globality—the process of obtaining information from the diagram being similar to that conveyed by the verbal text.

For the purpose of teaching, the foregoing may be represented by a language block diagram that has been derived in part from the schematic heat flow diagram and in part from information an experienced reader brings to this diagram. The sequence of components in the language block diagram follows in general the flow of the working fluid in the schematic diagram. This diagram is in fact a combination of two media of presentation, the nonverbal and the verbal form of information.

By analyzing the language block diagram in greater detail, the reader in fact manipulates the technical terms that are required; that is, the names of the given components in the system and of those language items that will express the characteristic features of the working fluid at each operational part. These language items may be considered as the reader's guidelines to be used for the purpose of understanding the functioning of the system.

There is, however, an additional problem that should be pointed out and taken into consideration. Namely, every schematic diagram includes in itself two forms of information: explicit and implicit. While the geometry of the diagram conveys explicit information, the implicit information appears to involve a prerequisite technical knowledge that, in my view, should be mastered before the reader is able to tackle the problem of reading a diagram. This may be called *technical presupposition* that permits the reader to understand the diagrammatic information.

As far as language is concerned, implied technical knowledge may be transferred to the student in teaching in such a way that the functions and operations of included components are expressed in statements, definitions, or descriptions; these must again be expressed in full sentences suitable for use in oral or written reproduction.

In our case, the student has to learn to use technical terminology as guidelines and incorporate them into sentences. The most important language items required in this process are verb forms of different kinds, by means of which the functions of operational parts are expressed. When constructing individual sentences, it is advisable to formulate them in such a way that all the most important verb forms commonly appearing in technical English are present. Usually, these are the present simple in the active or passive voice, participles, gerunds, and infinitives. To illustrate this, consider the following sentences, which again follow the sequence of operations given in Figures 14-1 and 14-2.

1. The steam generator *converts* high-pressure feed water to steam (i.e., it *produces* steam).
2. The function of the superheater is *to increase* the temperature level (i.e., it *produces superheated* steam).
3. The steam turbine *uses* the energy of steam (i.e., heat energy) for the purpose of *converting* it to mechanical work. Thus the heat energy *is converted* to mechanical energy, which in turn *is converted* to electrical energy in the generator.
4. The condenser *takes* the exhaust steam from the turbine. The condenser is *to maintain* a low temperature and pressure of the exhaust steam, thus *increasing* the amount of work that may *be obtained* per pound of steam. This *is obtained* by *cooling* the steam and *converting* it to the condensate.
5. The circulating pump *supplies* the condenser with *cooling* water for the purpose of *cooling* the exhaust steam.
6. The condensate pump *increases* the pressure of the condensate and *forces* it into the low-pressure heater.
7. The function of the low-pressure heater is *to heat* the condensate.

8. The deaerator *receives* the condensate *discharged* from the condenser. Its function is *to deaerate* the condensate and *make* it suitable for *feeding* to the steam generator.
   A certain quantity of water (the make-up water) *is added* to the deaerator for *making up* for the losses *existing* in the system. In this way the deaerated water *becomes* suitable for *feeding* the boiler.
9. The *deaerated* feed water then *flows* to the feed water pump, which *increases* the pressure at its outlet.
10. The high-pressure feed water *is* then *heated* in the heater before *being forced* into the steam generator.
11. The whole system *is connected* by water pipes and steam lines, which *ensure* the proper circulation of the working fluid in the system of the steam power plant.

In the following stage of teaching, paragraph building from the given sentences may be applied if written reproduction is to be practiced. The sentences should be connected in a "logical" way, which here means that the logic of the paragraph is based upon the sequence of the operations given by the diagram. In doing this, a close control of logical coherence and language cohesion should be maintained. In addition, it is proposed that the verb forms should be changed if possible. This can be done in our case, since the sequence given in the diagram can be taken as a time sequence expressing the anteriority or posteriority of the given events. For this purpose the perfect tense, active or passive, and the future tense, active or passive, may be introduced.

As an approximate guide, the following paragraphs are offered:

> The steam generator produces high-pressure saturated steam, which *will be superheated* in the superheater to the rated level. The superheated steam is used in the steam turbine, which converts it to the required mechanical work. Thus the heat energy is converted to mechanical energy, which in turn is converted to electrical energy in the generator.
> The exhaust steam then flows to the condenser where it is cooled and converted to the condensate. The condensate pump forces the condensate into the low-pressure heater. The heated condensate *will be deaerated* in the deaerator. In addition, make-up water *has* also *been added* and supplied to the deaerator for making up for the losses existing in the system. In this way the deaerated water becomes suitable for feeding the boiler
> The feed water pump increases the pressure of the feed water and forces it into the high-pressure heater before being forced into the steam generator.
> The whole system is connected by steam lines and water pipes, which ensure the proper circulation of the working fluid in the system of the steam power plant.

Finally, the proposed procedure may be further developed by including a summary of the information given by the diagram. The summary reduces the volume of information and involves only the condensed explicit information conveyed by the diagram. Again, as an approximate guide:

> The diagram shows the operational parts included in a steam power plant system as well as the functional interrelationship of these parts. The steam power plant is used for the purpose of generating electrical energy and is arranged as a closed flow of the working fluid in which the regenerative heating of the feed water is provided.

References

Bartolić, L. 1975. "Technical English: a Method of Teaching the Cause-Effect Relation as Applied to a Diagram." *English Language Teaching Journal* 29. 156-163.

Widdowson, H. G. 1978. *Teaching Language as Communication.* Oxford Univ. Press.

Editorial Comments

Bartolić here treats the process of "information transfer" (term coined by Widdowson) in application to a practical problem and shows in very specific terms how teaching materials might be developed. This is obviously an important area of ESP work, since, as Trimble has pointed out, some genres of EST writing (e.g., technical manuals) have as much as 50% of their pages devoted to nonprose diagrams and other illustrations. Intuitively, it seems to us that the student in this case must learn how to manipulate the often crucial information that occurs in the material. (This process is linked to grammar and rhetoric by Swales [chap. 4].)

Since the problem of "translating" the information presented in diagrams into acceptable English rhetoric in a scientific or technical report appears to be a very real need for many students of ESP, the kind of practical study for teachers presented here is truly needed. Trimble has worked extensively on EST problems in Yugoslavia and the focus here on the rhetorical problems of information ordering and tense choice, we believe, shows his influence.

Bartolić brings the background of many years teaching in one highly specialized area of ESP work—engineering and naval architecture—to bear on this study, and this background is reflected in the material presented. Unfortunately, it is rare in our experience to find an ESP person with a deep background in the subject specialism under discussion. Many people (e.g., Crofts, chap. 11) have noted difficulties when we do not understand the subject matter of our students' specialism. We hope our field begins to attract more people like Bartolić, people who have deep experience with a subject specialism, as well as insights into the difficulties of teaching in an ESP context.

We particularly like the linking up of units in a mechanical process with language teaching units (called here *language blocks*). The next step in this research might be a "special-purpose acquisition study" to see what second-language acquisition processes might be operating here.

L.S.
E.T.

15 Needs Assessment in English for Specific Purposes: The Case Study

Maxine F. Schmidt

In designing curriculum materials for ESP, assessing the non-native speaker's needs is a first step. If we do not take this as our point of departure we run the risk as Candlin (1978) puts it, "of producing a course for an audience which does not exist, or if it did, for an audience who would not require this type of course" Candlin 1978:203-4). Drobnic (1978) also discusses this problem. Thus, needs assessment is recognized as the desirable starting point. This chapter proposes that the case study can serve as an important preliminary step in the process of ESP curriculum design. It is itself a case study of the needs in lecture comprehension and essay test writing for a non-native speaker of English studying business administration in an American university.

METHODS OF NEEDS OF ASSESSMENT

There are various methods the curriculum developer can begin with to assess the needs of a given population of students. One way is to rely on past research. To design ESP curriculum materials in listening comprehension for Saudi Arabian engineering students, Candlin and Murphy (1976) begin by reviewing two surveys of problems in listening comprehension for foreign students studying in British universities. Candlin and Murphy cite Morrison (1974) and Holes (1972) as identifying the lecture as a language context of major difficulty for foreign students. Morrison rank-orders the linguistic features that cause difficulty as: (1) referentials, (2) lexis, (3) phonology. Holes finds two major obstacles to student comprehension: (1) lack of awareness about culture-bound information and (2) inability to interpret the speaker's intentions.

Candlin and Murphy take the findings of Morrison and Holes on the needs of foreign students in Britain to be a good approximation of the communicative needs of engineering students in Saudi Arabia on the basis of the fact that the lecture will be an important mode of instruction in their university study. On the other hand, Candlin and Murphy state that the level of English of the Saudi Arabian students is much below that of the students in the Morrison and Holes studies. Therefore, it is not clear that materials in lecture comprehension based on needs assessment done for foreign students in Britain will also conform to the immediate needs of Saudi Arabian students. Past research, then, that has been done on a population that is different from the one for whom one is designing curriculum materials seems to be a general way of assessing needs but relies on the curriculum developer's intuitions about the similarity of needs between two different student populations.

A second way to assess needs is through direct research on a given population. Two specific techniques that may be used in this case are the questionnaire and the proficiency test. Morrison uses the questionnaire as a technique in assessing which language situations are most important for students and then in establishing what their order of difficulty is. The questionnaire is advantageous in that it may be administered to a large group of students. It also relies totally on the intuitions of the student about his or her own needs. This, however, is not always enlightening to the curriculum developer in terms of isolating certain communicative features that are primary causes of difficulty, since the student is not always able to identify his or her troubles in terms of linguistic forms or functions. Both Morrison and Holes, therefore, also use tests to assess a student's ability to deal with certain features of the communicative setting. Morrison uses both the test and questionnaire in determining the linguistic features that cause difficulty, and Holes uses a listening comprehension test to assess students' ability to process lecture content and lexical items. The specific design of these tests, however, is not described in Candlin and Murphy's summary.

Mackay (chap. 10) also uses the questionnaire in assessing student needs for developing a reading curriculum for English for Specific Purposes. He finds the questionnaire to have disadvantages, such as a low rate of return and the risk of student misinterpretation of the questions. The oral interview, another method of needs assessment, is thus subsequently added by Mackay as it allows for personal explanation of questions. The interview is found to be a more reliable albeit more time-consuming method than the questionnaire.

The case study, in contrast with the methods mentioned above, is a unique tool for the curriculum developer in assessing the language needs of a non-native speaker in a particular setting. The advantages of this method over the others are the possibility of an in-depth study over a period of time, the opportunity to appeal to the student's intuitions about his or her difficulties and needs in more detail than in the oral interview or questionnaire, and the occasion for the curriculum developer to do direct observation of the student in the classroom and study situation to gain insight into the student's own methods of learning. That is, most importantly, the case study provides the curriculum developer with information he or she cannot obtain through other methods about how the learner goes about acquiring knowledge in the student's own field of specialization (or perhaps not acquiring that knowledge). Widdowson makes the important distinction between a "goal-oriented" definition of needs and a "process-oriented" definition of needs (chap. 1). A goal-oriented approach focuses on describing the special language that a learner needs to know. That description in turn defines the content of the language course. A process-oriented approach focuses instead on describing the way a learner appears to acquire knowledge and allows that process to define course content. Widdowson argues that the goal-oriented approach is ineffective in that it attempts to implant language as an end product in the learner rather than activating strategies in the learner that allow him or her to acquire that language. It seems then that needs assessment based solely on the questionnaire or test is useful for the goal-oriented definition of needs since they help to isolate problematic language contexts and linguistic forms within those contexts.

On the other hand, the case study as a means of needs assessment not only identifies difficult linguistic features but provides information to support a process-oriented definition of needs as well. The case study, in its careful observation of the learner's strategies for processing classroom lectures, reviewing notes, and taking exams provides the curriculum developer with knowledge about both the "means of learning" and the "language abilities" the learner must have to gain knowledge in his or her field. The case study, therefore, makes a unique contribution to the area of needs assessment in English for specific purposes.

The disadvantages of the case study are, of course, the time it takes to do such a study and its obvious lack of generalizability. A very critical problem involves the risk of defining one individual's problem *only*, rather than those we can expect any given non-native speaker to have in that particular situation. However, on the basis of the observations made through the case study it is possible to speculate about what student needs are for a given situation and what kinds of language strategies students may need to have access to a particular body of knowledge. From these speculative generalizations it is also possible to design other tools of needs assessment such as the questionnaire, question battery, and skills test that will test our generalizations for a larger population.

Procedure

The following account will suggest a methodology and illustrate the kinds of information a case study might generate as a method of needs assessment. The procedure followed was to select one non-native speaker essentially beginning her study in business administration. Yvonne (Y) was an advanced ESL student who had studied for one year in an American high school, had taken several ESL courses in the United States, and had also studied in a commercial school in her own country where she took such courses as typing, shorthand, and accounting, all in English.

I attended one upper-division transportation class (her first transportation class) with her for three weeks. The class dealt primarily with the legal aspects of transportation and models for inventory planning. During the time I attended the class I took notes and observed her. I also conducted study sessions with her to compare our note-taking techniques and to question her on her understanding of the notes. I also obtained her notes for the classes prior to my three weeks of observation. Since the class made little use of a text, it was an excellent course to take as an example, since it depended heavily on her ability to get the main points from the lecture to understand the course content.

Several interviews with the instructor of the course were also conducted to question him on his expectations of the students, his perception of Y's problems, and his testing and grading techniques. He also provided me with a key for the midterm essay exam he had given that I was able to use to analyze Y's test-taking strategies. I did this by going over her midterm exam with her, collecting data on her intuitions about her difficulties with the test. In addition, I was able to check her notes on that information to see how she had perceived it originally.

Data and Analysis

The observations I made can be divided into two parts: those pertaining to the lectures and note-taking and those pertaining to the midterm essay exam. In the following sections I will discuss the language needs that emerged.

Lectures

First of all, the lectures for this class were of two types, which I will call the *prose type* and the *mathematical-model type*. The prose type essentially uses the verbal message as its principle means of conveying information and does not lend itself to a concise graphic or mathematical representation that can easily be placed on the board. This type of lecture predominated in the first half of this course and was very difficult for the student. This type seems to be more difficult for the non-native speaker because it relies heavily on his or her ability to understand the stream of speech, condense it, and record the "kernel" or main ideas in the notes. It often is less conducive to blackboard support information than the mathematical-model type lecture and relies heavily on the listener's language abilities to be effective as a teaching tool. The mathematical-model type, on the other hand, appears to rely less heavily on the hearer's language abilities since it has a graphic or quantitative representation that is put on the board in most cases and frequently can be understood by students with limited English abilities. The students are able to copy the representation directly into their notes without worrying about the necessity to condense information since the model has already done so for them. This lecture type would then seem to be less difficult for the non-native speaker with limited English. Y felt that this was the case for her. This was the type of lecture given during the three weeks I attended the class. However, I observed that even though this type of lecture condenses kernel information through the use of a mathematical model, the connecting prose that serves to explain the entire concept of the model is still extremely important. Though a student may succeed in taking down all the information on the board in the way of charts, graphs, formulas, and such, he or she may fail to understand the connecting prose. This hidden learning problem is not likely to be revealed through the use of a questionnaire, test, or interview unless it is specifically designed with this purpose in mind. The case study, then, is a more effective tool in bringing such a problem to light.

Thus, even though a student may have the essential points of the mathematical-model lecture, I hypothesize that he or she will not have an overall picture unless the student has understood the connecting prose. Along these lines I categorize Y's difficulties as follows:

Category 1: Misses the point; misses an entire concept.
Category 2: Understands the concept but cannot record it in English.
Category 3: Misses vocabulary the instructor does not define because he or she assumes it to be part of the student's basic knowledge.
Category 4: Time pressure.

These topics are dealt with below.

Missing the Point. The explanation for category 1 above seems to involve a complex interaction of vocabulary problems, phonology problems, and problems with implicit cues. An example of this is the interpretation of Table 15-1, which is taken from the class notes:

Y seems to understand everything about this table except for the relationship between the first two columns. What she does not understand is that the MV value stands for the whole range of volumes between itself and the next highest volume in the column; that is, MV of 60 cwt means any volume from 60 to 179 cwt. This is partly due to phonological problems; the words *value* and *volume* are hard for her to distinguish. Their phonetic representations [vælju] and [valjum] respectively are very close. In this case she heard "minimum value" and not "minimum volume" and was confused. In addition, the interpretation of this relationship is implicit in the word *minimum* for a native speaker, who understands that minimum volume in this context implies a range of volumes without being explicitly told. The lecturer did not give a definition of this but rather proceeded to explain the table taking the understanding of the term *minimum volume* as a given. It is also implicit (at least for me as a native speaker) that a transportation "rate" has a particular relationship to a shipment volume that can be expressed in terms of one another; that is, the volume determines the rate, so that as volume increases, rates go down. All this is implicit in reading this table and knowing why things are lined up the way they are. For that reason, though Y may understand the actual arithmetic involved in the calculations, she

TABLE 15-1.   STUDENT NOTES:
              TRANSPORTATION TABLE A

TR = transportation rate		TC = total cost	
TL = truck load		IZ = indifferent zone	
CR = commodity rate		PP = purchase price	
MV = minimum volume		D = discount	

	TR	MV	TC	IZ
<TL	$26/cwt	none	— —	— —
TL	$20/cwt	60 cwt	$1200	46-60
CR	$18/cwt	180 cwt	$3240	162-180
	PP			
D_2	$170/cwt	200 cwt	$34,000	148-200

Source: Student's notebook (checked with teacher)

does not always seem to be aware of the underlying relationships between the factors. This is not to say that she is not capable of deriving these relationships by carefully doing the problems and studying the tables; she probably is. It is that this information is not implicitly at her finger tips the way it appears to be for the native speaker. She will have to spend much more time to get it this way. And in many cases she simply resorts to memorization of the notes as a study technique. This puts her at a grave disadvantage on the essay exam that tests her knowledge of and ability to express relationships.

Another example of category 1 difficulties is represented in the notes in Table 15-2:

Part of the implicit information is that the left column is different from the right column, and the right column is *not* a detailed breakdown of the column on the left (the mistaken interpretation of Y). This relationship of separate columns that do not subsume one another in any way is implied by the words *compared with* and by the physical layout of the table. Though I would need more data to confirm it, I propose that in a table used in a lecture, subordinate details are not lined up in one column next to a larger generalization but are placed under the generalization so as to imply the subordinate relationship unless some special convention (e.g., "wavy line") is used. In this case Y misunderstood the relationship, apparently due to her ignorance of the implicit relationships between the parts. Though she understands what each of the parts is in itself, she does not understand the whole concept that ties them together[1].

It is important to note that a mere examination of the subject's notes does not reveal this problem since Y's notes are seemingly complete, in fact much more complete than my own. All the important information is there. What is not there is the invisible thread that links each of the parts together in the mind of the student. This perhaps should serve as a caveat to those of us who teach the techniques of note-taking to our students. After they have mastered the grammar

TABLE 15-2. STUDENT NOTES: TRANSPORTATION TABLE B

Transportation is a subset of logistics in business compared with staff/service/support. Logistics is defined as one of the three line functional areas.

Line Functional Areas	Staff/Service/Support Areas
1. production	1. legal department
2. marketing	2. credit "
3. logistics	3. accounting
	4. finance

Source: Student's notebook (checked with teacher)

of the lecture and can recognize the varying "moves"[2] and write it all down, will they understand more than the mechanics of taking the information down in the proper form? Will they understand what the form itself implies? These are important things to keep in mind for the curriculum developer.

Another consideration is that this type of problem is not one that emerges through the use of the questionnaire or interview that relies on a student's intuitions about his or her own learning difficulties. A student is not likely to be aware of this difficulty because he or she "apparently" has all the information in the notes. Therefore, the student thinks he or she understands. The case study is much more effective in that it allows the observer to burrow in and ask the type of question that reveals such a problem. One of the implications of such a case study is that it can aid in the design of a skills-text that conceivably could test for such implicit knowledge.

Difficulty in recording "understood" information. The second type of difficulty (category 2) the subject had with the mathematical-model lecture, was in writing down a new concept in unfamiliar English terms. Faced with the double task of processing both a new idea and new language, Y often resorts to translation into her native language to get the new idea down in her notes. An illustration of this has to do with the concept of the "indifferent zone" as represented in Table 15-1. In Table 15-1 there are three indifferent zones. If we were to plot these zones on a line we would have the representation shown in Figure 15-1.

IZ_2 "lies within" IZ_3. This concept is a key one for the calculations involved in this model. However, both the concept and the vocabulary to express it, namely *lies within*, are new to Y. Therefore, the explanation is in her native

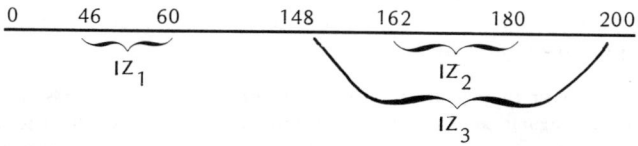

FIGURE 15-1.

language in her notes. While she can draw a diagram similar to figure 15-1 to indicate her understanding, she cannot express it well in English. There is an obvious implication here for difficulty in an essay exam where one is frequently asked to explain a concept in English.

Vocabulary. Thirdly, there is the obvious problem of vocabulary that is particular to the field (category 3). At times it seems that Y misses such vocabulary because the lecturer assumes this to be part of the background knowledge of the students. "Opportunity cost" and "rate break" are cases in point. The lecturer does not define these terms, since they are presented in basic business courses that he assumes his students to have had. Y was not familiar with these terms, however. This is not a problem particular to the non-native speaker. It is easy to see how the native speaker could find himself or herself in the same situation. However, the difference may lie in the native's willingness to question the lecturer on it. The non-native speaker often lets a term go unexplained. This problem, of course, can feed into the first problem of missing an entire concept. If an unexplained term is used as the keystone of an explanation of a whole new concept, nothing may be understood by the listener. Teaching the student when he or she can ask questions is imperative in solving this problem.

Time Pressure. Finally, a constant problem, complicated by the difficulties discussed above, is time pressure in note-taking and study. Reviewing the notes becomes a laborious effort. For example, Y tapes every lecture, goes home and plays the tape while reading the day's notes, fills in the missing information, and then often copies over the entire set of notes and memorizes them. The disadvantages of time are obvious; however, the disadvantages of simply memorizing rather than being able to restate the ideas in one's own words are more grave.

Problems with the Essay Exam

Problems with lecture comprehension and note-taking directly affect the taking of essay exams. By comparing a test key for the midterm prepared by the instructor (and explained in detail to me by him) and Y's own test, I was able to distinguish two types of essay questions.[3] One type such as (a) below asks essentially for recall of notes:

(a) Describe the legal classifications of carriers. (10 points)

Since the answer for (a) is contained within the notes, language and all, this type of question does not pose any problem for Y.

The second type of question, as illustrated in (b), does in fact pose a problem for Y. It demands that the student be able to synthesize the information of the lectures and apply it to an individual case:

(b) Governments wish to regulate transportation carriers for many reasons. The normal objectives of regulation are usually to protect both the public and the carriers. However, in addition, regulations are often designed to achieve certain social and economic goals.

What specific goals can governments achieve by regulating transportation? Why does regulating *transportation*, rather than some other industry, help in achieving them? (10 points)

I compared Y's notes on this particular subject with the answer key and found her notes to be spread over three or four pages, half in English and half in her native language. They were embedded in a discussion of the pros and cons of regulating transportation from the first half of the quarter where the prose-type lecture predominated. In this instance memorization of the notes is made difficult by the inclusion of native language explanations. Answering the question on the test is made difficult because it does not ask the student to reproduce information in the same form as in the notes. Rather the student must not only recall the information but must also decide what is relevant and what is not for the particular case in point and apply that to answering the question. An essay question that calls for synthesis of information presented in a mathematical-model lecture would presumably cause similar difficulties. In this case a student would not only have to recall the information directly given but the implicational information as well. In addition, he or she would be required to be able to fill in the connecting prose as it applied to any graphic or quantitative representation in the notes. I have anecdotal evidence that this is the case. Engineering students have told me that they are confident if all they have are calculations on an exam, but once they are asked to explain the theory behind the mathematics they have extreme difficulty in finding the words to do so and organizing it in coherent form.[4] Essay questions of this type are made more difficult for both these engineering students and Y, because the time pressure does not allow the non-native speaker with language limitations to think out the phrasing of the answer.

Phrasing an answer is difficult for Y in particular because she seems to have great difficulty expressing generalizations in English. She will often substitute an example for a definition or generalization. Since some native speakers also have this problem, it is not clear whether this is an individual problem or a second-language learning problem. Nonetheless, language undoubtably plays a role, since to generalize Y must have the English vocabulary to do so. It is likely that she needs to learn both the form and specific vocabulary items in English that are used to express general relationships between terms such as: A *acts independently* of B; A is *dependent on* B; A is increasing *as opposed to* B, which is decreasing; and so on. This would ease the task of phrasing on the essay exam.

In summary, we can see how the problems experienced in lecture note-taking feed into the problems of taking exams. Y does not find interpreting the questions too difficult; she has trouble expressing herself. However, if she has missed whole concepts in the notes, missed vocabulary for expressing general concepts, and missed key terminology, it is easy to see how an essay exam could be devastating. In a course such as this where the instructor is most concerned in testing for knowledge of the concepts underlying the mathematical model, memorization will not aid the student on the exam. The overriding problems are then time and expressing oneself in English when a mere recapitulation of the notes is not enough.

SUMMARY OF NEEDS

In summary, I find the needs of my subject in both note-taking and exam-writing to be:

1. The need to understand the implicit relationships between terms in a table or outline presented in lectures.
2. The need to be able, in reviewing the notes, to understand the implicit relationship in order to fill in the connecting prose that ties the main parts of an entire concept together.
3. The need to be able to deal simultaneously with a new concept and new vocabulary presented in a lecture in order to express that concept in her notes in English.
4. The need to be able to express generalizations or definitions in an essay exam, instead of simply giving an example.
5. The need to be able to do all of the above under time pressure.

HOW THE CASE STUDY FITS INTO NEEDS ASSESSMENT OF THE GENERAL POPULATION

The above description of needs is a generalization about the needs of one non-native speaker studying business administration. In this sense it describes the difficulties for this student. Without further study it is impossible to determine if the findings of the case study are unique to the subject or if they express the general needs of the non-native speaker in this language context. Nonetheless, the case study has value as a point of reference from which to begin to design the questionnaire or interview question battery. It eliminates some of the danger of beginning from the preconceived ideas an educator or researcher has about what ought to be difficult in a particular language context. It avoids total reliance on the learner's intuitions about where difficulties lie and what their causes are. The case study also serves as input into the design of a test to measure skills in a particular area. In these ways the generalizations may be tested to see if the difficulties are indeed individual or more generalized in the non-native population.

Most importantly, however, the case study provides information to support a process-oriented definition of needs. It furnishes the curriculum developer with information he or she cannot obtain through other methods about how the learner attempts to gain knowledge in his field. Through observation over a period of time the curriculum developer not only has first-hand access to what the content of the learner's field of study is, but also the process through which that content is presented orally by the instructor and assimilated by the learner. Thus the case study makes a unique contribution to the area of needs assessment in English for special purposes.

Notes

1. This appears similar to the reading problems of non-native speakers of English discussed by Selinker, Todd Trimble, and Trimble (1976 and 1978). They hypothesize that students are often unable to understand the "total meaning" of a piece of discourse in English for Science and Technology (EST) though they may understand all the words. (For a criticism of this study, see Urquhart 1976, appendix 2.)

2. See Candlin and Murphy (1976) for an analysis of the organization of several engineering lectures.

3. These questions tested the students on information that was largely presented in the form of the prose-type lecture rather than the mathematical-model type. Nonetheless, I feel that there is an analogous distinction in exams on information supplied by the mathematical-model type of lecture. Formulas or replication of graphs and charts is analogous to the simple recall question (a) whereas a question that demands an explanation of theory is analogous to the synthesis question (b).

4. This may also be a problem for native speakers; a comparative study would be revealing.

References

Candlin, C. N., J. M. Kirkwood, and H. M. Moore. 1978. "Study Skills in English: Theoretical Issues and Practical Problems." *English for Specific Purposes*, ed. R. Mackay and A. Mountford. Longmans.

Candlin, C. N., and D. F. Murphy. 1976. *Engineering Discourse and Listening Comprehension*. Univ. of Lancaster.

Drobnic, K. 1978. "Mistakes and Modification in Course Design: An EST Case History." Todd Trimble, Trimble, and Drobnic.

Holes, C. 1972. "An Investigation into Some Aspects of the English Language Problems of Two Groups of Overseas Postgraduate Students at Birmingham University." Unpublished master's dissertation.

Mackay, R. 1979. "Developing a Reading Curriculum for ESP." (Chap. 10, this vol.)

Morrison, J. 1974. "An Investigation of Problems in Listening Comprehension Encountered by Overseas Students in the First Year of Postgraduate Studies in Science in the University of Newcastle upon Tyne." Unpublished master's dissertation.

Selinker, L., M. Todd Trimble, and L. Trimble. 1976. "Presuppositional Rhetorical Information in EST Discourse." *TESOL Quarterly* 10. 281-90.

———. 1978. "Rhetorical Function-Shifts in EST Discourse." *TESOL Quarterly* 12.311-20.

Todd Trimble, M., L. Trimble, and K. Drobnic, (Eds.) 1978. *English for Specific Purposes: Science and Technology*, English Language Institute: Oregon State Univ.

Urquhart, A. H. 1976. *KAAU English for Academic Purposes Project*. Edinburgh Univ.

Widdowson, H. G. 1979. "English for Specific Purposes: Criteria for Course Design." (Chap. 1, this vol.)

Editorial Comments

This chapter points to the value of the case study approach to "needs analysis", as providing new information about the process of lecture comprehension, and the problems that may arise in this process for foreign students. In this respect, as the author points out, this small study relates to what Widdowson (chap. 1) refers to as a "process-oriented" approach to ESP.

Further, this study is part of a new and increasing emphasis in ESP on *oral* English for Specific Purposes—an emphasis most strongly represented in the work of Candlin and colleagues at Lancaster (see Candlin, chap. 9).

One of the contributions here is the proposal of a new classification of types of lecture: the prose type and the math-model type, and the suggestion that these two types of lecture provide distinctly different kinds of learning problems for the non-native speaker of English in an academic context. In particular, Schmidt observes first-hand the problems of "information transfer" (see Bartolić, chap. 14) from figures written on the board to notes and, ultimately, to an essay exam.

Additionally, the data in this chapter that concerns "connecting prose" should question seriously the apparently widespread belief that in a class where math is heavily used, the learner needs "no language." The four categories of Y's difficulties (p. 203) are particularly interesting here; this discussion points the way to a range of studies that could be done in the untapped area of "the acquisition of special-purpose skills."

L.S.
E.T.

Operating on Learning Texts

16

A. H. Urquhart

In a famous paper first published in 1917, the American psychologist E. L. Thorndike remarks that, up to that time, "little attention has been paid to the dynamics whereby a series of words whose meanings are known singly produces knowledge of the meaning of a sentence or a text" (Thorndike 1972:20). He argues that "understanding a paragraph is like solving a problem in mathematics. It consists in selecting the right elements of the situation and putting them together in the right relations" (Thorndike 1972:27). This chapter[1] is concerned with the dynamics of reading introductory learning-texts in subjects such as biology and mechanics. Lacking Thorndike's confidence, I discuss, not "right elements" or "right relations" but rather how a reader may operate with statements and such to impose what appears to be a satisfactory intepretation on a text.

The chapter falls into three main parts. First I examine types of inferencing and related activities that are postulated as being involved in the comprehension of a number of short texts. Next, I suggest how some very general maxims relating to (a) knowledge of the world and (b) the interpretation of verbal messages may be helpful to the reader in arriving at a satisfactory interpretation. Finally, I attempt to show how a reader might make use of these mental operations and maxims when processing two very different learning-texts, one from the field of biology and the other from mechanics.

TYPES OF INFERENCE AND DEDUCTION

Carroll has observed that "presuppositions and/or covert semantic assumptions invade the structure of discourse at every conceivable level" (Carroll 1972:362), and adds, "it would be satisfying to break down and classify these presuppositions further, thus giving structure to the several operations of mind which have produced these structures in the first place." What follows is not intended as a serious attempt to provide such a classification. Rather, it is a very limited attempt to classify some types of inference and such that I have found in learning-texts.

Type 1: Contrastive Inferences

Certain elements in sentences have the effect of contrasting the sentence, or parts of it, with another sentence or sentence-part that either has occurred or will occur in the same context, or can be taken as assumed. For example, the utterance,

1. Only John turned up.

is likely to occur in contexts where it has either been stated or is assumed that at least one other person was expected. In speech, contrasts of this kind are generally marked by intonation. In reading, unless special orthographic devices such as underlining are employed, the reader must often guess that a contrast is intended. Consider the following text:

2. Children with mongolism are known to have an increased risk of developing leukaemia, a type of cancerous proliferation of white blood cells. The general relationship of chromosomal abnormalities and a tendency to develop cancer is also interesting.

The reader may take "general" here as contrastive and thus look for the assumed "particular" relationship. The obvious one in the context seems to be that between "children with mongolism" and "leukaemia." From this, he or she may deduce that such children exhibit chromosomal abnormalities.

In the texts discussed later in the chapter, most contrastive inferences are signaled by adverbs (directly, completely, etc.) or by adjectives.

Type 2: Relationship-Justifying Inferences

I use this clumsy term to describe inferential information readers may use to justify to themselves a relationship (e.g., that of cause and effect) that has been overly imposed on two or more statements by the writer. A good example is reported in Bransford and Johnson (Ms.). Subjects shown the sentence:

3. The floor was dirty because she used the mop.

later recalled that they had seen the sentence, "The mop was dirty." Consider the next example:

4. Because atmospheric haze worsens scatter, mountain sites are best for coronagraphs.

The causal relationship imposed on the two statements can reasonably be justified by the inference that there is *less* atmospheric haze on mountains.

Type 3: Relationship-Assigning Inferences

It frequently happens that two or more statements may be juxtaposed in the same context without any formal marking of relationships. The reader may still impose an inferred relationship on them. For example, consider the following text:

> 5. The cells of your body are alive. Cells need energy, and they take in food and oxygen supplied to them by the blood.

The reader may well infer the following information:

> 5a. Cells need energy *because* they are alive.
> 5b. Cells take in food and oxygen *because* they need energy.

Inference (5a) may itself then trigger off a third inference, in this case a relationship-justifying inference, namely:

> 5c. Cells get energy from food and oxygen.

I would not, however, like to appear to be arguing for the psychological reality of a unique sequential train of inferencing operations.

Type 4: Projective or Extrapolative Inferences

The previous two types concerned cases where inferences were required to handle two or more statements existing in the same text. The third type is liable to be triggered off independently, although the information contained may later be assumed in the text. Consider again example (4):

> 4. Because atmospheric haze worsens scatter, mountain sites are best for coronagraphs.

The second clause is likely, by itself, to justify the inference:

> 4b. Coronagraphs are (usually) built on mountains.

This information, however, is never asserted in the source text.

Type 5: Deductions

The following example of this type of operation is taken from Carroll (1972):

> 6. John isn't as tall as Mary, but he is taller than Tom.

From this, we can deduce that Mary is the tallest of the three.

Carroll classes this as an inference or related reasoning process. Leaving aside the question of the relationship between different forms of reasoning, I prefer to distinguish between *inferences,* on the one hand, and *deductions,* on the other. My reason is that "inferences," as discussed here, are regarded as hypotheses, often dependent on the knowledge of a particular reader, or on a particular physical juxtaposition of statements in a text. Deductions, on the other hand, appear to be carried out in terms of fixed rules or conventionally accepted premises. In (6) above, the rules are those of algebraic logic; that is:

$$X < Y$$
$$X > Z$$
$$\therefore Y > X > Z.$$

Type 5 includes all kinds of syllogisms, either fully or partly expressed in a text, for example:

All forms of life require energy.
Plants are a form of life.
∴ Plants require energy.

BACKGROUND "OPERATING PRINCIPLES"

Knowledge of the World

In asserting above that inferential information will be supplied to make an asserted relationship "reasonable" or to supply such a "reasonable" relationship, I glossed over what criteria were likely to be used by the reader in judging reasonableness. At this point, I think one must appeal to readers' knowledge of the world. The question that arises is just how detailed that knowledge must be before the reader can begin inferencing sensibly. That such an appeal may be made at very general levels can be illustrated by the following sentence:

7. Since the sun is too blinding to study with the naked eye, astronomers have learned to make special solar telescopes.

From this, we can form the following Type 2 inference:

7a. Solar telescopes are used to study the sun.

A question we might ask, however, is: Is there any background knowledge that is likely to make the above inference seem reasonable? Apart from lexical knowledge (that "astronomers" study objects like the sun and that "solar" = "relating to the sun"), it seems to me that the reader can fall back on the following very general principle or maxim relating to his or her knowledge of the world:

If people (scientists, etc.) are unable to perform a particular operation without the help of a tool or instrument, then they are highly likely to *construct* such a tool or instrument.

Thus in the case of (7) above, on being told that:

Since X cannot be done naturally, astronomers have learned to construct Y.

it becomes reasonable to infer that instrument Y is used to perform task X. Some very similar knowledge principle seems to lie behind the interpretation of example (4):

4. Since atmospheric haze worsens scatter, mountain sites are best for coronagraphs.

It was argued above that from this, the reader is likely to draw the projective inference that coronagraphs are usually built on mountains. It seems reasonable to claim that this inference is based on the following knowledge principle:

> Given a choice between something that appears suitable and something that does not, people can generally be assumed to choose the former. That is, it can be assumed for ordinary purposes that people will act rationally and will not willingly make things difficult for themselves.

The principles above relate to the reader's imposing on the text his or her knowledge of human behavior. Rather similar principles appear to underlie our interpretation of texts relating to nonhuman, and even nonanimate beings. Consider again example (5):

> 5. The cells of your body are alive. Cells need energy and they take in food and oxygen supplied to them by the blood.

As argued above, we are probably justified here in inferring causal relationships. The second causal inference, however, that cells take in food and oxygen because they need energy, seems to be just a particular instance of a much more general case whereby, given a juxtaposition of (a) a statement of *Need*, and (b) a statement of *Action*, we are likely to infer that the Action is taken to satisfy the Need. And this seems to rest on a knowledge principle that can be stated as follows:

> If X has a need, then, all other things being equal, it can be assumed that X will take steps to satisfy that need.

Whether it is possible to reduce the elements of world knowledge required to make sense of texts to a finite number of general maxims such as, "Need tends to lead to Action," I do not know. Certainly, rather similar maxims seem to underlie parts of very different texts. If such maxims are cross-cultural, then their significance for EFL reading courses may be considerable. Widdowson has drawn attention to the need to allow the learner to make use of his or her previous knowledge when attempting to learn a foreign language (Widdowson 1976). It is possible that if the learner's attention is directed towards such principles of background knowledge as have been discussed here, he or she will be more confident in attempting to make sense of texts whose syntax and lexis the learner does not fully understand.

Reading Principles

Readers may refer to their background knowledge to construct inferences or deductions. It is relevant to ask here what prompts them to behave in such a fashion. One answer to this is given by Freedle and Carroll, when they remark, "One (assumption) is that the message as a whole is to 'make sense' and exhibit a certain consistency . . . ." (Freedle and Carroll 1972:361). Readers, then, may impose relationships on statements in the text on the assumption that the juxtaposition of these statements in the same text can and should be made "reasonable" and "consistent." Another, closely related way of answering the question put above is to refer to Grice's 'Relevance Maxim' (Grice 1975) and hypothesize that in a text consisting of Statement A, Statement B, Statement C, and so forth, B and C will be taken as relevant in the context of A and interpreted accordingly. If we put this together with what was said above about inference formation, then we can describe the reading process as consisting *at times of* the following steps:

1. Assume that Statement E is relevant to/consistent with Statement D (and ultimately with Statements A, B and C).
2. If the relevance/consistency is not immediately obvious, assume a missing connection.
3. Appeal to background knowledge, either general principles or particular knowledge items.
4. Use this knowledge to construct an inference that appears to match the missing connection.

It may be necessary to refine Grice's Relevance Maxim at times, to account for the fact that readers seem to operate sometimes on the principle of imposing *maximum* relevance. For example, consider again example (2):

> 2. Children with mongolism are known to have an increased risk of developing leukaemia, a type of cancerous proliferation of white blood cells. The general relationship of chromosomal abnormalities and a tendency to develop cancer is also interesting.

It was suggested above that the reference in sentence 2 of a *general* relationship would have the effect of making the reader look for a previously mentioned *particular* relationship and hence to deduce that children with mongolism suffer from chromosomal deficiencies. This is not, however, the only possible interpretation. Another might be summarized as follows:

> X is interesting.
>
> Y is also interesting.

That is, the text exhibits consistency because both sentence 1 and sentence 2 describe interesting facts. The notion of "interesting" may satisfy some readers on some occasions, but it seems likely that many readers, at least, will not be content with such a level of relevance.

TEXT ANALYSIS

In this section, two longer texts are examined to show how the inferential operations and principles discussed above may be used in the interpretation of extended texts. The passages used, one from biology and the other from mechanics, are both fairly typical of learning-texts at the high-school level. Sentences are numbered for convenience of reference.

> Text 1: Photosynthesis.
>
> 1. The term photosynthesis literally means building up or assembly by light. 2. As used commonly, photosynthesis is the process by which plants synthesize organic

compounds from inorganic raw materials in the presence of sunlight. 3. All forms of life in this universe require energy for growth and maintenance. 4. Algae, higher plants and certain types of bacteria capture this energy directly from the solar radiation and utilize the sunlight for the synthesis of essential food supplies. 5. Animals cannot use sunlight directly as a source of energy. 6. They obtain the energy by eating plants or by eating other animals which have eaten plants. 7. Thus the ultimate source of metabolic energy in our planet is the sun and photosynthesis is essential for maintaining all forms of life on earth.

This text is remarkable for the number of lacunae in the information structure. For example, at no point is it stated that the "organic compounds" (S2) supply the plant with energy, that these compounds are the "food supplies" mentioned in (S4), or that the process by which plants capture and utilize energy is known as photosynthesis. All these items of information have to be constructed by the reader, on the basis of the information the text *does* contain.

It may therefore be instructive to examine *one possible path* by which a reader might arrive at such conclusions: We will imagine him or her proceeding sentence by sentence through the text.

(S1) The term photosynthesis literally means building up or assembly by light.
Comments: From this, the reader can construct the following contrastive inference:
Inference 1: There is another, nonliteral use of the term.

(S2) As used commonly, photosynthesis is the process by which plants synthesize organic compounds from inorganic raw materials in the presence of sunlight.
Comments: This confirms Inference 1. It is probably also confirmation of a very general assumption that this text is going to be "about Photosynthesis."

(S3) All forms of life in this universe require energy for growth and maintenance.
Comments: This looks like a new move, in an informal sense. "Energy has not been mentioned up to this point. The only obvious relationship between (S2) and (S3) lies in the reader's knowledge that plants are a form of life. From this, the reader can construct:
Deduction 1: Plants require energy for growth and maintenance.

(S4) Algae, higher plants and certain types of bacteria capture this energy directly from the solar radiation and utilize the sunlight for the synthesis of essential food supplies.
Comments: (S4) can be brought together with Deduction 1 by appeal to the general knowledge principle, "Need leads to Action," resulting in the following Type 3 inference:
Inference 2: Plants capture energy from the sun because they need it for growth and maintenance.
The reader may also form the next Type 3 inference:
Inference 3: The energy for growth and maintenance is derived from the food supplies.

(S5) Animals cannot use sunlight directly as a source of energy.
Comments: Together with (S3) this leads to:
Deduction 2: Animals require energy for growth and maintenance.
(S5) also gives rise to the next contrastive inference:
Inference 4: Animals use sunlight indirectly.

(S6) They obtain the energy by eating plants or by eating other animals which have eaten plants.
Comments: This can be taken as confirming Inference 4.

(S7a) Thus the ultimate source of metabolic energy in our planet is the sun . . . .
Comments: This would appear to follow from sentences 4, 5, and 6.

(S7b)... and photosynthesis is essential for maintaining all forms of life on earth.

Comments: Photosynthesis was last mentioned in (S2). The reader now has two related tasks: (a) He or she must find a justification for the presence of "thus," the scope of which seems to apply to (S7b) as well as to (S7a). More generally, (b) he or she must achieve overall consistency by making (S7b) relevant to what has gone before. This includes finding a connection between sentences 1, 2, and 7b, on the one hand, and the other sentences in the text on the other. One way in which these tasks might be achieved is as follows. By assuming that (S3) is directly relevant in the context of (S2), the reader may be led to forming the following Type 3 inference:

Inference 5: Plants synthesize organic compounds because they need energy.

From this, he or she can form the next, Type 2 inference:

Inference 6: Plants derive energy from organic compounds.

If this is put together with Inference 3, that is:

Inference 3: The energy for growth and maintenance is derived from the food supplies.

we are only a short step from *equating* the "essential food supplies" and the "organic compounds," and hence to deducing that the energy required by all forms of life is derived from organic compounds produced by means of photosynthesis.

Another way of arriving at the same conclusion would be for the reader to extract from the text and relate together the following two statements:

(i) Plants synthesize organic compounds in the presence of sunlight.
(ii) Plants synthesize essential food supplies by utilizing sunlight.

assuming that they were relevant to each other *because they referred to the same process.*[2] After this, it is quite simple to impose a consistency on the entire text by the same operations of inferencing and deducing described above.

The ways in which different readers arrive at interpretations of texts, the different standards of relevance they require, the effect on interpretation of the different knowledge structures they appeal to are all interesting areas of research. What is important at this point, however, is that the text discussed above seems to require inferential reasoning *before* the reader can discern the relevance to each other of its component parts.

Text 2: Vectors.

1. A vector quantity is one which can be completely defined only by stating the direction in which it acts, as well as its magnitude.   2. Many quantities can be defined simply in terms of magnitude.   3. For example, we may indicate the quantity of bolts in a storage bin as 150, their length as 40 mm, the angle of the thread as 60° and the temperature of the room as 20°C.   4. All these quantities, and many others, are known as scalar quantities.

5. In stating that the movement of an aeroplane is 500 km, we have omitted an important part of the definition by not stating the direction of the movement or displacement.   6. The full statement "500 km due east" includes both magnitude and direction.

7. We can state the size or magnitude of a force as 50 units, but, in order to define the force completely, we must know the direction in which it is acting.

8. Quantities which are defined by magnitude only are known as scalar quantities.

9. Quantities which are defined by magnitude and direction are known as vector quantities.

My procedure for discussing this text will be different from the discussion of the Photosynthesis text, in that I will concentrate initially on (S1), discussing inferences that can be drawn from it and some paraphrases of the sentence, before attempting to relate the other sentences of the text to these inferences and paraphrases.

> (S1) A vector quantity is one which can be completely defined only by stating the direction in which it acts, as well as its magnitude.

From this, the reader may draw the following contrastive inference:

> *Inference 1*: There are quantities which can be completely defined by stating their magnitude.

Comments: Inference 1 is actually the result of drawing two contrastive inferences, namely:

> *Inference 1a*: There are quantities which are not vector quantities.

This is taking "vector" as contrastive with an as yet unnamed term, which can also qualify "quantities." Apart from falling back on the Relevance Maxim (any qualifier should be relevant), we can justify drawing the inference on the grounds that (S1) is a definition and that typically definitions assert that (a) an item belongs to a larger class and (b) the item can be distinguished from other classes by X characteristics. In (S1), the larger class is "quantities," and the subsets "vector quantities" and Y quantities.

> *Inference 1b*: The characteristic that marks off "vector quantities" from Y quantities is the need to include *direction* in the description.

This inference is more debatable. I justify drawing it on the grounds (which some speakers of English may dispute) that in instances of the construction "A as well as B," in which both A and B are NP's, "B" tends to be, or is, "given." That is, I would claim that the difference between:

> 8. John and Mary came.

and

> 9. John came, as well as Mary.

is that (9) is appropriate in a context in which the information "Mary came" has already been given. More particularly, it may occur in a context in which the information "Mary came alone" has been asserted or assumed.

If this is correct, then the following sentence is not a complete paraphrase of (S1):

> (S1c) A vector quantity is one which can be completely defined only by stating its magnitude and the direction in which it acts.

Moreover, the following sentence should verge on being anomalous to anyone who knows about quantities in mechanics:

> (S1d) A vector quantity is one which can be completely defined only be stating its magnitude as well as the direction in which it acts.

The reader may also be able to draw from (S1) another contrastive inference, depending mainly on the contrastive nature of "completely":

Inference 2: A vector quantity can be defined by stating its magnitude alone, but the resulting definition will be incomplete.

Let us now examine the rest of the text, sentence by sentence.

(S2) Many quantities can be defined simply in terms of magnitude.

Comments: This is mainly a spelling out of Inference 1, with the added information that the so far unnamed quantities are numerous.

(S3) For example, we may indicate the quantity of bolts in a storage bin as 150, their length as 40 mm, the angle of the thread as 60° and the temperature of the room as 20°C.

Comments: (S3) gives examples of such quantities.[3] If we wanted, we could produce *deductions* such as:

Deduction 1: Length can be defined simply in terms of magnitude.

(S4) All these quantities, and many others, are known as scalar quantities.

Comments: (S4) names all the quantities that can be defined in terms of magnitude. By combining (S2) and (S4), the reader can produce the following sentence:

Quantities which can be defined simply in terms of magnitude are known as scalar quantities.

Clearly, then, this text contains what Selinker et al. (1976) have referred to as "implicit definitions."[4]

(S5) In stating that the movement of an aeroplane is 500 km, we have omitted an important part of the definition by not stating the direction of the movement or displacement.

Comments: (S5) is rather odd in that it looks as if it should be equivalent to a sentence beginning, "We have stated that...." This is not, however, the case, so presumably the structure is being used as a covert "imagine" instruction, equivalent to "Suppose we state that..." or "If we state that...."

In its relationship with (S1), (S5) must be handled together with (S6):

(S6) The full statement "500 km due east" includes both magnitude and direction.

The reader can use (S6) to deduce the following:

Deduction 2: 500 km = the magnitude of the movement.

It thus becomes possible to rephrase (S5) as follows:[5]

(S5a) The movement of an aeroplane can be defined by stating its magnitude alone, but the definition is incomplete because we have not stated its direction.

This restatement now relates very obviously to Inference 2, permitting the following deduction:

Deduction 3: The movement of an aeroplane is a vector quantity.

(S7) We can state the size or magnitude of a force as 50 units, but, in order to define the force completely, we must know the direction in which it is acting.

Comments: Again, this can be rephrased, making its similarity to Inference 2 more obvious:

(S7a) A force can be defined by stating its magnitude but the definition will be incomplete because we have not stated its direction.

As in the last example, we can deduce that a "force" here is an example of a "vector quantity."

(S8) Quantities which are defined by magnitude only are known as scalar quantities.

Comments: This is a very clear restatement of the naming sentence constructed above from (S2) and (S4).

(S9) Quantities which are defined by magnitude and direction are known as vector quantities.

Comments: If (S1) is classed as a "defining" statement, then (S9) is its "naming" equivalent. While (S9) is, in many respects, a paraphrase of (S1), it differs in an important way from (S1) in that neither Inference 1 or Inference 2 can be drawn from it. An obvious explanation of the differences between the two sentences is that (S1) "raises" inferential information, which can then be made overt in the subsequent text. Once these inferences have been raised and then made overt, there is no reason to raise them again in the concluding sentence.

GENERAL CONCLUSIONS

The two texts examined above differ radically in the function of the inferential reasoning they require from the reader. In the *Photosynthesis* text, inferential reasoning is necessary to fill in gaps in the information structure. In the *Vectors* text, the inferences appear to set up expectations on the part of the reader, which are then satisfied when the inferred information is later explicitly asserted. The actual types of reasoning, as set out earlier in this chapter, also differ: The *Vectors* text seems to require only Type 1, contrastive reasoning, whereas the *Photosynthesis* text requires Type 2 and Type 3 inferences for its decoding. Whether these differences can be correlated with a difference in overall rhetorical purpose of the two texts—while both function as learning-texts, *Photosynthesis* presents an argument, whereas *Vectors* presents definitions—or whether the differences can be correlated with different stages in the respective teaching curricula is a matter for further research.

Notes

1. Most of the underlying work was done as part of the KAAU Research Project on Reading for Academic Purposes, funded by the King Abdul Azziz University, Jeddah, and supervised at Edinburgh University by H. G. Widdowson.
2. Such an assumption may well be an important reading principle.
3. Teachers of EST might like to notice that "quantity" in (S.3) is used synonymously with "number" (e.g., it contrasts in this context with "length," "angle of thread," etc.). This is clearly not the case in other sentences of the text, where it includes terms such as "number."
4. Selinker et al. (1976) argue that in the case of an EST text they examine, failure on the part of the reader to recognize implicit definitions, and such would lead to failure to grasp the "total meaning." This is *not* so in the case of the "Vectors" text, since, as will be seen, implicit naming or defining sentences are later explicitly asserted in the text. Such "later assertions" might be one factor that sets off some very introductory texts from some more specialized ones.
5. The syntactic and semantic complexities involved in the construction of these restatements are ignored in this analysis.

References

Bransford, J. D., and M. K. Johnson. 1973. "Considerations of Some Problems of Comprehension." *Visual Information Processing,* ed. W. G. Chase. Academic Press. pp. 383-438.
Carroll, J. B. 1972. "Defining Language Comprehension: Some Speculations." pp. 1-29. Freedle and Carroll.

Freedle, R. O. and J. B. Carroll. 1972. *Language Comprehension and the Acquisition of Knowledge.* V. H. Winston and Sons.
Grice, H. P. 1975. "Logic and Conversation." *Speech Acts: Syntax and Semantics 3,* ed. P. Cole and J. Morgan. pp. 43-58. Academic Press.
Melnik, A. and J. Merritt. 1972. *Reading Today and Tomorrow.* Univ. of London Press.
Selinker, L., M. Todd Trimble, and L. Trimble. 1976. "Presuppositional Rhetorical Information in EST Discourse." *TESOL Quarterly* 10. 281-90.
Thorndike, E. L. 1972. "Reading as Reasoning: A Study of Mistakes in Paragraph Reading." Melnik and Merritt, pp. 20-30.
Widdowson, H. G. 1976. "Discourse Analysis, Interpretive Procedures and Communicative Language Teaching." *Bulletin CILA* 23. 56-64.

Editorial Comments

We present as the final chapter in this Festschrift, a contribution to practical reading research. Urquhart distinguishes ESP texts in terms of the types of logical "operations" a reader appears to need to use to arrive at a "reasonable" interpretation of said texts. Urquhart builds on a point Trimble has stressed again and again: the importance of implicit information in this process. The data here, at the high-school level, is taken from the language of introductory science—called here, "learning-texts."

Urquhart's use of the structure of the deductive logical syllogism to characterize the Type 5 operation needed by a reader to interpret a text seems to us to be closely related to Lackstrom's focus (chap. 2) on the close parallelism between the rhetorical structure of the logical argument in EST and the deductive syllogism.

Urquhart suggests that future research may be able to correlate the differing logical operations needed to interpret differing texts with the rhetorical functions of those texts, which seems to us to be an intriguing possibility. The author's specific taxonomic suggestions in this regard should aid future researchers in coming to grips with these unobservable "mental operations."

Finally, we end where we began—with one of the insightful distinctions made by Widdowson (chap. 1): text/textualization. Urquhart's chapter focuses on an important area of reading research based on a textualization approach to discourse, with rhetoric playing a central role in the analysis.

In conclusion, we have seen in this volume a textualization approach to several genres of EST discourse:

Lackstrom:	Introductory scientific textbooks (university level).
Godman and Payne:	(Same as Lackstrom)
Swales:	(Same as Lackstrom)
Wingard:	Medical research papers.
Tyma:	Introductory engineering textbooks.
Oster:	Electrical engineering journal articles.
Mage:	(Same as Lackstrom)
Candlin:	Oral medical interviews.
Huckin and Olsen:	(Same as Lackstrom), (same as Tyma), and popular science.
Bartolić:	(Same as Tyma)
Schmidt:	Oral business-administration lectures.
Urquhart:	Introductory scientific textbooks (high-school level).

As a result, we are left richer in our understanding of the relationship of EST genre to EST texts, to rhetorical processes, to grammatical forms, and to practical applications.

L.S.
E.T.

PART THREE

Bibliography of Louis Trimble's Works: Fiction Books and Academic Studies

Fiction Books and Academic Studies

1938

Trimble, Louis. *Sports of the world.* Los Angeles: Golden West Publishing Co.

1941

———. *Fit to kill.* New York: Phoenix Press.

1942

———. *Date for murder.* New York: Phoenix Press.
——— (Gerry Travis, nom de plume). *Tarnished love.* New York: Phoenix Press.
———. *Tragedy in turquoise.* New York: Phoenix Press.

1945

———. *Design for dying.* New York: Phoenix Press.
———. *Murder trouble.* New York: Phoenix Press.

1946

———. *Give up the body.* Seattle: Superior Publishing Co.
———. *You can't kill a corpse.* New York: Phoenix Press.

1948

——— (Stuart Brock, nom de plume). *Death is my lover.* New York: M.S. Mill Co.
——— (Stuart Brock, nom de plume). *Just around the coroner.* New York: M.S. Mill Co.
———. *Valley of violence.* Philadelphia: Macrae Smith.

1949

———. *The case of the blank cartridge.* New York: Phoenix Press.
——— (Stuart Brock, nom de plume). *Railtown sheriff.* New York: Thomas Bouregy.
———. *The tide can't wait.* New York: Thomas Bouregy.

1950

———. *Blonds are skin deep.* New York: Lion Books.
———. *Gaptown law.* Philadelphia: Macrae Smith Co.
———. *Gunsmoke justice.* Philadelphia: Macrae Smith Co.

1952

———. *Fighting cowman.* New York: Popular Publishing.

1953

———. *Bring back her body.* New York: Ace Books.
———. *Crossfire.* New York: Bouregy and Curl (Avalon Press).

1954

———. *Bullets on bunchgrass.* New York: Bouregy and Curl (Avalon Press).
——— (Stuart Brock, nom de plume). *Double-cross ranch.* New York: Bouregy and Curl (Avalon Press).

1955

——— (Stuart Brock, nom de plume). *Action at Boundary Peak.* New York: Bouregy and Curl (Avalon Press).
——— (Stuart Brock, nom de plume). *Whispering canyon.* New York: Bouregy and Curl (Avalon Press).

1956

——— (Stuart Brock, nom de plume). *Forbidden range.* New York: Bouregy and Curl (Avalon Press).
——— (Stuart Brock, nom de plume). *Killer's choice.* New York: Graphic Publishers.

——— (Gerry Travis, nom de plume). *A lovely mask for murder.* New York: Thomas Bouregy.
———. *Stab in the dark.* New York: Ace Books.
———. *The virgin victim.* New York: Mercury Books Mag.

1957

——— (Gerry Travis, nom de plume). *The big bite.* New York: Thomas Bouregy.
———. *Nothing to lose but my life.* New York: Ace Books.
——— (Stuart Brock, nom de plume). *Railtown sherrif.* New York: Thomas Bouregy.
———. *The tide can't wait.* New York: Thomas Bouregy.

1958

———. *Mountain ambush.* New York: Thomas Bouregy.
———. *The smell of trouble.* New York: Ace Books.

1959

———. *Cargo for the Styx.* New York: Ace Books.
———. *Corpse without a country.* New York: Ace Books.
———. *Obit deferred.* New York: Ace Books.
———. *Til death do us part.* New York: Ace Books.

1960

———. *Duchess of Skid Row.* New York: Ace Books.
———. *Girl on a slay ride.* New York: Avon Books.
———. *Love me and die.* New York: Ace Books.

1961

———. *Deadman Canyon.* New York: Ace Books.
———. *Montana gun.* New York: Hillman Books.
———. *The surfside caper.* New York: Ace Books.

1962

———. *Siege at High Meadow.* New York: Ace Books.

1963

———. *The dead and the deadly.* New York: Ace Books.
———. *The man from Colorado.* New York: Ace Books.
———. *Wild Horse Range.* New York: Ace Books.

1964

———. *Trouble at Gunsight.* New York: Ace Books.

1965

———. *Desperate deputy of Cougar Hill.* New York: Ace Books.
———. *Holdout in the Diablos.* New York: Ace Books.

1966

———. *Showdown in the Cayuse.* New York: Ace Books.

1967

———. *Standoff at Massacre Buttes.* New York: Ace Books.

1968

———. *Anthropol.* New York: Ace Books.
———. *Marshal of Sangaree.* New York: Ace Books.
———. *West to the Pecos.* New York: Ace Books.

1969

———. *The hostile peaks.* New York: Ace Books.

1970

Lackstrom, John, Larry Selinker, and Louis Trimble. "Grammar and Technical English: English as a Second Language." *Current Issues,* 101-33. Philadelphia: Chilton.
Trimble, Louis, *The lonesome mountains.* New York: Ace Books.
———. *The noblest experiment in the galaxy.* New York: Ace Books.
———. *Trouble Valley.* New York: Ace Books.

1971

———. "Phonemic change and the growth of homophones in Maltese." *Journal of Maltese Studies* 7.92-98.

1972
Selinker, Larry, Louis Trimble, and Robert Vroman (=Bley-Vroman). *Working papers in English for Science and Technology*. Seattle: University of Washington Press.
Trimble, Louis, *The city machine*. New York: Daw Books.
———. *Guardians of the gate*. New York: Ace Books.
———. *The ragbag army*. New York: Ace Books.
———. *The wandering variables*. New York: Daw Books.

1973
Lackstrom, John, Larry Selinker, and Louis Trimble. "Technical rhetorical principles and grammatical choice." *TESOL Quarterly* 7.127-36.
Trimble, Louis. "Some linguistic comments on religious terms in Maltese." *Journal of Maltese Studies* 9.59-67.

1974
Huckin, Thomas, Larry Selinker, and Louis Trimble. *An annotated bibliography of research in scientific and technical language*. Reports 9: The Yugoslavian Serbo-Croatian English Contrastive Project, 108-18. Univ. of Zagreb, Institute of Linguistics.
Selinker, Larry and Louis Trimble. "Formal written communication and ESL." *Journal of Technical Writing and Communication* 4.81-91.
Selinker, Larry, Louis Trimble, and Robert Vroman (=Bley-Vroman). "Presupposition and technical rhetoric." *English Language Teaching Journal*, 59-65.
Trimble, Louis. *The Bodelan way*. New York: Daw Books.
———. "Sociolinguistics in the ESL classroom." *Štrani Jezici* 3.166-73.

1975
Celmić, Davorka, Mia Gottwald, Zlata Kipčić, Nevenka Murgić, and Louis Trimble. *New horizons: a reader in Scientific and Technical English*. Zagreb: Školska Knjiga.

1976
Selinker, Larry, Louis Trimble, and Mary Todd Trimble. "Presuppositional rhetorical information in EST discourse." *TESOL Quarterly* 10.281-90.

1977
Trimble, Louis, "An approach to reading Scientific and Technical English." *Edutec* 4.1-15. Mexico City.
Trimble, Louis and Mary Todd Trimble. "Course materials for non-native speakers planning to enter U.S. universities to study science or technology." San Francisco: Pacific American Institute.
———. "The development of EFL Materials for occupational English." International English for Specific Purposes Seminar, proceedings, 52-70. Bogota, Colombia: The British Council.
———. "Literary training and the teaching of Scientific and Technical English to non-native speakers." *English Teaching Forum* 15.11-17.

1978
Selinker, Larry, Louis Trimble, and Mary Todd Trimble. "Rhetorical function shifts in EST discourse." *TESOL Quarterly* 12.311-20.
Todd Trimble, Mary, Louis Trimble, and Karl Drobnic, eds. *English for Specific Purposes: Scientific and Technical English*. Corvallis: Oregon State Univ. Press.
Trimble, Louis and Mary Todd Trimble. *English for multinational business*. Washington, D.C.: International Communication Agency. (Intermediate level materials for non-native speakers, specifically businessmen in their native countries.)